DECEMBER **2006**

The SMALL
BUSINESS
ECONOMY
For Data Year 2005

A REPORT TO THE PRESIDENT

United States Government Printing Office

Washington: 2006

United States Government Printing Office

Washington: 2006

For sale by the Superintendent of Documents, U.S. Government Printing Office
Internet: bookstore.gpo.gov Phone: toll free (866) 512-1800; DC area (202) 512-1800
Fax: (202) 512-2250 Mail: Stop IDCC, Washington, DC 20402-0001

ISBN 0-16-076750-4

Dear Mr. President:

The Office of Advocacy of the U.S. Small Business Administration is pleased to present *The Small Business Economy: A Report to the President*. In 2005, the American economy continued to expand, adding 2 million new jobs, and ended the year with the seventeenth consecutive quarter of real gross domestic product growth. Based on Office of Advocacy research, we know that small business owners contributed to this expansion by continuing to invest in their companies, hire additional workers, and develop innovative products and services.

For many Americans, the resilience of the U.S. economy was tested with Hurricanes Katrina and Rita in August and September 2005. The affected regions will grapple with the devastation and aftermath for many years. In April 2006, the Office of Advocacy cosponsored a conference, "Entrepreneurship: The Foundation for Economic Renewal in the Gulf Coast Region," in New Orleans with the Ewing Marion Kauffman Foundation, the Public Forum Institute, and the Gulf Coast Urban Entrepreneur Partnership. Speaker after speaker discussed the challenges they face as small business owners, yet the prevailing sentiment was one of hope and opportunity. Alabama, Louisiana, and Mississippi have the opportunity to reinvent their economies—something that could bring long-term economic benefits once accomplished. To view the conference proceedings, please visit http://www.sba.gov/advo/research/.

The U.S. economy was also affected by the devastating hurricanes. Growth in real GDP fell in the fourth quarter; the retail and travel and leisure industries experienced decreased employment; oil prices increased dramatically; and overall optimism declined. Many of the hurricane-related challenges, though, were short-term phenomena. The economy bounced back and continues to grow briskly, a sign of its resilience.

Previous reports have discussed technology transfer and the importance of small firm innovation to new firm formation (see chapters by Scott Shane in the 2004 edition and William Baumol in the 2005 volume). This year's report features two chapters that build on that concept. In discussing technology transfer, we dealt with the importance of university-based research and development and its linkages to new entrepreneurial ventures. Mark Weaver, Pat Dickson, and George Solomon write in this report of the benefits of education in general to new startups and their success.

Also, we often discuss the vital role that small business owners play in the economy. Implicit in this discussion is that small businesses can play a role in economic development. That was the focus of the April New Orleans conference and of a "best practices" conference the Office of Advocacy cosponsored in 2005. Economic development officials must decide whether to focus their resources on attracting large firms or to devote their energies toward growing the small businesses they already have. In this report Steve Quello and Graham Toft address these challenges, focusing on the benefits of "economic gardening" over "chasing smokestacks."

Economic development can take many forms, and in addition to the normal basket of incentives, the perceived business environment can have an impact on economic activity. Many states have begun adopting regulatory flexibility laws and executive orders modeled after the federal Regulatory Flexibility Act (RFA). Since the Advocacy state regulatory flexibility model legislation initiative was introduced in December 2002, 34 state legislatures have considered the model bill, and 19 states have implemented regulatory flexibility through either legislation or executive order. Meanwhile, Advocacy involvement in federal agency rulemakings helped secure $6.62 billion in first-year cost savings and $966 million in recurring annual savings for small entities in fiscal year (FY) 2005. Advocacy conducted 21 training sessions on the RFA, in accordance with the requirements of Executive Order 13272, as reported in the chapter on this topic.

This report also summarizes the economic and small business financial climate in 2005, and examines progress on small business procurement. Generally, the economy and financial markets were supportive of small business growth in 2005. And in the context of efforts to improve small business access to the federal procurement markets, small businesses won a significant share of FY 2005 contracts. A chapter on women's business ownership takes advantage of newly released data from the U.S. Bureau of the Census.

In summary, of the nearly 26 million firms in the United States, most are very small—97.5 percent of employer and nonemployer firms have fewer than 20 employees. Yet cumulatively, these firms account for half of our nonfarm real gross domestic product, and they have generated 60 to 80 percent of the net new jobs over the past decade. Entrepreneurs rightly command enormous respect, and their contributions to the U.S. economy are followed by academics and policymakers alike.

Fortunately, small business owners, many of whom are too busy running their businesses to ponder their own importance to the macroeconomy, continue to provide the vitality needed to spur new innovation and continued economic expansion for years to come.

Chad Moutray
Chief Economist & Director
of Economic Research

Acknowledgments

The Small Business Economy: A Report to the President was prepared by the U.S. Small Business Administration, Office of Advocacy. The Chief Counsel for Advocacy is Thomas M. Sullivan; the Chief Economist is Chad Moutray. The project was managed by Kathryn J. Tobias. Specific chapters were written or prepared by the following staff and outside contributors:

Chapter 1   Brian Headd

Chapter 2   Vicky Williams with Charles Ou

Chapter 3   Major Clark

Chapter 4   Ying Lowrey

Chapter 5   Mark Weaver, Rowan University; Pat Dickson, Wake Forest University; and George Solomon, George Washington University

Chapter 6   Steve Quello, CCS Logic; and Graham Toft, Growth Economics

Chapter 7   Claudia Rogers and Sarah Wickham

The Office of Advocacy appreciates the interest of all who helped prepare the report. Thanks are also extended to the U.S. Government Printing Office for their assistance.

Contents

Executive Summary

The Small Business Economy is a review of how small businesses fared in the economy in 2005, in the financial markets, and in the federal procurement marketplace, as well as new information about women in business. Chapters 6 and 7 offer guest contributors' studies of, respectively, links between education and entrepreneurship, and an approach to economic development that has been called "economic gardening." In its 25th year of overseeing the implementation of the Regulatory Flexibility Act of 1980, the Office of Advocacy takes a look back and ahead at ways to improve the regulatory environment for small firms. Appendices provide additional data on small businesses and background information on the Regulatory Flexibility Act.

The Small Business Economy in 2005

Three economic indicators key to an analysis of the economy's performance are output, productivity and unemployment. From 2004 to 2005, all three were up, and 2005 was generally a good year for the economy, although a deceleration occurred in the aftershocks of the late summer hurricanes. The estimated number of small business starts in 2005, at 671,800, was higher than the estimated number of closures, at 544,800, contributing to an estimated total of 5.99 million employer firms—a new high. The estimated number of nonemployer firms also reached a new high, at 19.86 million. The number of self-employed individuals continued to increase. Over the 1995–2004 decade, about 0.3 percent of adults per month became primarily self-employed. Nonfarm sole proprietorship income was up 7.5 percent in 2005, and corporate income, representing a mixture of large and small firm business returns, was also up, by 16.4 percent.

Small Business Financing

Favorable financial conditions supported U.S. economic growth in 2005, in spite of the effects of hurricanes and increases in energy prices. Real gross domestic product grew at a rate of 3.1 percent in 2005 compared with 3.75

percent in 2004. Growth was supported by a relatively stimulative fiscal policy combined with a tightening monetary policy. Long-term interest rates remained fairly stable, and by the end of the year, both short- and long-term rates were at about the same level. Net domestic borrowing by all sectors increased by 19 percent—a pace comparable to the 17 percent growth from 2003 to 2004. Business borrowing was at an all-time high, primarily as a result of borrowing by the nonfinancial corporate sector, but also reflecting high levels of borrowing by nonfarm, noncorporate businesses. Commercial banks expanded lending in 2005 and eased lending standards and terms on commercial and industrial loans in response to competition from nonbank lenders. The relative importance of banks of different sizes continued to evolve. Very large banks accounted for 71 percent of total domestic bank assets and 39 percent of small business loans under $1 million. Finance companies increased their lending by 6.8 percent in 2005. Public equity and initial public offering (IPO) markets were active, although down somewhat from 2004. Total IPO offerings were valued at $39.7 billion in 2005.

Federal Procurement from Small Firms

A number of efforts were under way in 2005 to improve the market for small businesses contracting with the federal government. For example, regulations promulgated with small business support in 2004 provided guidance to "other than small" contractors about subcontracting with small businesses. Changes in the subcontracting rule set the stage for the new Electronic Subcontracting Reporting System, which became operational in October 2005. Efforts continued to provide greater transparency in federal contracting. Changes to the Central Contractor Registration process implemented in April 2005 are expected to improve accuracy and reduce previously required data input. The Office of Advocacy was also asked to participate in a supporting role with the U.S. Small Business Administration (SBA) in the Service Acquisition Advisory Panel, which will review laws and regulations regarding the use of commercial practices, performance-based contracting, the performance of acquisition functions across agency lines of responsibility, and the use of government-wide contracts. As efforts to improve the small business contracting marketplace continued, small businesses were awarded $79.6 billion in contracts in fiscal year (FY) 2005, according to the SBA Office of Government Contracting report based on the second year of data from the Federal Procurement Data

System-Next Generation (FPDS–NG). This represented 25.36 percent of the $314 billion in federal prime contract dollars available for small business competition.

Women in Business

Recently released statistics offer new information about women in the work force and in the business community. Data from sources that include the Current Population Survey, the American Community Survey, the Economic Census, and the Survey of Business Owners are the basis for a review of the characteristics of women-owned business and women's participation in the labor force. More than 51 percent of the population and nearly 47 percent of the labor force are women. Between 1997 and 2002, the number of women-owned firms overall increased by 19.8 percent, and the number of women-owned employer firms rose by 8.3 percent. In 2002, women owned 6.5 million or 28.2 percent of nonfarm U.S. firms. More than 14 percent of these firms were employers, with 7.1 million workers and $173.7 billion in annual payroll. Minority groups in the United States had larger shares of women business owners than did the non-Hispanic White population: 31 percent of Asian American and 46 percent of African American business owners were women. Almost 80 percent of women-owned businesses in both 1997 and 2002 had receipts under $50,000; most of women-owned business receipts were in the wholesale and retail trade and manufacturing industries. In 2002 significant proportions of women-owned businesses were in the professional, scientific, and technical services.

Entrepreneurship and Education

A review of recent research on the impact of general education on entrepreneurship suggests three generalizations, according to guest contributors Mark Weaver, Paul Dickson, and George Solomon. First, the evidence suggests a positive link between education and entrepreneurial performance. Second, when the forms of entrepreneurship examined are divided into "necessity entrepreneurship" and "opportunity entrepreneurship," the relationship between entrepreneurship and education becomes clearer. Third, the education-entrepreneurship link is not linear—the highest levels of entrepreneurship are linked to individuals with at least a bachelor's degree, but higher levels of education are not generally found to be positively linked to entrepreneurship. A review of research specific to entrepreneurship education suggests a link, although no definitive evidence, between such education and venture creation. The precursors of entrepreneurial activity can be important and measurable outcomes for entrepreneurship education, the researchers find.

Economic Gardening

"Economic gardening" is an entrepreneur-centered growth strategy that balances the more traditional economic development approach of business recruitment. The approach examined here by researchers Steve Quello of CCS Logic and Graham Toft of Growth Economics, was developed by the city of Littleton, Colorado, in 1989 in conjunction with the Center for the New West. It began as a demonstration program to deal with the sudden erosion of economic conditions following the relocation of the city's largest employer. The economic best practices that evolved in Littleton were associated with one of three critical themes: infrastructure—building and supporting the community assets essential to commerce and overall quality of life; connectivity—improving the interaction and exchange among business owners and critical resource providers; and market information—accessing competitive intelligence on markets, customers, and competitors comparable to the resources historically available to larger firms. Economic gardening is finding application in a number of community settings, especially in the Western states.

The Regulatory Flexibility Act in Fiscal Year 2005

Enacted in 1980, the Regulatory Flexibility Act (RFA) reached a 25-year anniversary in 2005. The SBA's Office of Advocacy oversees implementation of the law, which requires federal agencies to determine the impact of their rules on small entities, consider alternatives that minimize small entity impacts, and make their analyses available for public comment. President Bush's Executive Order 13272, signed in August 2002, gave agencies new incentives to improve their compliance with the RFA. Advocacy efforts to implement the law resulted in FY 2005 regulatory cost savings to small entities of $6.62 billion in first-year and $966 million in recurring annual savings. Pursuant to E.O. 13272, Advocacy trained federal agencies in implementation of the law in FY 2005.

In response to Advocacy's model state legislation initiative, 18 states introduced regulatory flexibility legislation in 2005. The importance of state regulatory flexibility for small businesses is demonstrated in a real life example from Colorado. The Colorado Department of Revenue proposed an amendment to a rule that would require hotels and restaurants offering resealing of opened bottles to purchase commercially manufactured stoppers and sealable containers such as bags or boxes. The overall cost of compliance for this regulatory proposal was estimated at approximately $1.8 to $3.3 million. After discussions with small business representatives and before going further with the rulemaking process, the Department of Revenue agreed to revise its initial proposal. The revised rule was a success for small businesses as it provided a more economical way for them to comply with the rule while meeting Colorado's policy objective. The example demonstrates how agencies, as well as small businesses in other states, would benefit greatly by implementing a comprehensive regulatory flexibility system.

1 *The* SMALL BUSINESS ECONOMY

Synopsis

The year 2005 saw a sustained economic expansion, which in many ways was a continuation of the previous few years. Output rose and equity markets inched upward while unemployment was down over the course of the year. The estimated number of firms and self-employed climbed. Growth was decelerating in the fourth quarter, most likely related to the devastating effects of Hurricanes Katrina and Rita.

Introduction

The small business universe is often hidden from view. Businesses in retail trade, an industry that is among the most visible of those inhabited by small firms, constituted just 12.9 percent of employer firms in 2003.[1] Often small firms are difficult to view statistically as well: much of current federal data are in aggregate business statistics that do not separate out small and large firm sectors.

Both small and large businesses are important in the provision of goods and services. Most large businesses were once small, and many small business owners once worked in large businesses. The constant movement across size classes makes it difficult to determine the status of the small business sector from any one piece of data. Key indicators in taking the pulse of small business include the number of business starts and stops, and the availability of small business "fuel"—bank financing.

For research purposes, the Office of Advocacy often defines a small business as one with fewer than 500 employees.[2] This definition results in about an even split between large and small businesses of private sector employment

---

1   U.S. Department of Commerce, Bureau of the Census.

2   For government program purposes, the U.S. Small Business Administration's Office of Size Standards, www.sba.gov/size, lists criteria for small business size designation by industry.

and output, with small businesses employing 50.7 percent of the private sector work force and generating about half of nonfarm private gross domestic product. This 500-employee threshold also means about 99.9 percent of businesses are small. The size difference between the average (mean) small and large businesses was stark in 2003, according to the latest U.S. Census Bureau data. The average small employer had one location and 10 employees, while the average large employer had 61 locations and 3,300 employees.[3]

Although small and large firms differ by definition in size, they are affected by economic conditions in similar ways. A series of devastating hurricanes, increasing fuel costs, and an ongoing war had important effects on both groups in 2005.

The information presented here opens a window on the status and role of small business in 2005 and on government statistics available for further exploration. Additional numerical and historic data in Appendix A provide a further look at the small business marketplace.

Small Business in 2005

It is often said that a rising tide lifts all boats. In the business community, the tide overwhelms about 10 percent of firms annually; these businesses are replaced by a slightly larger number. The smaller businesses come and go, and it is this turnover that is a great virtue of the small business sector, where struggling ventures are replaced by new ideas. Good economic news and strong economic indicators from small businesses do go hand in hand.

In analyzing the economy's annual performance, three statistics—output, productivity, and unemployment—are key. From 2004 to 2005, output and productivity were up—as was unemployment (Table 1.1). So 2005 was a good year for the economy, although a deceleration was occurring; trends in these indicators were better in the 2003–2004 period than in 2004–2005. This is not surprising considering the economic aftershocks of Hurricanes Katrina and Rita in 2005. Real GDP in the fourth quarter of 2005 was half

---

3 For more basic details on small business, see the SBA Office of Advocacy's *Frequently Asked Questions* at www.sba.gov/advo/stats/sbfaq.pdf.

Table 1.1 Quarterly Economic Measures, 2004–2005 (percent)

	2004				2005			
	Q 1	Q 2	Q 3	Q 4	Q 1	Q 2	Q 3	Q 4
Real GDP change (annual rates)	4.3	3.5	4.0	3.3	3.8	3.3	4.1	1.7
Unemployment rate	5.7	5.6	5.5	5.4	5.2	5.1	5.0	5.0
GDP price deflator (annual rates)	3.7	3.9	1.3	2.7	3.0	2.6	3.3	3.5
Productivity change (annual rates)	3.7	3.7	1.6	2.7	3.4	1.1	4.9	0.2
Establishment births	0.3	-1.7	3.2	7.1	-9.0	7.5	1.1	NA
Establishment closures	1.9	0.6	4.5	-7.2	8.4	-2.0	-0.3	NA

NA = Not available.

Source: U.S. Small Business Administration, Office of Advocacy, from figures provided in *Economic Indicators* by the U.S. Department of Commerce, Bureau of Economic Analysis, and the U.S. Department of Labor, Bureau of Labor Statistics.

the increase of the third quarter. Unemployment did not decline from the third to the fourth quarter.

Small businesses, representing half of private sector employment, were at the center of output, productivity, and unemployment changes; but as these figures are not broken out by firm size on a timely basis, other indicators offer more insight into the small business sector. In 2005 the estimated number of employer firm births, at 671,800, was higher than the number of closures, at 544,800 (Table 1.2).[4] The net gain contributed to an estimated total of 5.99 million employer firms—a new high. The number of smaller ventures also reached a new high: the estimated number of nonemployers was 19.86 million in 2005.[5] The number of self-employed individuals also increased.

Even with the prime rate climbing throughout 2005, financing was sought after to start and grow small firms. Bank commercial and industrial loan dollars were up 12.6 percent from 2004 to 2005. Bank loan officers reported stronger loan demand throughout 2005 and the loosening of credit standards.[6]

---

4   Note that business bankruptcies were up in 2005; however, it is believed that the increase is in part the result of more individuals attempting to file before more restrictive bankruptcy rules were to be in place.

5   Employer size data in Census's Statistics of U.S. Businesses have been available since 1988; nonemployer data have been available annually since 1997.

6   National private sector loan demand did decelerate from the third quarter to the fourth quarter, again most likely related to the effects of the hurricanes.

Table 1.2 Business Measures, 2004–2005

	2004	2005	Percent change
Employer firms (nonfarm)	e 5,865,400	e 5,992,400	2.2
Employer firm births	e 642,600	e 671,800	4.5
Employer firm terminations	e 544,300	e 544,800	0.0
Self-employment, nonincorporated	10,400,000	10,500,000	1.0
Self-employment, incorporated	5,200,000	5,300,000	1.9
Business bankruptcies	34,317	39,201	14.2

e = estimate

Sources: U.S. Small Business Administration, Office of Advocacy, from data provided by the U.S. Department of Commerce, Bureau of the Census; the U.S. Department of Labor; and the Administrative Office of the U.S. Courts.

Wages are important to small businesses because payroll represents a very large share of their costs; moreover, high wages may entice owners away from business ownership and into wage work. Wage statistics for the year are mixed, with aggregate figures showing solid gains while average figures showed declines. Aggregate wages and salaries were up 6.0 percent from 2004 to 2005, while inflation-adjusted average hourly earnings were down 0.7 percent.[7] Benefits, which continue to be difficult for many small businesses to offer, saw gains that continued to outpace wage gains, and were up 4.1 percent for 2004–2005.

Even against a backdrop of rising energy prices, real estate costs, wages, and interest rates, nonfarm sole proprietorship income was up 7.5 percent. Corporate income, a mix of small and large business returns, was also up substantially during the year, by 16.4 percent.

Although the equity markets are dominated by large firms, they are home to an important group of small firms, often referred to as gazelles: these nascent entrepreneurs and companies are often the recipients of seed investments in the equity markets. In line with the increases in sole proprietorship income and corporate profits, the S&P 500 Index was up 6.8 percent and the NASDAQ

---

7   Aggregate wage-and-salary data are from the U.S. Department of Commerce, Bureau of the Census; adjusted average hourly earnings are from the U.S. Department of Labor, Bureau of Labor Statistics. These figures are not comparable as the first figure is not adjusted for inflation, but the divergent trends show that there are "facts" for both critics and supporters to tout.

was up 5.7 percent over the course of the year—solid increases, although still below their 2000 levels.

Demographics

Overall, self-employment (as a primary occupation and including incorporated ventures) rose 12.2 percent from 1995 to 2004, with 10.2 percent of the 2004 work force choosing self-employment.[8] The number of self-employed overall declined somewhat from 1995 to 2000, and then increased considerably from 2000 to 2004 (Table A.10). Over the 1995–2004 decade, about 0.3 percent of adults per month became primarily self-employed.[9]

Women's self-employment rate was below the overall rate but increased more than men's self-employment over this period. Men represented two-thirds of the self-employed in 2004.

Large self-employment gains occurred in all nonwhite race and ethnic origin categories; however, self-employment rates remained low for Black and Hispanic populations. By 2004, White Americans still constituted most of the self-employed—88.3 percent.

Trends in business ownership by veterans moved in the opposite direction, with large declines in self-employment—22 percent over the 1995–2004 decade—but a high self-employment rate of 14.8 percent in 2004. Most of the declines in veterans' self-employment were over the 1995 to 2000 period.

Individuals with disabilities that restrict or prevent some types of work sought self-employment opportunities at rates higher than the national average. These business owners had a 14.3 percent self-employment rate. The number that were self-employed changed little over the 1995 to 2004 period, gaining 3.8 percent.

---

8   Owner characteristics are available through the Bureau of the Census's Economic Census Survey of Business Owners (SBO) and the joint Census/Bureau of Labor Statistics (BLS) Current Population Survey (CPS). Recently the SBO released very detailed 2002 figures by owner type, industry, and location (www.census.gov/csd/sbo/.) While this program produces invaluable geographic and industry figures, this section will employ the CPS figures in an attempt to focus on more current figures.

9   Robert W. Fairlie, *Kauffman Index of Entrepreneurial Activity* (Ewing Marion Kauffman Foundation, 2006); see www.kauffman.org/items.cfm?itemID=703.

Patterns in the age of the self-employed population matched findings from years past. Few younger workers are self-employed; self-employment rates increase with age; most of the self-employed are middle-aged; and in line with population shifts, self-employment is climbing substantially in the older age categories.

With respect to education as a component of human capital: like the general population, most of the self-employed—38.5 percent—have high school diplomas or less schooling. Self-employment rates increase with educational attainment, reaching 13.9 percent for individuals with master's degrees or above. The increase in the self-employed from 1995 to 2004 was also in the higher education categories.

The Amazing Maze of Federal Data

The federal government provides scores of statistical resources that can be accessed by small business owners, even from home.[10] Many datasets are based on surveys such as BLS's price indices; others are based on administrative data, such as the Internal Revenue Service's Statistics of Income tax return counts; still others are based on a combination, such as Census's Economic Census.

Finding the right source is often the challenge, with data dissemination scattered among the various federal agencies. The tried and true method of starting with the Census Bureau's *Statistical Abstract of the United States*, which contains basic information from many federal and nonfederal sources, still works today.[11] Researchers who need more detail can conduct follow-up work on the sources listed in tables with similar data. Umbrella government websites, in addition to general Internet searches, are other good methods to find data.[12]

---

10 For working from home statistics that include the self-employed, see www.bls.gov/news.release/homey.toc.htm.

11 For the *Statistical Abstract of the United States*, see www.census.gov/prod/www/statistical-abstract.html. Other useful publications include *Economic Indicators* (www.gpoaccess.gov/indicators) and the *Economic Report of the President* (www.gpoaccess.gov/eop).

12 See www.fedstats.gov, www.firstgov.gov, and the Federal Reserve Board of Governors's FRED at http://research.stlouisfed.org/fred2/.

Multiple "quick glance" products from the government combine various data sources and provide state-level data. See Census's state profiles (http://quickfacts.census.gov/qfd/), BLS's state profiles (http://www.bls.gov/eag/home.htm), the Bureau of Economic Analysis's state profiles (http://www.bea.gov/bea/regional/bearfacts/statebf.cfm) and the SBA Office of Advocacy's state and territory profiles (www.sba.gov/advo/research/profiles). Many government agencies also have electronic push technologies to inform users of newly released data.[13]

The hunt is not necessarily over if the information is not published. For the truly adventurous, Census makes basic data from CPS available so individuals can create their own cross-tabulations.[14] But the adventurous are advised to view the number of responses used to create tables to make sure that the results are representative.[15] Census also will produce special aggregate data requests at cost, as in the Statistics of U.S. Business program, but users should recognize that they will not release figures that violate companies' privacy concerns.[16]

Users may be looking for one simple number or for large electronic datasets: both are available, but often the historic data are not in the desired format. Because data producers strive to provide statistics that are comparable over time, new data sources are rare and changes occur infrequently. With respect to business statistics, manufacturing and agriculture grabbed the lion's share of resources years ago and have not been good at sharing. Data on small businesses or by size of firm have had an uphill battle ever since and many of the data programs are relatively new, making acquiring historical data from a few decades ago challenging.[17]

---

13   The Federal Reserve Board's email notification (www.federalreserve.gov/generalinfo/subscribe/notification.htm), BLS' news service (www.bls.gov/bls/list.htm) and Advocacy's listservs (http://web.sba.gov/list/) are good examples.

14   See http://dataferrett.census.gov/.

15   Calculating average figures across a few time periods can help mitigate this issue.

16   See http://www.census.gov/csd/susb/susb.htm.

17   Even obtaining the number of firms can be daunting. From 1929 to 1963, the precursor to the U.S. Department of Commerce, Bureau of Economic Analysis (BEA), the Office of Business Economics, produced the number of firms by major industry, but, "The last substantial revision was made in January 1963 and revealed errors in the earlier estimates for absolute number and rate of growth ..." (*The Historical Statistics of the United States, Colonial Times to 1970*, U.S. Department of Commerce, Bureau of the Census, 1975, 909.)

Fortunately, the Kauffman Foundation and the National Academy of Sciences are collaborating in an examination of currently produced small business statistics: a committee report is expected to be released in the fall of 2007 with recommendations. Efforts to close some of the data gaps are currently under way with the expansion of the Bureau of Labor Statistics' Business Employment Dynamics to include geographic data and of the Census Bureau's Nonemployer Statistics to include dynamic (business entry and exit) data.

Continued Growth?

The Office of Advocacy does not attempt to read the tea leaves, but provides current small business statistics in *Small Business Quarterly Indicators*.[18] Past quarterly indicators and information about firm size show that the small business sector has grown steadily if sometimes slowly over time, so deviations from this pattern would be unusual.

Somewhat surprisingly, a National Federation of Independent Business (NFIB) poll found that only 51 percent of small employers wanted to grow their firms; fewer than 10 percent aspired to become "growth firms."[19] This 10 percent is a small percentage of all firms, but certainly the group of firms largely responsible for changing the competitive nature of markets and developing new markets.

NFIB's monthly survey found a 1.7 percent decline between 2004 and 2005 in the number of firm owners who thought it was a good time to expand. The lower level continued into the first few months of 2005. The surveys have also found that health care issues top small business concerns in recent years.[20]

---

18 See www.sba.gov/advo/research/sbei.html.

19 National Federation of Independent Business, *Success, Satisfaction and Growth*, NFIB National Small Business Poll, Volume 1, Issue 6, 2001, www.nfib.com/object/sbPolls.

20 National Federation of Independent Business, *Small Business Economic Trends*, see www.nfib.com/page/sbet.

2 SMALL BUSINESS FINANCING in 2005

Synopsis

The U.S economy grew at a slower pace in 2005 as the economy entered the fourth year of recovery from a relatively mild recession in 2001. The Federal Open Market Committee continued to tighten monetary policy by raising the target federal funds rates at each of its scheduled committee meetings. Financial markets, however, accommodated the financing needs of all sectors—the federal and state governments, housing, and business. Pressure on inflation caused by high energy prices and global demand remained subdued. Equity markets remained unstable and dipped in 2005, while the level of new small initial public offerings was limited.

Economic and Credit Conditions in 2005

Despite the effects of devastating hurricanes and increases in energy prices, the U.S. economy maintained moderate growth in 2005. Spending by the household sector (consumer spending and housing investment) remained strong because of high household wealth and high housing prices. With historically high and continuous increases in oil prices placing a squeeze on disposable spending and with a rising debt burden, real gross domestic product grew at a slower rate—at 3.1 percent in 2005, compared with 3.75 percent in 2004, while core inflation remained contained.

Favorable financial conditions supported U.S. economic growth in 2005. Credit conditions remained supportive for financing business expansions, even though the Federal Open Market Committee (FOMC) gradually tightened monetary policy. The target federal funds rate was increased by 25 basis points at each of the FOMC meetings beginning in June 2004. In a nutshell, economic growth in 2005 proved to be resilient based on a relatively stimulative fiscal policy combined with a tightening monetary policy.

Interest Rate Movements

The FOMC continued a steady tightening of monetary policy through eight consecutive rate increases during the year in an effort to curtail pressure on inflation. The target funds rate increased by 2 percentage points over the period—from 2.25 percent at the beginning of the year to 4.25 percent at year's end. The demand and supply of funds available in the financial markets determine the movements in long-term interest rates. Long-term interest rates remained fairly stable, and by the end of the year both short- and long-term interest rates were at about the same level, resulting in a flat yield curve. Corporate bond rates with AAA ratings declined further during the first half of the year and reached their lowest level in the summer, at 4.96 percent, then began a gradual increase during the second half of the year, ending at 5.37 percent (Chart 2.1).

The prime rate, the base index rate for most small firm loans, moved up steadily throughout the year, from 5.25 percent at the beginning of the first quarter to 7.00 percent toward the end of the year. In general, interest rates paid by small firms followed a similar pattern, in line with overall interest rate movements in the capital and credit markets. Over the past three years, loan rates charged by banks for small business borrowing—mostly adjustable rates—moved in parallel with money market rates. Rates paid by small business owners for variable-rate loans with 2- to 30-day repricing periods rose about 2.0 percent from November 2004 to November 2005. This is comparable to the increases in money market rates for one- to two-month commercial paper or for four-week Treasury bills. For example, rates for loans of $100,000 to less than $500,000 rose from 4.69 percent in November 2004 to 6.65 percent in November 2005 (Table 2.1; see the appendix to this chapter for all quarters). Rates for fixed-rate loans with a year or more in maturity for all three loan size categories moved up throughout the year, but at a slightly slower pace.

The Nonfinancial Sector's Use of Funds in Capital Markets

The slow but continued growth in the economy was reflected in the use of funds by the nonfinancial sectors. For example, net domestic borrowing in the financial markets by all nonfinancial sectors increased by 19 percent—from $1,933 billion in 2004 to $2,295 billion in 2005—a pace comparable to the 17 percent growth in borrowing from 2003 to 2004. The ongoing increases in borrowing can be attributed to continued heavy borrowing by households and

Chart 2.1 Interest Rate Movements, 2000 to 2005

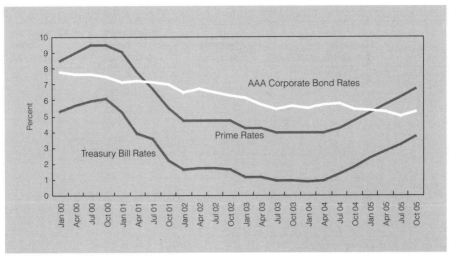

Source: Board of Governors of the Federal Reserve System, *Federal Reserve Bulletin*, various issues.

increased borrowing by state and local governments and the business sector (Table 2.2).

Federal, State, and Local Government Borrowing

While federal government spending continued to increase, although at slower rates than in 2004, federal budgetary deficits declined as a result of increased federal revenues in 2005. According to the national income account estimates, the federal budget deficit in 2005 declined to $318 billion compared with $413 billion in 2004.[1] Borrowing by the federal government followed a pattern similar to that of 2004, declining further to $307 billion in 2005 from $362 billion in 2004—a 15 percent decrease—but still accounting for more than 10 percent of total net borrowing by nonfinancial sectors in the financial markets (Table 2.2).

The level of borrowing by state and local governments in 2005 increased significantly, to $177 billion, from a two-year average of $118 billon (Table 2.2). State and local governments expanded borrowing in the financial markets for

---

1   See Federal Reserve Bank of St. Louis, "Government revenues, spending, and debt," *National Economic Trends*, April 2006, 16.

Table 2.1 Loan Rates Charged by Banks by Loan Size, November 2000–November 2005

	Loan size (thousands of dollars)	Fixed-rate term loans	Variable-rate loans (2–30 days)	Variable-rate loans (31–365 days)
November 2005	1–99	8.07	6.69	7.72
	100–499	7.48	6.65	7.41
	500–999	6.70	6.38	7.00
	Minimum-risk loans	4.98	4.51	4.88
November 2004	1–99	6.76	4.52	6.53
	100–499	6.21	4.69	5.75
	500–999	4.80	4.41	5.08
	Minimum-risk loans	4.42	2.62	2.96
November 2003	1–99	6.53	4.27	6.11
	100–499	5.68	3.79	5.03
	500–999	4.99	3.22	3.94
	Minimum-risk loans	5.50	1.59	1.81
November 2002	1–99	7.34	5.14	7.11
	100–499	6.21	4.42	5.51
	500–999	5.99	3.93	4.91
	Minimum-risk loans	2.84	3.85	3.19
November 2001	1–99	7.97	5.53	7.59
	100–499	6.83	4.79	6.23
	500–999	6.30	4.29	4.56
	Minimum-risk loans	5.71	2.59	3.20
November 2000	1–99	10.33	9.95	10.18
	100–499	9.96	9.24	9.77
	500–999	8.66	8.63	8.68
	Minimum-risk loans	9.25	7.12	7.82

Source: Board of Governors of the Federal Reserve System, *Survey of Terms of Lending*, Statistical Release E.2, various issues, and special tabulations prepared by the Federal Reserve Board for the U.S. Small Business Administration, Office of Advocacy.

Table 2.2 Credit Market Borrowing by the Nonfinancial Sector, 1995–2005 (billions of dollars)*

	1995	1996	1997	1998	1999	2000	2001	2002	2003	2004	2005
Total domestic borrowing	712.0	731.4	804.7	1,041.9	1,026.6	825.1	1,095.3	1,319.0	1,649.4	1,932.7	2,294.6
Government											
Federal	144.4	145.0	23.1	-52.6	-71.2	-295.9	-5.6	257.6	396.0	361.9	306.9
State and local	-51.5	-6.8	56.1	67.7	38.5	15.5	105.8	143.9	117.8	118.2	177.3
Business											
Farm	2.9	4.8	6.2	8.0	5.5	11.3	10.5	7.8	7.7	11.8	15.4
Nonfarm noncorporate	30.6	81.4	94.7	159.7	189.4	197.1	162.7	148.5	96.9	243.0	301.1
Nonfinancial corporate	243.7	148.8	291.1	408.4	371.6	346.0	221.4	25.0	84.7	174.5	289.3
Total	277.2	235.0	392.0	576.1	566.5	554.4	394.6	181.3	189.3	429.3	605.8
Households	350.3	358.1	332.7	450.8	492.8	551.1	600.5	736.2	946.3	1,023.4	1,204.7
Foreign borrowing in the United States	71.1	88.4	71.8	31.2	13.0	63.0	-43.8	70.8	54.3	82.2	95.0

* Annual revision for statistics from 2000 to 2005.

Note: Downward revisions and adjustments were made to the data in 2002.

Source: Board of Governors of the Federal Reserve System, Flow of Funds Accounts, Fourth Quarter 2005: Z1, Flows and Outstandings, March 2006.

capital projects such as school construction, as the budgetary position for most state governments improved significantly in 2005.

Borrowing by the Household Sector

Borrowing by the household sector reached a new high of $1.205 trillion in 2005, as households continued to dominate borrowing by nonfinancial sectors. Household borrowing accounted for slightly over 50 percent of total net borrowing in the U.S. financial markets. Household sector borrowing grew by 18 percent, from $1.023 trillion in 2004 to $1.205 trillion in 2005 (Table 2.2). Rising household wealth sustained the housing market along with still relatively low mortgage rates. These rates encouraged borrowing by households, which lowered personal savings rates.[2]

Business Borrowing

Business borrowing reached an all-time high of $606 billion in 2005, up from $429 billion in 2004. Most of the increase was the result of increased borrowing by the nonfinancial corporate sector. The increase in capital expenditures was supported by a large increase in internal sources of funds (Table 2.3).[3] Net business borrowing by nonfinancial corporations continued to increase in 2005, soaring by 66 percent to an annual rate of $289 billion from $175 billion in 2004. Nevertheless, corporate borrowing remained below the high levels reached in the late 1990s.

Net borrowing by nonfarm, noncorporate businesses increased to a record high, accounting for 50 percent of total business borrowing in 2005. Borrowing by this sector has, until the recent past, been at lower levels and less volatile than corporate borrowing; however, it increased significantly in 2004 and 2005. High levels of borrowing in commercial mortgages over this period contributed to the large increases (Table 2.4).

---

2   See Board of Governors of the Federal Reserve System, Flow of Funds Accounts, Fourth Quarter 2005: Z1, Flows and Outstandings, F.8 Savings and Investment, March 2006.

3   Before-tax corporate profits rose from an annual rate of $574 billion in 2004 to $868 billion in 2005.

Table 2.3 Major Sources and Uses of Funds by Nonfarm, Nonfinancial Corporate Businesses, 1995–2005 (billions of dollars)*

	1995	1996	1997	1998	1999	2000	2001	2002	2003	2004	2005
Before-tax profit	437.7	458.8	494.5	460.1	456.7	421.9	309.9	336.4	448.1	573.8	867.5
Domestic undistributed profit	111.7	108.3	120.2	65.1	63.2	2.5	-45.0	-12.9	28.7	49.4	383.3
Depreciation with inventory valuation adjustment	430.7	504.2	548.2	570.6	598.1	617.7	643.8	718.7	752.2	814.1	1,027.6
Total internal funds, on book basis	542.4	612.5	659.9	635.7	660.4	631.8	632.5	720.9	765.5	853.7	1,051.3
Net increase in liability	390.8	398.5	283.5	616.0	987.6	1,237.4	95.2	84.9	13.4	378.8	156.0
Funds raised in credit markets	218.6	148.8	291.9	408.4	371.6	346.0	221.4	25.0	84.7	174.5	289.3
Net new equity issues	-58.3	-69.5	-114.4	-215.5	-110.4	-118.2	-48.1	-41.6	-57.8	-141.1	-366.0
Capital expenditures	567.7	684.7	760.2	826.5	866.7	928.6	800.4	737.1	751.5	861.0	925.3
Net financial investment	42.7	4.8	-11.1	-46.1	-17.7	-28.2	82.4	45.2	69.2	122.5	151.5

* Annual revision for statistics from 2000 to 2005.

Source: Board of Governors of the Federal Reserve System, Flow of Funds Accounts, Fourth Quarter 2004: Flows and Outstandings (March 2006).

Table 2.4 Major Sources and Uses of Funds by Nonfarm, Noncorporate Businesses, 1995–2005 (billions of dollars)*

	1995	1996	1997	1998	1999	2000	2001	2002	2003	2004	2005
Net income	534.2	569.7	609.9	656.5	710.6	767.3	820.0	817.4	835.8	900.2	942.8
Gross investment	56.4	110.8	118.5	125.0	148.7	168.7	149.2	151.5	161.9	177.4	204.8
Fixed capital expenditures	99.2	109.6	118.8	123.9	185.8	215.3	197.0	182.0	193.6	208.6	232.9
Changes in inventories	1.9	1.1	3.0	3.6	3.5	2.9	-1.6	0.07	0.08	2.6	1.2
Net financial investments	-44.7	0	-3.3	-2.5	-40.6	-49.5	-46.3	-31.2	-32.4	-33.8	-29.4
Net increase in credit market debt	23.9	81.4	94.7	159.7	189.4	197.1	162.7	148.5	96.9	243.0	301.1
Mortgages	-2.2	50.9	47.7	117.7	135.1	137.5	121.2	121.0	80.2	217.8	258.8
Net Investment by proprietors	51.9	-18.1	-55.1	-64.8	-82.3	-45.1	-14.9	-85.4	21.0	-62.2	-37.6

* Annual revision for statistics from 2000 to 2005.

Source: Board of Governors of the Federal Reserve System, Flow of Funds Accounts, Fourth Quarter 2004: Flows and Outstandings (March 2006).

Lending by Financial Institutions to Small Businesses

With ample liquidity available in the financial markets and in spite of large increases in money market rates, commercial banks expanded their lending activities in 2005. As the economy continued to improve, banks eased their lending standards and terms on commercial and industrial (C&I) loans throughout the year in response to competition from nonbank lenders and increased tolerance for risk.[4] According to the Federal Reserve Board's Senior Loan Officer Survey, banks reported rising demand for C&I loans, with a few reporting an increase in demand for C&I loans from small firms. The survey noted that, on net, banks had narrowed the spreads of loan rates, reduced the cost of credit lines, and increased the maximum maturities and sizes of loans or credit lines. Profits of U.S. commercial banks were moderately high because of generally favorable financial and economic conditions in 2005.[5] Net operating income for all FDIC-insured institutions reached $130.4 billion in 2005, compared to $117.0 billion the previous year.[6]

Lending to Small Businesses by Commercial Lending Institutions

The Office of Advocacy's study of lending by commercial banks has been expanded for 2005 to include federal and state savings banks and savings and loan associations (S&Ls), in addition to the commercial banks covered in previous bank studies. The total number of institutions included in the study was

---

4   See "Profits and Balance Sheet Developments at U.S. Commercial Banks in 2005," *Federal Reserve Bulletin*, 2006, and the Federal Reserve Board's Senior Loan Officer Opinion Survey on Bank Lending Practices, February 2006.

5   Return on assets (ROA) was slightly down from 2004 by 3 basis points to 1.31, but was still in the upper half of its range for the last 10 years, while return on equity (ROE) reached its lowest level in more than 10 years, of 13.01 percent. The decline can be attributed to an increase in equity relative to assets because of the accumulation of good will acquired as a result of some recent large mergers. See "Profits and Balance Sheet Developments at U.S. Commercial Banks in 2005," *Federal Reserve Bulletin*, June 2006, A77-A95, or visit http://www.federalreserve.gov/Pubs/Bulletin/2006/bank-profits/default.htm.

6   See Federal Deposit Insurance Corporation, "Quarterly Banking Profile," Table II-A, or visit the agency's web page, http://www2.fdic.gov/qbp/2006mar/qbp.pdf.

7,624 as of June 2005.[7] It is important to note that the overall trend of institutional consolidation follows the pattern that has appeared in previous studies.

The dollar amount of business loans outstanding increased steadily for most loan sizes between June 2003 and June 2005. Increases were larger for larger small business loans (loans between $100,000 and $1 million), up 12.3 percent over the 2003–2005 period, compared with a very small increase in micro business loans, of 1.4 percent.

In contrast to the previous year's pattern, total business borrowing by large businesses increased more than small business borrowing. Total business loans increased by 11.1 percent, from $1.51 trillion in June 2004 to $1.68 trillion in June 2005, compared with 4.6 percent over the previous one-year period. Large corporations increased their bank borrowing when they moved away from higher-rate commercial paper and as they continued to finance mergers and acquisitions.

Total small business loans (loans under $1 million) amounted to $600.8 billion in June 2005—$23.7 billion more than in the previous year (Table 2.5). The dollar value of the smallest business loans grew only slightly, by 1.9 percent, while the number increased by 24.8 percent, from 15.2 million in June 2004 to 19.0 million in June 2005. The 19.0 million loans represented outstanding micro business loans valued at $138.4 million.

As discussed in the 2004 report on *The Small Business Economy*, declines in both the dollar amount and number of loans under $100,000 over the June 2003 to June 2004 period represented mostly an accounting phenomenon.[8] Large increases in the number of these loans between June 2004 and June 2005 confirmed large banks' continued promotion of small business credit cards. Small increases in the dollar amount reflect the small account balances maintained by small business owners.

---

7   As reported in Table 2.10 of the 2005 edition of *The Small Business Economy*, the total number of banks and banking holding companies (BHCs) in June 2004 was 6,423. The 2004 total shown in Table 2.6 of this edition is 7,737, so approximately 1,300 additional institutions are included in this edition (for 2004).

8   Data used in the analysis are adjusted to reflect the consolidation of banking institutions for the years 2003, 2004, and 2005 in an effort to provide a more accurate report of lending in the banking industry. Without adjustment, statistics from the call reports for June 2004 showed an even larger decline. Continued efforts by banks to consolidate credit card accounts held by employees under the same employer contributed to the adjustments.

Table 2.5 Total Assets and the Number, Dollar Amount, and Change in Business Loans of Reporting Institutions by Loan Size, June 2003–June 2005 (dollars in billions, numbers of loans in millions)

		2003	2004	2005	Percent change		
					2003–2004	2004–2005	2003–2005
Total assets	Dollars	8,106.7	8,772.9	9,494.5	8.2	8.2	17.1
Loan Sizes							
Under <$100,000	Dollars	136.6	135.9	138.4	-0.5	1.9	1.4
	Number	17.14	15.24	19.02	-11.1	24.8	11.0
$100,000–$1 million	Dollars	411.5	441.3	462.3	7.2	4.8	12.3
	Number	1.77	1.89	1.98	6.6	5.0	12.0
Under $250,000	Dollars	245.4	249.8	255.2	1.8	2.1	4.0
	Number	18.06	16.21	20.03	-10.2	23.6	10.9
Under $1 million	Dollars	548.1	577.1	600.8	5.3	4.1	9.6
	Number	18.91	17.13	21.00	-9.4	22.6	11.1
Total business loans	Dollars	1,446.0	1,512.6	1,680.8	4.6	11.1	16.2

Source: U.S. Small Business Administration, Office of Advocacy, special tabulations of call reports (*Consolidated Reports of Condition and Income for U.S. Banks*) prepared for the Office of Advocacy by James Kolari, A&M University, College Station, Texas.

Table 2.6 Number of Lending Institutions by Asset Size, June 2003–June 2005

Institution asset size	2003	2004	2005
Under $100 million	3,705	3,529	3,345
$100 million–$500 million	3,154	3,183	3,188
$500 million–$1 billion	499	491	541
$1 billion–$10 billion	405	430	449
Over $10 billion	96	104	101
Total	7,859	7,737	7,624

Source: U.S. Small Business Administration, Office of Advocacy, special tabulations of call reports (Consolidated Reports of Condition and Income for U.S. Banks) prepared for the Office of Advocacy by James Kolari, A&M University, College Station, Texas.

The relative importance of lending institutions of different sizes in the small business loan markets continued to evolve as the lending industry continued to grow and consolidate through mergers and acquisitions. The total number of depository institutions decreased by 113, from 7,737 in June 2004 to 7,624 in June 2005 (Table 2.6). Again, most of the declines over this period were in the smallest institutions, with assets of less than $100 million.

Lending institutions with total domestic assets in excess of $10 billion numbered 101 in June 2005. These large institutions accounted for 73.8 percent of total domestic assets of these institutions, 62.4 percent of total business loans, and 43.8 percent of small business loans under $1 million (Table 2.7). While their share of assets increased between June 2003 and June 2005, their share of small business loans overall remained the same over this period. These giant institutions have been more active in the market for micro business loans (loans under $100,000) than for larger small business loans (loans of $100,000 to $1 million). They accounted for almost 50 percent of total micro business loans and 42 percent of larger small business loans as of June 2005. The large institutions' micro business loans outstanding were valued at $60.3 billion, and larger small business loans totaled $194.1 billion.

The dominance of large lending institutions in the micro business loan market is even more apparent when their participation in C&I loans is examined separately from commercial mortgages. Large institutions accounted for more than

Table 2.7 Share of Small Business Loans, Total Business Loans, and Total Assets by Asset Size of Lending Institution, 2003–2005 (percent)

Institution asset size / year	Share of small business loan dollars			Share of total business loan dollars	Share of total assets
	Under $100,000	$100,000 to $1 million	Under $1 million		
Assets under $100 million					
2005	8.5	4.1	5.1	2.1	1.8
2004	9.2	4.4	5.6	2.4	2.1
2003	10.4	4.8	6.2	2.6	2.3
Assets between $100 million and $500 million					
2005	20.0	22.0	21.5	11.2	7.4
2004	21.2	22.2	22.0	12.0	8.0
2003	21.7	22.4	22.2	11.6	8.4
Assets between $500 million and $1 billion					
2005	6.6	9.9	9.2	6.1	3.9
2004	6.4	9.1	8.5	6.0	3.9
2003	7.2	9.6	9.0	6.1	4.3
Assets between $1 billion and $10 billion					
2005	15.0	22.0	20.4	18.2	13.1
2004	13.9	20.9	19.3	18.1	13.3
2003	13.8	20.4	18.8	17.0	13.8
Assets over $10 billion					
2005	49.8	42.0	43.8	62.4	73.8
2004	49.2	43.3	44.7	61.5	72.8
2003	47.0	42.8	43.8	62.7	71.2

Source: U.S. Small Business Administration, Office of Advocacy, special tabulations of call reports (*Consolidated Reports of Condition and Income for U.S. Banks*) prepared for the Office of Advocacy by James Kolari, A&M University, College Station, Texas.

Table 2.8 Profile of Small Business Lending by Institution Size and Loan Type, June 2005

	Asset size of institution					
	Over $10 billion	$1 billion to $10 billion	$500 million to $1 billion	$100 million to $500 million	Less than $100 million	Total
Commercial and industrial loans						
Under $100,000	57.4	14.2	5.9	15.8	6.6	100
$100,000 to $1 million	48.4	20.9	8.1	18.5	4.0	100
Mortgages						
Under $100,000	22.4	18.1	9.2	35.0	15.4	100
$100,000 to $1 million	38.0	22.6	11.1	24.1	4.2	100

Source: U.S. Small Business Administration, Office of Advocacy, special tabulations of call reports (*Consolidated Reports of Condition and Income for U.S. Banks*) prepared for the Office of Advocacy by James Kolari, A&M University, College Station, Texas.

half of all C&I loans made in the smallest loan amounts (less than $100,000) in June 2005 (Table 2.8). They also accounted for roughly 48 percent of C&I loans of $100,000 to $1 million. In contrast, large banking institutions were not as active as smaller ones in the nonresidential commercial mortgage markets—they accounted for only 22.4 percent of these micro business loans (under $100,000) and only 38.0 percent of the larger small business mortgage loans of $100,000 to $1 million.

Lending by Finance Companies

Business loans from finance companies have shown large increases since 2001, up 6.8 percent compared with an average of 0.78 percent over the previous four years. The increase in 2004 was 3.2 percent. Total business receivables outstanding reached $504 billion in 2005, up from $472 billion in 2004 (Table 2.9).

Equity Borrowing in the Public Issue Markets

The U.S. public equity and initial public offerings (IPO) markets were rather active in 2005, although the volumes declined from the 2004 level. The total value of IPO offerings was down by 17 percent from a high of $48.0 billion in 2004 to $39.7 billion in 2005 (Table 2.10). IPO offerings in 2005 were

**Table 2.9 Business Loans Outstanding from Finance Companies,
December 31, 1980–December 31, 2005**

	Total receivables outstanding		Annual change in chain-type* price index for GDP (percent)
	Billions of dollars	Change	
December 31, 2005	504.2	6.8	3.5
December 31, 2004	471.9	3.2	4.2
December 31, 2003	457.4	0.5	2.7
December 31, 2002	455.3	1.9	1.6
December 31, 2001	447.0	-2.5	0.8
December 31, 2000	458.4	16.3	3.7
December 31, 1999	405.2	16.6	4.5
December 31, 1998	347.5	9.1	4.2
December 31, 1997	318.5	2.9	4.5
December 31, 1996	309.5	2.6	3.7
December 31, 1995	301.6	9.7	2.4
December 31, 1994	274.9	NA	2.5
December 31, 1993	294.6	-2.3	2.3
December 31, 1992	301.3	1.9	2.5
December 31, 1991	295.8	0.9	2.6
December 31, 1990	293.6	14.6	3.4
December 31, 1989	256.0	9.1	4.6
December 31, 1988	234.6	13.9	3.9
December 31, 1987	206.0	19.7	4.0
December 31, 1986	172.1	9.3	3.2
December 31, 1985	157.5	14.3	2.5
December 31, 1984	137.8	21.9	3.5
December 31, 1983	113.4	12.9	3.8
December 31, 1982	100.4	0	5.3
December 31, 1981	100.3	11.1	8.5
December 31, 1980	90.3		

* Changes from the fourth quarter of the year before.

NA = Not available.

Source: Board of Governors of the Federal Reserve System, *Federal Reserve Bulletin Statistical Supplement*, Table 1.52 (or 1.51), various issues; U.S. Department of Commerce, Bureau of Economic Analysis, *Business Conditions Digest*, various issues; and idem., *Survey of Current Business*, various issues.

Table 2.10 Common Stock Initial Public Offerings by All and Small Issuers, 1995–2005

		Common stock	
	Number	**Amount (millions of dollars)**	**Average size (millions of dollars)**
Offerings by all issuers			
2005	227	39,667.4	174.7
2004	249	48,003.4	192.8
2003	84	15,956.9	190.0
2002	86	25,716.3	299.0
2001	95	37,194.7	391.5
2000	385	60,782.2	157.9
1999	508	62,801.5	123.6
1998	363	37,895.1	104.0
1997	621	46,175.6	74.4
1996	850	52,190.3	61.4
1995	570	32,786.1	57.5
Offerings by issuers with assets of $25 million or less			
2005	10	570.9	57.1
2004	19	763.8	40.2
2003	6	514.4	85.7
2002	10	410.4	41.0
2001	14	477.2	34.1
2000	56	3,323.9	59.4
1999	205	10,408.9	50.8
1998	128	4,513.7	35.3
1997	241	5,746.1	23.8
1996	422	10,642.0	25.2
1995	248	5,603.1	22.6
Offerings by issuers with assets of $10 million or less			
2005	5	412.9	82.6
2004	9	378.3	42.0
2003	2	16.9	8.5
2002	4	150.9	37.7
2001	5	54.9	11.0
2000	13	407.2	31.3
1999	86	3,525.9	41.0
1998	62	2,208.0	35.6
1997	132	2,538.6	19.2
1996	268	5,474.4	20.4
1995	159	2,545.2	16.0

Note: Excludes closed-end funds. Registered offerings data from the Securities and Exchange Commission are no longer available: data provided by Securities Data Company are not as inclusive as those registered with SEC.

Source: Special tabulations prepared for the U.S. Small Business Administration, Office of Advocacy, by Thomson Financial Securities Data, May 2006.

roughly two-thirds of the volume reached in 1999, but were much higher than the 2002 and 2003 levels. The IPO market remained very selective—limited to higher quality and larger offerings. Offerings by smaller issuers with assets of $25 million or less showed insignificant increases over the 2001–2003 period.

IPO offerings by venture-backed companies mirrored the 2005 IPO market. Venture-backed companies numbered 56 and raised a total of $4.5 billion—a 40 percent decline in volume from 2004.

Venture Capital Funds

Venture capital companies' performance remained flat, and matched that of 2004. Funds invested by venture capitalists totaled roughly $22 billion in 2005, about the same amount as in 2004.[9] However, the number of deals in 2005 totaled 2,939, up from 2,399 in 2004. The venture capital industry continued a shift toward later-stage investing, a trend in place for the last five years. As a result, funding for early-stage companies dipped slightly to $4.1 billion in 2005 from $4.4 billion the previous year. Later-stage funding rose by 22 percent from $8 billion in 2004 to $9.7 billion in 2005 and accounted for 952 deals. Funds raised by venture capital firms increased to $25.2 billion.

Angel Investment

The angel investor market grew modestly in 2005, by 2.7 percent from the previous year, with total investments of $23.1 billion.[10] A total of 49,500 entrepreneurial ventures received angel funding in 2005, up 3.1 percent from 2004.[11] Active investors numbered 227,000, with an average of four or five joining forces to fund an entrepreneurial startup in 2005. Angels are the largest source of seed and startup capital; they provided $12.7 billion—55 percent of their total investment—to seed and startup companies.[12]

---

9   See Pricewaterhouse Coopers and the National Venture Capital Association, *Money Tree Report, Full-year & Q4 2005 Results*, http://www.pwcmoneytree.com/exhibits/05Q4MoneyTreeReport_FINAL.pdf.

10 Jeffrey Sohl, professor, Whittemore School of Business and Economics, and director, University of New Hampshire, Center for Venture Research.

11 Jeffrey Sohl, press release, "The Angel Investor Market in 2005: The Angel Market Exhibits Modest Growth," March 2006.

12 Investment by venture capital companies in seed and early-stage companies was $4.1 billion in 2005.

Conclusion

Overall, borrowing in the financial markets showed slight increases in 2005, primarily as a result of borrowing by household and government sectors, despite continued increases in interest rates. The FOMC steadily tightened monetary policy over the course of the year.

Large lending institutions continue to dominate in the small business and commercial and industrial lending markets. In 2005, angel investing continued to be the largest source for seed and startup capital. Equity capital markets were active but weak, and venture-backed IPOs continue to favor later-stage investing.

Appendix 2A

**Table 2A.1 Loan Rates Charged by Banks by Loan Size,
February 1998–November 2005**

	Loan size (thousands of dollars)	Fixed–rate term loans	Variable–rate loans (2–30 days)	Variable–rate loans (31–365 days)
November 2005	1–99	8.07	6.69	7.72
	100–499	7.48	6.65	7.41
	500–999	6.70	6.38	7.00
	Minimum-risk loans	4.98	4.51	4.88
August 2005	1–99	7.90	6.09	7.09
	100–499	6.89	6.23	6.52
	500–999	6.39	5.82	5.65
	Minimum-risk loans	4.24	4.12	4.15
May 2005	1–99	7.48	5.74	7.13
	100–499	6.44	5.71	6.27
	500–999	5.74	5.49	5.27
	Minimum-risk loans	3.90	3.79	3.83
February 2005	1–99	7.05	5.25	6.61
	100–499	6.38	5.08	6.09
	500–999	5.82	4.52	5.05
	Minimum-risk loans	6.58	3.24	4.42
November 2004	1–99	6.76	4.52	6.53
	100–499	6.21	4.69	5.75
	500–999	4.80	4.41	5.08
	Minimum-risk loans	4.42	2.62	2.96
August 2004	1–99	6.71	4.59	6.25
	100–499	5.81	4.06	5.06
	500–999	4.54	3.99	4.45
	Minimum-risk loans	5.52	2.07	3.33
May 2004	1–99	6.49	4.21	6.05
	100–499	5.77	3.73	4.90
	500–999	5.24	3.50	3.62
	Minimum-risk loans	5.42	1.67	2.54
February 2004	1–99	6.80	4.29	6.05
	100–499	5.31	3.76	4.58
	500–999	3.73	3.41	4.81
	Minimum-risk loans	5.50	1.59	1.81

**Table 2A.1 Loan Rates Charged by Banks by Loan Size,
February 1998–November 2005—continued**

	Loan size (thousands of dollars)	Fixed–rate term loans	Variable–rate loans (2–30 days)	Variable–rate loans (31–365 days)
November 2003	1–99	6.53	4.27	6.11
	100–499	5.68	3.79	5.03
	500–999	4.99	3.22	3.94
	Minimum-risk loans	5.50	1.59	1.81
August 2003	1–99	6.68	4.15	6.34
	100–499	6.01	3.49	4.74
	500–999	5.67	3.69	3.97
	Minimum-risk loans	4.85	1.58	2.33
May 2003	1–99	6.84	4.78	6.49
	100–499	6.13	3.92	5.56
	500–999	5.83	3.34	4.21
	Minimum-risk loans	5.62	1.87	2.41
February 2003	1–99	6.80	4.29	6.05
	100–499	5.31	3.76	4.58
	500–999	3.73	3.41	4.81
	Minimum-risk loans	4.08	2.64	2.40
November 2002	1–99	7.34	5.14	7.11
	100–499	6.21	4.42	5.51
	500–999	5.99	3.93	4.91
	Minimum-risk loans	2.84	3.85	3.19
August 2002	1–99	7.75	5.05	7.32
	100–499	6.51	4.32	5.14
	500–999	5.92	3.69	3.88
	Minimum-risk loans	6.94	3.74	2.58
May 2002	1–99	7.75	5.06	7.09
	100–499	6.81	4.46	6.08
	500–999	6.39	3.69	5.13
	Minimum-risk loans	4.58	3.05	2.43
February 2002	1–99	7.91	5.26	7.28
	100–499	6.57	4.31	5.89
	500–999	6.41	3.73	4.45
	Minimum-risk loans	7.11	2.23	2.70

Table 2A.1 Loan Rates Charged by Banks by Loan Size, February 1998–November 2005—continued

	Loan size (thousands of dollars)	Fixed–rate term loans	Variable–rate loans (2–30 days)	Variable–rate loans (31–365 days)
November 2001	1–99	7.97	5.53	7.59
	100–499	6.83	4.79	6.23
	500–999	6.30	4.29	4.56
	Minimum-risk loans	5.71	2.59	3.20
August 2001	1–99	8.73	7.15	8.60
	100–499	7.72	6.46	7.29
	500–999	6.63	6.81	6.06
	Minimum-risk loans	7.47	4.34	4.83
May 2001	1–99	9.12	7.91	8.87
	100–499	8.34	7.25	8.06
	500–999	7.40	6.55	6.24
	Minimum-risk loans	7.23	5.20	5.24
February 2001	1–99	9.84	9.10	9.89
	100–499	8.88	8.24	9.11
	500–999	8.08	7.51	7.75
	Minimum-risk loans	8.13	6.18	6.63
November 2000	1–99	10.33	9.95	10.18
	100–499	9.96	9.24	9.77
	500–999	8.66	8.63	8.68
	Minimum-risk loans	9.25	7.12	7.82
August 2000	1–99	10.44	9.98	10.18
	100–499	9.70	9.45	9.32
	500–999	8.87	9.31	8.52
	Minimum-risk loans	9.23	7.07	7.56
May 2000	1–99	10.01	9.66	9.68
	100–499	9.24	9.04	8.90
	500–999	8.77	8.68	8.24
	Minimum-risk loans	7.90	7.16	7.17
February 2000	1–99	9.64	9.31	9.41
	100–499	8.81	8.44	8.70
	500–999	9.24	7.88	7.88
	Minimum-risk loans	7.80	6.88	7.70

**Table 2A.1 Loan Rates Charged by Banks by Loan Size,
February 1998–November 2005—continued**

	Loan size (thousands of dollars)	Fixed–rate term loans	Variable–rate loans (2–30 days)	Variable–rate loans (31–365 days)
November 1999	1–99	9.44	8.90	9.32
	100–499	8.84	8.03	8.38
	500–999	8.41	7.50	7.50
	Minimum-risk loans	6.51	6.19	7.01
August 1999	1–99	9.19	8.79	9.15
	100–499	8.71	7.91	8.00
	500–999	7.86	7.55	7.55
	Minimum-risk loans	6.74	5.76	6.48
May 1999	1–99	8.90	8.36	9.03
	100–499	8.28	7.70	8.23
	500–999	7.62	7.20	7.77
	Minimum-risk loans	6.33	5.26	5.91
February 1999	1–99	8.99	8.77	9.05
	100–499	8.41	7.68	8.12
	500–999	7.90	6.90	6.97
	Minimum-risk loans	5.62	6.12	5.83
November 1998	1–99	9.45	9.15	9.21
	100–499	8.51	8.01	8.28
	500–999	7.81	7.10	7.04
	Minimum-risk loans	5.90	5.69	6.16
August 1998	1–99	9.62	9.62	9.60
	100–499	8.29	8.66	8.29
	500–999	7.97	7.82	7.28
	Minimum-risk loans	6.77	6.25	7.06
May 1998	1–99	9.88	9.81	9.76
	100–499	8.77	8.78	8.58
	500–999	8.57	7.72	7.64
	Minimum-risk loans	7.77	6.27	6.20
February 1998	1–99	9.81	9.83	9.77
	100–499	8.92	8.44	8.72
	500–999	8.08	7.47	7.78
	Minimum-risk loans	8.96	5.97	6.38

Source: Board of Governors of the Federal Reserve System. *Survey of Terms of Lending,* Statistical Release E.2, various issues, and special tabulations prepared by the Federal Reserve Board for the U.S. Small Business Administration, Office of Advocacy.

3 FEDERAL PROCUREMENT *from* SMALL FIRMS

Synopsis

In 2002, President George W. Bush introduced his Small Business Agenda, which called for new efforts to create an environment in which small firms could flourish, among them ensuring that U.S. government contracts are open to all small businesses that can supply the government's needs. Since then, a number of efforts have been ongoing, including new guidance for large businesses subcontracting to small firms, improvements in small business size standards, clarification of the "novation" regulations relating to small businesses acquired by larger ones, initiatives toward more transparency in federal procurement data, and steps to reduce the contract bundling that can leave small firms out of the competition. In FY 2005, the SBA's Office of Advocacy was involved in a number of efforts to work with individual agencies and small firms to help move the federal procurement markets further along the path of increased small business participation.

Small businesses were awarded more than $79.6 billion in direct prime contract awards in fiscal year 2005, according to statistics from the Federal Procurement Data System-Next Generation (FPDS–NG). Based on that database, the SBA's Office of Government Contracting reported that the government had again exceeded its small business prime contract goal of 23 percent, awarding small firms 25.4 percent of the $314 billion in government prime contract dollars available for small business competition.

The Office of Advocacy continued to build on research efforts conducted in previous years as part of the effort to improve the climate for small business contracting. Advocacy procurement studies have focused on topics such as electronic procurement, contracting with veteran-owned businesses, the categorization/coding of businesses for procurement purposes, and contract bundling.

Federal Procurement Policy Initiatives in 2005

In his 2002 Small Business Agenda, President Bush directed the government to improve small business access to government contracts, specifically to:

- Ensure that government contracts are open to all small businesses that can supply the government's needs,
- Avoid unnecessary contract bundling, and
- Streamline the appeals process for small businesses that contract with the federal government.[1]

In FY 2005, the SBA's Office of Advocacy participated in a number of efforts to address concerns with respect to procurement from small firms by specific federal agencies and to broaden opportunities for small businesses in the federal procurement marketplace; for example:

- Advocacy was asked in February 2005 to participate in a staff supportive role with the SBA in an Acquisition Advisory Panel pursuant to the Services Acquisition Reform Act. The purpose of the panel was to review laws and regulations regarding the use of commercial practices, performance-based contracting, the performance of acquisition functions across agency lines of responsibility, and the use of government-wide contracts.
- In March, Advocacy joined the SBA in a letter to the House Appropriations Committee urging Congress not to renew a one-year provision that prohibited the Department of Defense (DOD), in a public-private A-76 competition, from giving an advantage to a private offeror that provides less comprehensive health care coverage than the federal government. The provision will have the unintended consequence of limiting small businesses' ability to compete, since small businesses often cannot afford the level of health care coverage provided to federal employees. Data show that small firms won about two-thirds of A-76 competitions between 1995 and 2004.[2]

---

1   See http:// www.whitehouse.gov/infocus/smallbusiness.

2   See http://www.sba.gov/advo/laws/comments/lewis05_0316.html.

- Advocacy provided comments in April 2005 to the Senate Committee on Small Business and Entrepreneurship concerning a subcontracting provision in the Iraq/Afghanistan Emergency Supplemental Appropriations Act for 2005. In part as a result of these and other concerns, the bill was modified to require Advocacy to be part of a Department of Energy (DOE) and SBA team to study DOE management and operating (M&O) contracts to encourage new M&O opportunities for small businesses and increase their role in prime contracting.[3]

- Advocacy worked with the DOD and the Office of Management and Budget (OMB) to address concerns regarding the impact of requiring small businesses to place Radio Frequency Identification Tags (RFID) for delivery of materiel. DOD performed a detailed cost-benefit analysis on the regulation's impact on small businesses and authorized extensive training for its small business suppliers on RFID technology. DOD will require that passive tags be applied to cases and pallets and to individual high-value items.

In the federal procurement arena, small businesses continued to make progress toward a more level playing field, as efforts were under way to increase small business subcontracting, reduce contract bundling, increase transparency in small business contracting data, and improve small business access to federal procurement opportunities.

Subcontracting

Regulations promulgated with small business support in 2004 provided guidance to "other than small" contractors—large businesses subcontracting with small businesses.[4] The final rule also authorized federal agencies to evaluate a contractor's past performance in meeting subcontracting goals as a source selection factor in placing orders through the Federal Supply Schedules, government-wide agency schedules, and multiple award contracts. These changes set the stage for the new Electronic Subcontracting Reporting System (ESRS), which became operational in October 2005. ESRS is a part of the President's

---

3 See http://www.sba.gov/advo/laws/comments/snowe05_0413.pdf.

4 See Small Business Government Contracting Programs; Subcontracting (RIN: 3245–AF12) published in the *Federal Register*, December 20, 2004, 69 *Federal Register* 75820.

Management Agenda for Expanding Electronic Government to provide greater transparency in federal procurement subcontracting data.

Contract Bundling

The practice of bundling contracts—combining two or more contracts into a large single agreement—most often pushes small firms out of the competition. An Office of Advocacy study found that contract bundling was at a ten-year high in 2001.[5] President Bush's 2002 Small Business Agenda requested agencies to stop the unnecessary bundling of contracts and required the OMB's Office of Federal Procurement Policy (OFPP) to develop a detailed plan to implement this objective.[6] The SBA and OMB/OFPP initiated regulatory action. The final regulation was published in the *Federal Register* on October 20, 2003.[7] In May 2004 the Government Accountability Office (GAO) published a report, *Contract Management: Impact of Strategy to Mitigate Effects of Contract Bundling*, which found that agency bundling data in the Federal Procurement Data System were miscoded because of confusion about the statutory definition of contract bundling, inadequate verification of information, and ineffective controls in the FPDS reporting process. Much of the work done by Advocacy in the area of contract bundling in FY 2005 was with specific agencies and specific small businesses to address individual case situations.

Small Business Procurement Data

An FY 2005 Advocacy-sponsored study published in December 2004, *Analysis of Type of Business Coding for the Top 1,000 Contractors Receiving Small Business Awards in FY 2002*, found coding problems with small business contracts.[8] The coding problems pertained to a number of companies found to be other than small among 1,000 businesses coded as small in the FY 2002 procurement data. The coding problems could have resulted from errors in the companies' size identification or from companies growing to—or having been acquired by—larger businesses during the course of the contract.

---

5   See http://www.sba.gov/advo/research/rs221tot.pdf.

6   The OMB/OFPP report is available at http://www.acqnet.gov.

7   67 *Federal Register* 47244, January 31, 2003, and 68 *Federal Register* 60015, October 20, 2003.

8   The report is available at http://www.sba.gov/advo/research/rs246tot.pdf.

Efforts to provide greater transparency in federal procurement data continue. In 2004, the General Services Administration and the OMB/OFPP introduced the fourth generation of the FPDS–NG. Work is ongoing to correct problems in the quality, timeliness, and accuracy of the data under the new system. The new FPDS–NG is designed to reduce the potential for human error in transferring data from the contractor to the contracting agency to the FPDS. When the system is fully operational, small business stakeholders will be able to retrieve federal small business procurement numbers in real time and make policy and marketing decisions more quickly and accurately.[9]

In April 2005, SBA continued to provide more transparency in counting small businesses by making changes to the Central Contractor Registration (CCR) process, using its Small Business Logic program to determine the small business status of companies registered in the CCR. This is expected to improve accuracy and reduce previously required data input. Companies are no longer required to populate the SBA-certified small disadvantaged business, SBA-certified 8(a), and SBA-certified HUBZone business type fields. The SBA will provide accurate data regarding the firms it has certified as HUBZone, 8(a), and small disadvantaged business, and will validate, for each North American Industry Classification System (NAICS) code listed in a trading partner profile, the small business and emerging small business status of the firm based on the employee and revenue data it provided to CCR.[10]

These and other regulatory changes in proposal stages are significant initiatives to improve the process of providing more transparency in counting small business contract awards.

Federal Contracting with Small Firms in FY 2005

In FY 2005, federal government awards exceeded those in the previous banner year of FY 2004, when the federal government awarded a total of $299.9 billion in contracts for the purchase of goods that were available for small business participation (Table 3.1). Of the $314 billion total in FY 2005, small businesses were the recipients of more than $79.6 billion in direct prime

---

9   See Amendment 2004–04, General Services Acquisition Regulations (GSAR) Case 2004–G509, Access to the Federal Procurement Data System, December 28, 2004.

10   Information on CCR is available at http://www.ccr.gov/.

Table 3.1 Total Federal Prime Contract Actions, FY 2004–FY 2005

Fiscal year	Thousands of dollars		Small business Share (percent)
	Total	Small business	
2005	314,002,424	79,624,883	25.35
2004	299,886,098	69,228,771	23.09

Note: In 2004, GSA and OMB/OFPP introduced the fourth generation of the FPDS. The FPDS–NG data shown here, unless otherwise noted, reflect all contract actions available for small business competition (excluding some categories), not just those over $25,000.

Source: General Services Administration, Federal Procurement Data System.

contract dollars, up from $69.2 billion in FY 2004, according to FPDS–NG data.[11] The small business share of the dollars available for small business competition again exceeded 23 percent, reaching 25.36 percent, following achievement of 23.09 percent in FY 2004, according to the database.

In FY 2003, small businesses were awarded approximately $45.5 billion in subcontracts from prime contractors. Subcontracting statistics for FY 2004 are not available, but it is estimated, based on the FY 2003 level of subcontracting, that small businesses were awarded nearly $50 billion. Based on previous trends, the estimate for small business subcontracting dollars in FY 2005 is about $60 billion, for a total of some $140 billion in small business prime contract and subcontracting dollars in FY 2005.

Sources of Small Business Awards by Department/Agency

The largest share of all federal purchases in contracts has historically come from the DOD (Tables 3.2-3.4). DOD's share of overall procurement dollars

---

11 The following disclaimers to the FY 2005 Small Business Goaling Report appear at the Small Business Administration's Office of Government Contracting website (http://www.sba.gov/GC/goals/index05.html). "Fiscal Year 2005 is the second year the FPDS–NG has produced the Small Business Goaling Report. There are three issues identified in this year's report. One is government-wide; the other two are agency-specific. Government-wide: 'The FY 2005 Small Business Goaling Report does not provide 8(a) credit for delivery orders against Indefinite Delivery Vehicles (IDVs). This issue will be fixed in time for the FY 2006 report.' USAID [U.S. Agency for International Development] specific: 'USAID is still in the process of entering their FY05 data into FPDS–NG; therefore this report is not a complete reflection of their small business achievement. USAID is working diligently to enter their data, and expect to be finished by the end of this summer.' DOD specific: 'The number of actions reported is fewer than it should be because DOD consolidates certain actions into single contract reports. This does not affect the dollar amount or small business percentages.'"

Table 3.2 Procurement Dollars in Contract Actions over $25,000 by Major Agency Source, FY 1984–FY 2003, and in Total, FY 2004–FY 2005

Fiscal year	Total (thousands of dollars)	Percent of total			
		DOD	DOE	NASA	Other
2005*	314,002,424	69.7	7.3	3.9	19.1
2004*	299,886,098	70.3	7.3	4.2	18.2
2003	292,319,145	67.9	7.2	4.0	20.9
2002	258,125,273	65.1	7.4	4.5	23.1
2001	248,985,613	58.2	7.5	4.5	29.8
2000	207,401,363	64.4	8.2	5.3	22.2
1999	188,846,760	66.4	8.4	5.8	19.4
1998	184,178,721	64.1	8.2	5.9	21.8
1997	179,227,203	65.4	8.8	6.2	19.5
1996	183,489,567	66.5	8.7	6.2	18.7
1995	185,119,992	64.3	9.1	6.3	20.2
1994	181,500,339	65.4	9.9	6.3	18.4
1993	184,426,948	66.7	10.0	6.4	16.8
1992	183,081,207	66.3	10.1	6.6	16.9
1991	193,550,425	70.2	9.5	6.1	14.2
1990	179,286,902	72.0	9.7	6.4	11.9
1989	172,612,189	75.0	8.8	5.7	10.6
1988	176,544,042	76.9	8.2	4.9	10.0
1987	181,750,326	78.6	7.7	4.2	9.5
1986	183,681,389	79.6	7.3	4.0	9.0
1985	188,186,597	80.0	7.7	4.0	8.3
1984	168,100,611	79.3	7.9	4.0	9.0

* In 2004, the General Services Administration and the Office of Federal Procurement Policy (OMB/OFPP) introduced the fourth generation of the FPDS. The FPDS–NG data shown here for FY 2004 and FY 2005 reflect all contract actions available for small business competition (excluding some categories) not just those over $25,000. The figures are not strictly comparable with those shown for previous years.

Note: Percentages shown are the agencies' percentages of total contract dollars, not just small business contract dollars. See Table 3.3 for the agencies' share of dollars in small business contracts.

Source: General Services Administration, Federal Procurement Data System.

Table 3.3 Distribution of Small Business Share of Dollars in Contract Actions by Procuring Agency Source, FY 2004 and FY 2005

	Total small business		Small business distribution (percent)		Rank	
	FY 2005	FY 2004	FY 2005	FY 2004	FY 2005	FY 2004
Total, all agencies	79,624,883,437	69,228,771,571	100.0	100.00		
Agency for International Development (1152, 7200)	8,796,457	51,944,280	0.01	0.08	31	18
Corporation for National and Community Service	13,952,752	—	0.02	—	29	—
Commodity Futures Trading Commission	3,280,930	3,537,943	0.00	0.01	37	34
Consumer Product Safety Commission	4,339,008	5,253,688	0.01	0.01	34	32
Department of Agriculture	1,955,655,108	1,957,587,894	2.46	2.83	5	5
Department of Commerce	985,368,031	794,439,680	1.23	1.15	10	12
Department of Defense	53,807,026,057	46,928,476,346	67.58	67.79	1	1
Department of Education	115,895,340	102,648,093	0.15	0.15	20	20
Department of Energy	939,320,963	918,251,981	1.18	1.32	11	11
Department of Health and Human Services	3,355,609,490	2,339,000,990	4.21	3.38	3	3
Department of Homeland Security	4,496,333,612	1,706,076,224	5.65	2.46	2	7
Department of Housing and Urban Development	681,735,427	686,939,213	0.86	0.99	14	14
Department of the Interior	1,490,829,122	1,240,593,866	1.87	1.79	8	9
Department of Justice	1,442,746,604	1,271,135,195	1.81	1.84	9	8
Department of Labor	557,101,909	587,813,760	0.70	0.85	16	16
Department of State	745,134,130	946,842,559	0.94	1.37	12	10
Department of the Treasury	718,026,760	714,322,403	0.90	1.03	13	13
Department of Transportation	665,685,246	677,934,185	0.84	0.98	15	15
Department of Veterans Affairs	2,788,525,148	2,263,843,279	3.50	3.27	4	4
Environmental Protection Agency	495,796,617	398,490,413	0.62	0.57	17	17
Equal Employment Opportunity Commission	21,393,992	13,726,398	0.03	0.02	28	30
Executive Office of the President	32,026,126	28,005,947	0.04	0.04	27	26

Agency						
Federal Election Commission	1,831,526	2,127,792	0.00	0.00	42	36
Federal Emergency Management Agency	242,544,990	17,619,592	0.30	0.03	19	29
Federal Maritime Commission	451,236	472,359	0.00	0.00	44	42
Federal Trade Commission	1,928,618	38,918	0.00	0.00	41	43
General Services Administration	1,518,062,263	3,161,604,640	1.91	4.57	7	2
International Trade Commission	3,319,351	4,992,441	0.00	0.01	36	33
Millennium Challenge Corporation	2,862,443	—	0.00	—	38	—
National Aeronautics and Space Administration	1,770,494,782	1,804,891,570	2.22	2.61	6	6
National Archives and Records Administration	2,145,942	40,454,930	0.00	0.06	40	23
National Foundation on the Arts and Humanities	555,148	1,664,093	0.00	0.00	43	38
National Labor Relations Board	5,909,354	1,074,647	0.01	0.00	33	40
National Mediation Board	103,816	—	0.00	—	45	—
National Science Foundation	35,219,784	22,343,855	0.04	0.03	25	28
National Transportation Safety Board	2,383,394	1,208,490	0.00	0.00	39	39
Nuclear Regulatory Commission	39,335,752	34,851,834	0.05	0.05	24	24
Office of Personnel Management	80,222,541	78,325,112	0.10	0.11	21	21
Peace Corps	8,884,590	5,950,269	0.01	0.01	30	31
Railroad Retirement Board	3,718,390	2,432,260	0.00	0.00	35	35
Securities and Exchange Commission	41,812,447	59,192,592	0.05	0.09	23	22
Small Business Administration	34,197,652	26,801,613	0.04	0.04	26	27
Smithsonian Institution	56,265,515	28,545,265	0.07	0.04	22	25
Social Security Administration	310,705,161	227,786,096	0.39	0.33	18	19
Trade and Development Agency	6,105,295	829,702	0.01	0.00	32	41
U.S. Information Agency	37,390	1,708,616	0.00	0.00	46	37

Note: The FPDS-NG data shown here reflect all contract actions available for small business competition (excluding some categories), not just those over $25,000. The figures for FY 2004 and 2005 are not strictly comparable with those for previous years.

Source: General Services Administration, Federal Procurement Data System, and Global Computer Enterprises, Inc...

Table 3.4 Small Business Share of Dollars by Top 25 Major Procuring Agencies, Fiscal Years 2004 and 2005

Agency	Contract dollars (thousands)				Small firm share (percent)		Share rank	
	FY 2005		FY 2004		FY 2005	FY 2004	FY 2005	FY 2004
	Total	Small business	Total	Small business				
Total	314,002,424	79,624,883	299,886,098	69,228,772	25.36	23.09		
Department of Defense	218,970,654	53,807,026	210,742,333	46,928,476	24.57	22.27	22	17
Department of Homeland Security	9,642,620	4,496,334	4,435,595	1,706,076	46.63	38.46	5	9
Department of Health and Human Services	9,210,072	3,355,609	7,892,963	2,339,001	36.43	29.63	12	13
Department of Veterans Affairs	9,800,420	2,788,525	8,472,953	2,263,843	28.45	26.71	20	16
Department of Agriculture	3,948,159	1,955,655	3,996,408	1,957,588	49.53	48.98	4	5
National Aeronautics and Space Administration	12,259,931	1,770,495	12,456,469	1,804,892	14.44	14.49	23	20
General Services Administration	4,342,817	1,518,062	7,470,718	3,161,604	34.96	42.32	15	8
Department of the Interior	2,698,843	1,490,829	2,323,773	1,240,594	55.24	53.39	2	2
Department of Justice	4,165,035	1,442,747	3,876,756	1,271,135	34.64	32.79	16	11
Department of Commerce	1,896,181	985,368	1,491,763	794,440	51.97	53.26	3	3
Department of Energy	22,855,579	939,321	21,987,386	918,252	4.11	4.18	25	23
Department of State	2,109,253	745,134	1,871,751	946,843	35.33	50.59	14	4

Agency								
Department of the Treasury	1,946,821	718,027	2,450,891	714,322	36.88	29.15	9	15
Department of Housing and Urban Development	1,072,524	681,735	946,938	686,939	63.56	72.54	1	1
Department of Transportation	1,493,316	665,685	1,572,426	677,934	44.58	43.11	7	7
Department of Labor	1,653,649	557,102	1,681,304	587,814	33.69	34.96	19	10
Environmental Protection Agency	1,468,353	495,797	1,352,085	398,490	33.77	29.47	18	14
Social Security Administration	864,844	310,705	523,150	227,786	35.93	43.54	13	6
Federal Emergency Management Agency	527,391	242,545	23,487	17,620	45.99	75.01	6	*
Department of Education	1,258,848	115,895	1,523,043	102,648	9.20	6.74	24	22
Office of Personnel Management	234,950	80,223	469,639	78,325	34.14	16.68	17	19
Smithsonian Institution	213,070	56,266	140,780	28,545	26.40	20.28	21	18
Securities and Exchange Commission	93,162	41,812	86,102	59,193	44.88	68.74	8	*
Nuclear Regulatory Commission	107,197	39,336	94,902	34,852	36.70	36.72	10	*
National Science Foundation	96,500	35,220	48,206	22,344	36.50	46.35	11	*

* Not ranked in 2005 report.

Note: The FPDS–NG data shown here reflect all contract actions available for small business competition (excluding some categories), not just those over $25,000. The figures are not strictly comparable with figures for previous years. All agencies are represented in the total dollars; the organizations listed are those agencies that awarded at least $35 million to small firms in FY 2005.

Source: General Services Administration, Federal Procurement Data System, and Global Computer Enterprises, Inc.

reached about 70 percent in both FY 2004 and FY 2005 (Table 3.2). In FY 2005, the DOD awarded $53.8 billion—24.57 percent—of its available dollars to small businesses, according to the FPDS–NG data (Table 3.4). Of the $79.6 billion awarded to small businesses, 67.6 percent were in DOD awards (Table 3.3). DOD's small business dollars seem to increase when its acquisition strategy shifts from major weapons systems as occurred in FY 2005.

The next largest source of federal contracting dollar awards to small businesses was the Department of Homeland Security, which awarded $4.5 billion or 46.63 percent of its dollars to small businesses in FY 2005. Third was the Department of Health and Human Services, which awarded $3.36 billion or 36.43 percent to small businesses. The Department of Housing and Urban Development sent the largest share of its contracting dollars to small firms— 63.6 percent of its $1.07 billion total, or $681.7 million (Table 3.4).

Small Business Innovation Research

The Small Business Innovation Development Act requires the federal departments and agencies with the largest extramural research and development (R&D) budgets to award a portion of their R&D funds to small businesses. Ten government agencies with extramural research and development obligations over $100 million initially participated in this program: the Departments of Agriculture, Commerce, Defense, Education, Energy, Health and Human Services, and Transportation, and the Environmental Protection Agency, the National Aeronautics and Space Administration, and the National Science Foundation. A total of about $17.9 billion has been awarded to small businesses over the 23 years of the Small Business Innovation Research (SBIR) program (Table 3.5).[12] Participating agencies received a total of 30,183 proposals in FY 2005 and made 6,171 awards totaling $1.87 billion.

The SBIR program continues to be successful not only for small businesses and participating federal agencies, but for the American public, which benefits from the new products and services developed. For example, fast flow pre-filter cartridges have 20 times greater capacity than conventional cartridges and offer extraordinary filtration efficiency and dirt holding capability. Broadband Acoustic Doppler Current Profiler (ADCP) products—ocean research instruments—are widely used by the DOD to measure physical properties of the

---

12   FY 2004 figures for the Small Business Innovation Research program are preliminary.

Table 3.5 Small Business Innovation Research Program, FY 1983–FY 2005

Fiscal year	Phase I Number of proposals	Phase I Number of awards	Phase II Number of proposals	Phase II Number of awards	Total awards (millions of dollars)
Total	435,330	64,510	51,452	24,743	17,985.84
2005*	*26,003	*4,300	*4,180	*1,871	*1,865.90
2004	30,766	4,638	3,604	2,013	1,867.44
2003	27,992	4,465	3,267	1,759	1,670.10
2002	22,340	4,243	2,914	1,577	1,434.80
2001	16,666	3,215	2,566	1,533	1,294.40
2000	17,641	3,172	2,533	1,335	1,190.20
1999	19,016	3,334	2,476	1,256	1,096.50
1998	18,775	3,022	2,480	1,320	1,100.00
1997	19,585	3,371	2,420	1,404	1,066.70
1996	18,378	2,841	2,678	1,191	916.3
1995	20,185	3,085	2,856	1,263	981.7
1994	25,588	3,102	2,244	928	717.6
1993	23,640	2,898	2,532	1,141	698
1992	19,579	2,559	2,311	916	508.4
1991	20,920	2,553	1,734	788	483.1
1990	20,957	2,346	2,019	837	460.7
1989	17,233	2,137	1,776	749	431.9
1988	17,039	2,013	1,899	711	389.1
1987	14,723	2,189	2,390	768	350.5
1986	12,449	1,945	1,112	564	297.9
1985	9,086	1,397	765	407	199.1
1984	7,955	999	559	338	108.4
1983	8,814	686	127	74	44.5

* Preliminary estimates.

Note: Phase I evaluates the scientific and technical merit and feasibility of an idea. Phase II expands on the results and further pursues the development of Phase I. Phase III commercializes the results of Phase II and requires the use of private or non-SBIR federal funding. The Phase II proposals and awards in FY 1983 were pursuant to predecessor programs that qualified as SBIR funding.

Source: U.S. Small Business Administration, Office of Innovation, Research, and Technology (annual reports for FY 1983–FY 2005).

Table 3.6 Prime Contract Awards by Recipient Category (billions of dollars)

	FY 2005		FY 2004	
	Dollars	Percent	Dollars	Percent
Total to all businesses	314.00	100.00	299.89	100.00
Small businesses	79.62	25.35	69.23	23.08
Small disadvantaged businesses (SDBs)	21.71	6.91	18.54	6.11
8(a) businesses	10.46	3.33	8.44	2.81
Non-8(a) SDBs	11.25	3.58	10.09	3.30
HUBZone businesses	6.10	1.94	4.78	1.58
Women-owned small businesses	10.49	3.34	9.09	3.03
Service-disabled veteran-owned small businesses	1.89	0.60	1.15	0.39

Source: General Services Administration, Federal Procurement Data System.

ocean in regions of interest to the Navy. Advanced magnetometers are for use in a hand-held electronic compass that has also now become a consumer product, the Wayfinder™ Electronic Automobile Compass.[13]

Procurement from Minority- and Women-owned Businesses

The participation of small women- and minority-owned businesses in the federal procurement marketplace continues to grow (Tables 3.6–3.8). Small women-owned businesses' share of federal procurement dollars grew from 3.03 percent in FY 2004 to 3.34 percent in FY 2005. (Table 3.6). Small disadvantaged businesses achieved their 5 percent goal, reaching 6.91 percent or $21.71 billion. Participants in the SBA 8(a) program were awarded 3.33 percent of the total FY 2005 procurement dollars or $10.5 billion in contracts.

Service-disabled veteran business owners are now among the socioeconomic groups monitored in the federal procurement marketplace. Public Law 106-50 established a statutory goal of 3 percent of all prime and subcontracting dollars to be awarded to service-disabled veterans. Public Law 108-183 fortified this requirement by providing the contracting officer with authority to sole-source and restrict bidding on contracts to serviced-disabled veteran-owned small businesses. In FY 2001 they were awarded 0.25 percent of direct federal

---

13 More extensive listings of SBIR accomplishments may be seen at these web sites: DOD, http://www.dodsbir.net/SuccessStories/default.htm; National Aeronautics and Space Administration, http://sbir.nasa.gov/SBIR/successes/techcon.html; Health and Human Services (National Institutes of Health), http://grants1.nih.gov/grants/funding/sbir_successes/sbir_successes.htm.

Table 3.7 Annual Change in the Dollar Volume of Contract Actions Over $25,000 Awarded to Small, Women-Owned, and Minority-Owned Businesses, FY 1980–FY 2003 and in Total, FY 2004–FY 2005* (thousands of dollars)

	Total, all business			Small business			Women-owned business			Minority-owned business		
	Total	Change from prior year		Total	Change from prior year		Total	Change from prior year		Total	Change from prior year	
	(Thousands of dollars)	Thousands of dollars	Per-cent	(Thousands of dollars)	Thousands of dollars	Per-cent	(Thousands of dollars)	Thousands of dollars	Per-cent	(Thousands of dollars)	Thousands of dollars	Per-cent
2005*	314,002,424	14,116,144	4.7	79,624,883	11,396,111	16.7	10,494,302	1,402,383	15.4	21,715,093	3,177,081	17.1
2004*	299,886,098	*	*	68,228,772	*	*	9,091,919	*	*	18,538,012	*	*
2003	292,319,145	47,740,664	19.5	59,813,330	12,587,280	26.7	8,212,453	1,534,833	23.0	18,903,087	3,595,020	23.5
2002	244,578,481	21,476,465	9.6	47,226,050	461,545	9.9	6,677,620	-3,595	—	15,308,067	754,369	5.2
2001	223,338,280	17,490,979	8.5	46,764,505	7,983,057	20.6	6,681,215	2,226,212	50.0	14,553,698	1,966,900	15.6
2000	205,847,301	20,722,610	11.2	38,781,448	3,036,256	8.5	4,455,003	427,264	10.6	12,586,798	727,575	5.8
1999	185,124,691	1,013,686	0.6	35,745,192	1,485,753	4.3	4,027,739	485,838	13.7	11,859,223	414,203	3.6
1998	184,111,005	5,186,111	2.8	34,259,439	-7,013,742	-17.0	3,541,901	-48,406	-1.3	11,445,020	312,398	2.8
1997	178,924,894	-4,558,799	-2.5	41,273,181	8,082,760	24.4	3,590,307	621,845	20.9	11,132,622	491,851	4.6
1996	183,483,693	-1,636,299	-0.9	33,190,421	1,383,158	4.3	2,968,462	148,214	5.3	10,640,771	121,302	1.2
1995	185,119,992	3,619,653	2.0	31,807,263	3,384,230	11.9	2,820,248	508,700	22.0	10,519,469	1,459,981	16.1
1994	181,500,339	-2,926,609	-1.6	28,423,033	475,592	1.7	2,311,548	262,828	12.8	9,059,488	255,468	2.9
1993	184,426,948	1,345,741	0.7	27,947,441	-282,308	-1.0	2,048,720	56,155	2.8	8,804,020	1,007,913	12.9
1992	183,081,207	-10,469,218	-5.4	28,229,749	-617,609	-2.1	1,992,565	227,399	12.9	7,796,107	1,309,818	20.2
1991	193,550,425	14,263,523	8.0	28,847,358	3,445,732	13.6	1,765,166	287,272	19.4	6,486,289	796,229	14.0
1990	179,286,902	6,674,713	3.8	25,401,626	1,685,455	7.1	1,477,894	74,955	5.3	5,690,060	356,172	6.7

Table 3.7 Annual Change in the Dollar Volume of Contract Actions Over $25,000 Awarded to Small, Women-Owned, and Minority-Owned Businesses, FY 1980–FY 2003 and in Total, FY 2004–FY 2005* (thousands of dollars)—continued

| | Total, all business | | | Small business | | | Women-owned business | | | Minority-owned business | | |
| | Total | Change from prior year | | Total | Change from prior year | | Total | Change from prior year | | Total | Change from prior year | |
	(Thousands of dollars)	Thousands of dollars	Percent	(Thousands of dollars)	Thousands of dollars	Percent	(Thousands of dollars)	Thousands of dollars	Percent	(Thousands of dollars)	Thousands of dollars	Percent
1989	172,612,189	-3,931,853	-2.2	23,716,171	-1,955,147	-7.8	1,402,939	75,215	5.7	5,333,888	141,382	2.7
1988	176,544,042	-5,206,284	-2.9	25,671,318	-2,256,401	-8.1	1,327,724	74,839	6.0	5,192,506	343,381	7.1
1987	181,750,326	-1,931,063	-1.1	27,927,719	-852,373	-3.0	1,252,885	56,034	4.7	4,849,125	563,200	13.1
1986	183,681,389	-4,505,240	-2.4	28,780,092	2,077,397	7.8	1,196,851	102,643	9.4	4,285,925	401,286	10.3
1985	187,985,466	20,085,235	11.9	26,702,695	1,196,672	4.7	1,094,208	238,077	27.8	3,884,639	-119,500	-3.0
1984	167,933,486	12,513,288	8.0	25,506,023	3,425,999	15.5	856,131	244,755	40.0	4,004,139	817,048	25.6
1983	155,588,106	3,190,222	2.1	22,080,024	-1,478,539	-6.3	611,376	60,775	11.0	3,187,091	328,180	11.5
1982	152,397,884	23,533,140	18.3	23,558,563	3,489,774	17.4	550,601	-534,772	-49.3	2,858,911	223,903	8.5
1981	128,864,744	27,971,359	27.7	20,068,789	4,742,668	30.9	1,085,373	297,844	37.8	2,635,008	813,087	44.6
1980	100,893,385			15,326,121			787,529			1,821,921		

— Less than 0.05 percent.

* For FY 2004 and subsequent years, the new FPDS–NG data reflect all contract actions available for small business competition (excluding some categories), not just those over $25,000. The figures are not strictly comparable with those shown for previous years; therefore, the FY 2003–FY 2004 change is not shown.

Source: Federal Procurement Data System, "Special Report S89522C" (prepared for the U.S. Small Business Administration, Office of Advocacy, June 12, 1989); and idem., *Federal Procurement Report* (Washington, D.C.: U.S. Government Printing Office, July 10, 1990, March 13, 1991, February 3, 1994, January 13, 1997, 1998, 1999, 2000). Eagle Eye Publishers, and Federal Procurement Data System, FPDS-NG.

Table 3.8 Contract Actions Over $25,000, FY 1984–FY 2003, FY 2004–FY 2005 Total*
with Annual 8(a) Set-Aside Breakout

Fiscal year	Thousands of dollars		8(a) share (percent)
	Total	8(a) set-aside	
2005*	314,002,424	10,464,083	3.3
2004*	299,886,098	8,438,046	2.8
2003	292,319,145	10,043,219	3.4
2002	258,125,273	7,868,727	3.0
2001	248,985,613	6,339,607	2.5
2000	207,537,686	5,785,276	2.8
1999	188,865,248	6,125,439	3.2
1998	184,176,554	6,527,210	3.5
1997	179,227,203	6,510,442	3.6
1996	183,489,567	6,764,912	3.7
1995	185,119,992	6,911,080	3.7
1994	181,500,339	5,977,455	3.3
1993	184,426,948	5,483,544	3.0
1992	183,081,207	5,205,080	2.8
1991	193,550,425	4,147,148	2.1
1990	179,286,902	3,743,970	2.1
1989	172,612,189	3,449,860	2.0
1988	176,544,042	3,528,790	2.0
1987	181,750,326	3,341,841	1.8
1986	183,681,389	2,935,633	1.6
1985	188,186,629	2,669,174	1.4
1984	168,101,394	2,517,738	1.5

* For FY 2004–FY 2005, the new FPDS–NG data shown here reflect all contract actions available for small business competition (excluding some categories), not just those over $25,000. The figures are not strictly comparable with those shown for previous years.

Source: General Services Administration, Federal Procurement Data System.

contract dollars, and in FY 2002 that percentage was 0.17 percent. In FY 2003 their share was $550 million or 0.20 percent, and in FY 2004 small service-disabled veteran-owned businesses were awarded contracts valued at $1.115 billion or 0.39 percent of federal contracting dollars. In FY 2005 this group was awarded $1.89 billion or 0.60 percent of federal procurement.

Historically underutilized business zone (HUBZone) small business owners were awarded $6.10 billion or 1.94 percent of the FY 2005 procurement dollars, up from $4.78 billion and 1.58 percent in FY 2004.

Conclusion

As leaders in innovation, net new job creation, and business formation, small businesses continue to be the economic backbone of the nation. As leaders, small businesses provide the best value for the taxpaper's dollar through an acquisition process commonly called competition. Small businesses are eager to compete for a share of the marketplace. The increase in federal dollars awarded to small businesses is an indicator that, with a level playing field, small businesses will win their share of the federal acquisition dollar. The FY 2005 increase in DOD dollars awarded to small firms is encouraging, as DOD spends nearly two-thirds of the government's acquisition dollars annually.

4 Women *in* Business

Synopsis

Recently released statistics provide new information on women in the work force and women-owned businesses, including women's population statistics, their labor force participation, age, education, occupation, work schedules, average personal and household income, business ownership, and business dynamics. Data sources here include, but are not limited to the Current Population Survey, the American Community Survey, the Economic Census, and the Survey of Business Owners.

Demographics

- Women constitute more than 51 percent of the American population, and nearly 47 percent of the labor force.

- Of women in the United States, 14.5 percent were in poverty in 2004. The poverty rate among unemployed women was more than double that, at 31.8 percent.

- Nearly one in four families, or more than 8.3 million, was headed by a single mother caring for her own children younger than 18. Families headed by single fathers totaled 2.3 million.

- Of the total labor force, more than 3.9 million people (less than 3 percent of total wage-and-salary earners and more than 32 percent of total self-employed workers) were "moonlighters" involved in both self-employment and wage-and-salary work.

- Three groups were categorized to compare the gender differences in their demographic profiles: the civilian labor force, professional workers, and moonlighters.

- More than 36.8 percent of the female labor force and 30.6 percent of the male labor force were in professional occupations as defined in the Standard

Occupational Classification (SOC) system (management, business, and financial occupations; professional and related occupations).

- Moonlighters were more likely than the civilian labor force overall and less likely than those in professional occupations to be married, with higher levels of education, in better paying occupations, and with higher personal and household income.

- Professional women were more likely than professional men, moonlighters, and the overall civilian work force to work full time. More than a quarter of professional women worked in government.

Women-owned Businesses

- In 2002, women owned 6.5 million or 28.2 percent of nonfarm U.S. firms. More than 14 percent of these women-owned firms were employers, with 7.1 million workers and $173.7 billion in annual payroll.

- Women-owned firms accounted for 6.5 percent of total employment in U.S. firms in 2002 and 4.2 percent of total receipts.

- Compared with non-Hispanic White business owners, of whom 28 percent were women, minority groups in the United States had larger shares of women business owners, ranging from 31 percent of Asian American to 46 percent of African American business owners.

- Of all women business owners, 8.33 percent claimed Hispanic heritage, 85.95 White, 8.43 percent African American, 1.23 percent American Indian and Alaska Native, 5.25 percent Asian, and 0.18 percent Native Hawaiian and Other Pacific Islander.

- Almost 80 percent of women-owned firms had receipts totaling less than $50,000 in both 1997 and 2002. Total receipts for firms in this under-$50,000 group constituted about 6 percent of total women-owned business receipts in both years.

- More than 84 percent of all women-owned employer firms had fewer than 10 employees in 2002. As a share of all women-owned firms with employees, these very small firms accounted for 29 percent of total business receipts, employed nearly 27 percent of the workers, and paid more than 26 percent of the total payroll.

- The 7,240 women-owned firms with 100 employees or more accounted for $275.0 billion in gross receipts or 34.2 percent of the total receipts of women-owned employer firms in 2002.

- The largest shares of women-owned business receipts were in wholesale and retail trade and manufacturing in both 1997 and 2002.

- According to 2002 data, significant proportions of women-owned businesses were in professional, scientific, and technical services, and in health care and social assistance, but the share of receipts in these businesses was smaller than in the trades and manufacturing.

Women-owned Business Dynamics

- Between 1997 and 2002, the numbers of women-owned firms overall increased by 19.8 percent and of women-owned employer firms, by 8.3 percent.

- Firms owned by women increased employment by 70,000; those owned by men lost 1 million employees; those owned jointly by men and women lost 2.6 million; and publicly held and other firms not identified by gender of ownership increased employment by 10.9 million between 1997 and 2002.

- Overall, neither women nor men saw the receipts and payroll of their firms increase as fast as those of large publicly held firms and other firms not classifiable by gender.

- A special Census tabulation allows a comparison of survival rates, as well as expansion and contraction rates, for employer businesses owned by women of various ethnic groups over three time spans—1997–1998, 1997–1999, and 1997–2000.

- Over the 1997–2000 period, the firms owned by Asian American women had the highest survival rate of 77 percent, compared with the other ethnic groups.

- There were significant expansions in women-owned establishments between 1997 and 2000. At the same time, more than 20 percent of each ethnic group of women-owned businesses lost employment because of contractions each year of the period studied.

- Of the ethnic groups examined, only American Indian and Alaska Native women-owned businesses registered a net gain in employment at the end of the three-year period after the combined effects of business expansions, contractions, and deaths or closings. (Not included in this calculation is the effect of business births or openings.)

Introduction

Women's business ownership has greatly influenced the economy in general and women's economic well-being in particular. This report presents demographic descriptions of the female population and labor force, followed by data on women-owned businesses. The report concludes with a look at the relationship between women-owned businesses and women's economic well-being in the United States.

Characteristics of Women in the Population and Labor Force

Women constituted more than 51 percent of the American population and nearly 47 percent of the labor force in 2004. Women's labor force participation rate was about 46.2 percent, approximately 10 percentage points less than that of men (Table 4.1).[1]

Of the female population, about 14.5 percent were in poverty in 2004, about 3 percentage points more than men.[2] The poverty rate among unemployed women was more than double the women's overall poverty rate, at 31.8 percent—a rate almost 8 percentage points higher than that of unemployed men (Table 4.2).

Women carry a large share of the responsibility for caregiving in the United States (Table 4.3). Of American families, 75 percent were headed by married couples. Married couples headed 69 percent of households with children

---

1 The labor force participation rate is the percentage of working age persons in a given cohort who are either working or looking for a job.

2 For the definition of poverty used in the American Community Survey, see http://www.census.gov/acs/www/UseData/Def/Poverty.htm.

Table 4.1 Total U.S. Population and Labor Force by Gender, 2004

	Estimated number	Share of total (percent)	Labor participation rate (percent)
Total U.S. population	284,577,956	100.0	NA
Male	139,214,726	48.9	NA
Female	145,363,230	51.1	NA
Total U.S. labor force	144,720,309	100.0	50.9
Male	77,559,334	53.3	55.7
Female	67,160,975	46.7	46.2

NA = Not applicable.

Data Source: U.S. Census Bureau, 2004 American Community Survey.

Table 4.2 Poverty Rates in the Total and Unemployed U.S. Populations by Gender, 2004 (percent)

	Poverty rate in the total population	Poverty rate in the unemployed population
Male	11.6	24.0
Female	14.5	31.8

Note: For the definition of poverty used in the American Community Survey, see http://www.census.gov/acs/www/UseData/Def/Poverty.htm.

Data Source: U.S. Census Bureau, 2004 American Community Survey.

of their own under 18 years of age. Seven percent of these households with children were headed by men with no wife present and more than three times that many—24 percent—were headed by women with no husband—a partial explanation for the higher poverty rate among unemployed women.

"Moonlighters" are people involved in more than one job that may be wage-and-salary work and/or self-employment. Of the total labor force, more than 3.9 million people—less than 3 percent of total wage-and-salary earners and more than 32 percent of total self-employed workers—took both self-employment and wage-and-salary work in 2004. Moonlighters accounted for about 2.9 percent of the male labor force and 2.4 percent of the female labor force.

Table 4.3 Households and Families by Gender of Family Householder, 2004

	Number of households	Number of families	Households with own children under 18 years
Total number of U.S. households	109,902,090	73,885,953	34,976,246
Married couple family household	55,223,574	55,223,574	24,319,914
Male householder, no wife present family household	4,811,462	4,811,462	2,348,065
Female householder, no husband present family household	13,850,917	13,850,917	8,308,267
Nonfamily household	36,016,137	—	—
Percent of total	100	100	100
Married couple family household	50	75	69
Male householder, no wife present family household	4	6	7
Female householder, no husband present family household	13	19	24
Nonfamily household	33	—	—

Note: Data are limited to the household population and exclude the population living in institutions, college dormitories, and other group quarters.

Data Source: U.S. Census Bureau, 2004 American Community Survey.

Like the civilian labor force, moonlighters take a variety of occupations that differ somewhat by gender (Table 4.4). "Management, business and financial occupations" constitute similar shares of the men's and women's occupations in the labor force. Almost 24 percent of women in the labor force held "professional and related occupations," 8 percentage points more than the share of the male labor force in these occupations. Many working women were also in the office and administrative support and service sectors.

In 2004, there were 53 million American professional workers: about 28 million women and 25 million men (Table 4.5). Professionals are defined here as those in the occupations of management; business and financial operations; computers and mathematics; architecture and engineering; life, physical, and social sciences; community and social services; law; education, training, and

Table 4.4 Occupations of Women in the Labor Force and Moonlighters, 2004 (percent)

Occupations	Civilian labor force[1]		Moonlighters[2]	
	Male	Female	Male	Female
Management, business, and financial	14.57	12.89	19.8	14.8
Professional and related	16.03	23.95	22.5	32.3
Service	13.15	20.45	9.7	15.8
Sales and related	11.03	12.13	12.7	13.0
Office and administrative support	6.26	22.36	4.5	19.0
Farming, fishing, and forestry	1.07	0.39	0.9	0.1
Construction and extraction	11.83	0.42	10.6	0.2
Installation, maintenance, and repair	6.56	0.33	6.0	0.1
Production	9.11	4.58	6.2	2.7
Transportation and material moving	9.85	2.05	7.3	2.1
Armed Forces	0.04	0.01	0.0	0.0
Not in universe, or children	0.51	0.45	0.0	0.0
Total	100.0	100.0	100.0	100.0

[1] The data universe for this group is A_CIVLF=2, i.e., civilian labor force. The "civilian labor force" did not include children or armed forces.

[2] The data universe for this group is WSAL_YN=1 (Yes—wage and salary earnings received in 2004) and SEMP_YN=1 (Yes—self-employment for any job in 2004).

Note: Occupational titles are defined in the Department of Labor's Standard Occupational Classification (SOC) system—see http://www.bls.gov/soc/.

Data Source: U.S. Census Bureau, 2005 Current Population Survey, March Supplement.

libraries; arts, design, entertainment, sports, and media; healthcare practitioners and technicians; and healthcare support. These professions are often considered desirable for their human capital intensity, social status, and/or earnings potential. Women were about as intensely involved as men in business and financial operations. In other fields there were distinct gender dif-

Table 4.5 Detailed Occupational Information for Professionals[1] by Gender, 2004 (percent)

Detailed occupations	Male	Female
Management	36.6	19.6
Business and financial operations	10.3	11.8
Computer and mathematical science	9.7	3.2
Architecture and engineering	9.6	1.3
Life, physical, and social science	3.1	2.0
Community and social services	3.6	4.5
Legal	3.3	2.8
Education, training, and library	9.0	22.3
Arts, design, entertainment, sports, and media	6.2	4.8
Healthcare practitioner and technical	7.2	17.6
Healthcare support	1.4	10.0
Total	100.0	100.0

[1] The data universe for this group is: A_DTOCC=1 through 11.

Note: Occupational titles are defined in the Department of Labor's Standard Occupational Classification (SOC) system—see http://www.bls.gov/soc/.

Data Source: U.S. Census Bureau, 2005 Current Population Survey, March Supplement.

ferences. Women were more concentrated in education, training, library, and healthcare occupations, while men were more likely to be in management, science, and engineering.

Three groups were compared for gender differences in their 2004 demographic profiles: the civilian labor force, professional workers, and moonlighters (Table 4.6). Of the professionals, 70 percent of men and about 61 percent of women were married, 10 percent and 7 percent, respectively, more than in the general labor force. Professionals were highly educated, concentrated in the 25–59 age groups, and more likely to have health insurance in their own name. Men continued to earn more than women: nearly 21 percent of men professionals were in the highest income bracket ($100,000 plus), compared with 5 percent of women, and more men were in the next two highest income brackets. Almost 42 percent of men and more than 33 percent of women lived in households with the top household income ($100,000 and over).

Table 4.6 Profiles of the Labor Force, Professionals, and Moonlighters by Gender, 2004 (percent)

Items	Civilian labor force[1] Male	Female	Professionals[2] Male	Female	Moonlighters[3] Male	Female
Marital status						
Married	59.1	53.4	70.3	60.5	69.3	57.8
Not married	11.1	19.4	9.4	17.8	11.7	19.3
Never married	29.7	27.2	20.3	21.6	19.0	22.8
Education level						
Less high school	14.6	10.8	2.6	2.8	6.5	5.1
High school degree	31.4	28.5	12.9	15.3	25.0	18.2
Some college	25.8	31.5	22.3	29.2	30.0	33.7
Bachelor's degree	18.3	19.8	35.2	32.2	22.5	26.1
Post graduate	9.9	9.5	27.1	20.4	16.0	16.9
Age groups						
15–24	14.6	15.4	7.1	8.4	8.7	10.6
25–39	33.8	32.0	32.9	35.5	31.5	32.9
40–49	25.0	25.6	27.0	27.6	29.6	27.7
50–59	18.3	19.3	22.6	21.5	19.6	20.2
60 and over	8.3	7.7	10.5	7.1	10.6	8.6
Health insurance in own name						
Not in universe	25.6	21.9	12.4	12.6	21.1	19.6
Yes	60.2	53.7	75.1	64.4	63.3	52.1
No	14.2	24.4	12.4	23.0	15.5	28.3
Personal income						
<$20,000	25.8	39.6	10.9	23.7	15.6	33.2
$20,000 to <$40,000	29.8	34.6	19.2	33.4	21.8	29.8
$40,000 to <$60,000	19.8	14.6	22.3	22.7	22.6	17.0
$60,000 to <$80,000	10.4	6.2	16.3	10.9	13.8	9.1

Table 4.6 Profiles of the Labor Force, Professionals, and Moonlighters by Gender, 2004 (percent)—continued

Items	Civilian labor force[1]		Professionals[2]		Moonlighters[3]	
	Male	Female	Male	Female	Male	Female
$80,000 to <$100,000	5.2	2.3	10.5	4.2	6.1	3.7
$100,000 and over	9.0	2.6	20.8	5.1	20.1	7.2
Household income						
<$20,000	7.4	9.6	3.4	5.0	4.9	7.2
$20,000 to <$40,000	17.6	19.2	9.6	13.4	12.0	16.3
$40,000 to <$60,000	19.9	19.4	14.5	17.5	17.3	16.7
$60,000 to <$80,000	17.3	16.8	16.2	16.9	16.2	19.0
$80,000 to <$100,000	12.5	11.7	14.5	13.7	13.8	10.9
$100,000 and over	25.3	23.2	41.8	33.4	35.7	29.9

[1] The data universe for this group is A_CIVLF=2, i.e., civilian labor force. The "civilian labor force" did not include children or armed forces.

[2] The data universe for this group is: A_DTOCC=1 through 11: occupations listed in table 4.5.

[3] The data universe for this group is WSAL_YN=1 (Yes—wage and salary earnings received in 2004) and SEMP_YN=1 (Yes—self-employment for any job in 2004).

Data Source: U.S. Bureau of the Census, 2005 Current Population Survey March Supplement.

Where did people work, and how many hours? While the overwhelming majority worked in the private sector in 2004, almost 26 percent of women professionals and more than 16 percent of their male counterparts worked for government (Table 4.7). Nearly 89 percent of women professionals worked full time, about 20 percentage points more than in the general civilian labor force. More men than women in all three groups—the labor force, professionals, and moonlighters—claimed self-employment as their major income earning source.

Tables 4.6 and 4.7 also give a complete profile of American moonlighters in 2004. In most of the characteristics discussed here, moonlighters fell between the general civilian labor force and the professionals. American moonlighters were more likely than the general civilian labor force and less likely than the professionals to be married and educated, to hold better-paying occupations,

Table 4.7 Employment Sector and Work Schedule by Gender, 2004 (percent)

Items	Civilian labor force[1] Male	Female	Professionals[2] Male	Female	Moonlighters[3] Male	Female
Employment sector						
Private sector	72.6	71.4	64.5	64.1	55.3	54.9
Self-employed	12.4	7.1	17.6	7.5	30.2	28.7
Government	11.3	17.0	16.2	25.9	14.4	16.4
Worked but unpaid	0.1	0.1	0.0	0.0	0.1	0.0
Never worked	3.8	4.5	1.7	2.6	0.0	0.0
Work schedule						
Full time	82.2	70.0	82.2	88.5	84.9	69.0
Part time for economic reasons, usually full time	1.3	0.7	0.6	0.7	1.4	1.2
Part time for noneconomic reasons, usually part time	9.0	21.8	12.8	6.9	8.8	25.0
Part time for economic reasons, usually part time	1.7	2.4	1.1	0.8	2.7	2.0
Unemployed full time	5.0	3.9	2.1	2.3	2.0	2.1
Unemployed part time	1.0	1.2	0.4	0.3	0.3	0.6
Not in labor force	0.0	0.0	0.8	0.6	0.0	0.0

[1] The data universe for this group is A_CIVLF=2, i.e., civilian labor force. The "civilian labor force" did not include children or armed forces.

[2] The data universe for this group is: A_DTOCC=1 through 11: occupations listed in Table 4.5.

[3] The data universe for this group is WSAL_YN=1 (Yes—wage and salary earnings received in 2004) and SEMP_YN=1 (Yes—self-employment for any job in 2004).

Data Source: U.S. Bureau of the Census, 2005 Current Population Survey March Supplement.

and to live in households with higher levels of household income. The fact that almost one-third of moonlighters earn their primary income from self-employment and that they are more educated than the average labor force participant may imply that self-employed workers benefit from higher levels of education.

Women-owned Businesses

In 2002, women owned 6.5 million nonfarm U.S. firms, of which more than 14 percent were employer firms with 7.1 million workers and $173.7 billion in annual payroll.[3] These women-owned firms accounted for 28.2 percent of all nonfarm firms in the United States, 6.5 percent of their employment, and 4.2 percent ($940.8 billion) of their total receipts of $22.6 trillion. Men owned more than 13 million firms, accounted for 57.4 percent of all U.S. firms, 31.3 percent of total U.S. business receipts, 38.4 percent of total business employment, and 34.7 percent of total business payroll (Table 4.8). The remaining employment, receipts, and payroll are accounted for by firms jointly owned by women and men, publicly owned, or otherwise not identified by gender of ownership. The number of firms owned equally by men and women totaled 2.7 million in 2002, down from 5.1 percent of the total in 1997 to 3.2 percent in 2002. The number of publicly held and other firms not classifiable by gender increased by 112,000, and their receipts soared by more than $3.67 trillion.

Race/Ethnicity of Women Business Owners

The rate of women's business ownership appears to be higher among minorities than among Whites: 28 percent of businesses owned by Whites were owned by women; the comparable figure was 46 percent for African Americans and 39 percent for American Natives (Table 4.9). American Indians and Alaska Natives had the lowest rate of male/female joint business ownership at 3 percent. Most business owners are White, but more than 14 percent of women business owners are minorities, compared with fewer than 10 percent of men business owners.

Size of Firm

Women-owned firms with paid employees accounted for 14 percent of the total number of women-owned firms and about 85 percent of gross receipts (see Table 4.8). Most women-owned businesses (86 percent) had no employment. More than 79 percent of women-owned firms made less than $50,000; their receipts totaled about 6 percent of all women-owned business receipts in both 1997 and 2002 (Table 4.10). There were 117,069 women-owned firms

---

3   The 2002 Survey of Business Owners (SBO) defines women-owned businesses as firms in which women own 51 percent or more of the interest or stock of the business. The 2002 SBO data were collected as part of the 2002 Economic Census from a large sample of all nonfarm firms filing 2002 tax forms as individual proprietorships, partnerships, or any type of corporation, and with receipts of $1,000 or more. Note that the preliminary 2002 SBO figures shown here were released in early 2006; final 2002 SBO figures released in August 2006 may differ slightly, but do not change the conclusions in this chapter.

Table 4.8 U.S. Nonfarm Firms by Gender of Ownership, 1997 and 2002

	All firms[*]		Firms with paid employees			
	Firms (number)	Receipts (millions of dollars)	Firms (number)	Receipts (millions of dollars)	Employees (number)	Annual payroll (millions of dollars)
Women-owned firms						
2002[1]	6,489,483	940,775	916,768	804,097	7,146,229	173,709
1997[2]	5,417,034	818,669	846,780	717,764	7,076,081	149,116
Growth (percent)	19.8	14.9	8.3	12.0	1.0	16.5
Men-owned firms						
2002[1]	13,184,529	7,073,165	3,525,299	6,576,056	42,502,789	1,322,192
1997[2]	11,374,194	6,635,375	3,485,921	6,270,253	43,532,114	1,187,721
Growth (percent)	15.9	6.6	1.1	4.9	-2.4	11.3
Equally men-/women-owned						
2002[1]	2,693,171	731,447	717,880	627,004	5,663,453	129,676
1997[2]	3,641,263	943,881	1,029,469	828,390	8,284,537	160,989
Growth (percent)	-26.0	-22.5	-30.3	-24.3	-31.6	-19.5
Publicly held and other firms not classifiable by gender						
2002[1]	494,253	13,833,816	352,697	13,810,783	55,358,624	2,184,984
1997[2]	381,519	10,161,242	NA	10,104,058	44,458,403	1,437,195
Growth (percent)	29.5	31.6	—	36.7	24.5	52.0

Table 4.8 U.S. Nonfarm Firms by Gender of Ownership, 1997 and 2002—continued

	All firms*			Firms with paid employees			
	Firms (number)	Receipts (millions of dollars)		Firms (number)	Receipts (millions of dollars)	Employees (number)	Annual payroll (millions of dollars)
All U.S. firms							
2002[3]	22,974,685	22,627,167		5,524,813	21,859,758	110,786,416	3,813,488
1997[4]	20,821,934	18,553,243		5,295,151	17,907,940	103,359,815	2,936,493
Growth (percent)	10.3	22.0		4.3	22.1	7.2	29.9
2002 percent of total U.S. firms**							
Women-owned	28.2	4.2		16.6	3.7	6.5	4.6
Men-owned	57.4	31.3		63.8	30.1	38.4	34.7
Equally men/women-owned	11.7	3.2		13.0	2.9	5.1	3.4
Publicly held and other firms not classifiable by gender	2.2	61.1		6.4	63.2	50.0	57.3

NA = Not available
* Includes firms with and without paid employees.
** Percentages may not add to 100 because of rounding.
Data Sources:
[1] 2002 Survey of Business Owners, Women-owned Firms.
[2] 1997 Survey of Women-owned Business Enterprises.
[3] 2002 Economic Census. Final published figures for 2002 may vary slightly from the preliminary figures shown here.
[4] 1997 Economic Census.

Table 4.9 Gender of Ownership of U.S. Nonfarm Firms by Race or Ethnicity, 1997 and 2002

Race or ethnicity of firm ownership	2002 Number of businesses				1997 Number of businesses			
	Women-owned	Men-owned	Equally men-/women-owned	Total[1]	Women-owned	Men-owned	Equally men-/women-owned	Total[1]
Total[1]	6,492,795	13,185,703	2,691,722	22,370,220	5,417,034	11,374,194	3,641,263	20,432,491
Hispanic	540,909	921,963	111,287	1,574,159	337,708	666,486	195,702	1,199,896
White	5,580,524	11,916,049	2,398,250	19,894,823	4,487,589	9,689,012	3,140,194	17,316,796
African American	547,341	571,670	78,978	1,197,989	312,884	443,643	66,972	823,499
Natives[2]	79,637	119,567	6,922	206,126	53,593	106,872	36,836	197,300
Asian American	340,556	641,032	123,740	1,105,328	242,202	487,329	164,059	893,590
Pacific Islander[3]	11,673	18,189	2,437	32,299	5,764	10,129	3,476	19,370
Gender share of total[1] (percent)								
Total[1]	29	59	12	100	27	56	18	100
Hispanic	34	59	7	100	28	56	16	100
White	28	60	12	100	26	56	18	100
African American	46	48	7	100	38	54	8	100
Natives[2]	39	58	3	100	27	54	19	100
Asian American	31	58	11	100	27	55	18	100
Pacific Islander[3]	36	56	8	100	30	52	18	100
Racial/ethnic share of total[1] (percent)								
Hispanic	8.33	6.99	4.13	7.04	6.23	5.86	5.37	5.87
White	85.95	90.37	89.10	88.93	82.84	85.18	86.24	84.75

Table 4.9 Gender of Ownership of U.S. Nonfarm Firms by Race or Ethnicity, 1997 and 2002—continued

Race or ethnicity of firm ownership	2002 Number of businesses				1997 Number of businesses			
	Women-owned	Men-owned	Equally men-/women-owned	Total[1]	Women-owned	Men-owned	Equally men-/women-owned	Total[1]
African American	8.43	4.34	2.93	5.36	5.78	3.90	1.84	4.03
Natives[2]	1.23	0.91	0.26	0.92	1.46	0.94	1.01	0.97
Asian American	5.25	4.86	4.60	4.94	4.47	4.28	4.51	4.37
Pacific Islander[3]	0.18	0.14	0.09	0.14	0.11	0.09	0.10	0.09

[1] The sum of all racial and ethnic groups does not equal the U.S. total, as multiple counts occur across racial and ethnic groups. Also, publicly held and other firms not classifiable by gender or ethnicity/race of the owner are not included in the total.

[2] Natives = American Indian and Alaska Native

[3] Pacific Islanders = Native Hawaiian and Other Pacific Islander

Note: Particular caution should be exercised in comparing the 1997 and 2002 figures for racial and ethnic variables, and for equally male- and female-owned businesses, as the methodology changed. For more detail, see the Appendix 4B section titled Comparability of the 2002 and 1997 SBO Data by Gender, Race, and Ethnicity.

Data Sources: U.S. Bureau of Census, 2002 Survey of Business Owners, Final and Preliminary Estimates of Business Ownership by Kind of Business, Gender, Hispanic or Latino Origin, and Race; 1997 Survey of Women-owned Business Enterprises.

Table 4.10 Receipts Sizes of All Women-owned Businesses, 1997 and 2002*

	2002		1997	
	Firms (number)	Receipts (thousands of dollars)	Firms (number)	Receipts (thousands of dollars)
All women-owned firms	6,489,483	940,774,986	5,417,034	818,669,084
Less than $5,000	1,831,238	4,371,785	1,630,833	3,849,564
$5,000–$9,999	1,167,913	7,876,084	976,085	6,553,733
$10,000–$24,999	1,405,378	21,641,615	1,115,180	17,219,946
$25,000–$49,999	731,950	25,408,375	571,368	19,827,640
$50,000–$99,999	495,519	34,580,259	399,326	27,941,867
$100,000–$249,999	422,596	66,300,101	355,804	55,586,538
$250,000–$499,999	197,309	69,001,805	169,337	59,126,765
$500,000–$999,999	121,510	84,699,002	100,230	69,398,077
$1,000,000 or more	117,069	626,895,960	98,870	559,164,953
Percent of all women-owned firms	100	100	100	100
Less than $5,000	28.2	0.5	30.1	0.5
$5,000–$9,999	18.0	0.8	18.0	0.8
$10,000–$24,999	21.7	2.3	20.6	2.1
$25,000–$49,999	11.3	2.7	10.5	2.4
$50,000–$99,999	7.6	3.7	7.4	3.4
$100,000–$249,999	6.5	7.0	6.6	6.8
$250,000–$499,999	3.0	7.3	3.1	7.2
$500,000–$999,999	1.9	9.0	1.9	8.5
$1,000,000 or more	1.8	66.6	1.8	68.3

* A flaw in this receipt-size classification is that the dollar value of each class is recorded in current rather than constant values.

Data Sources: 2002 Survey of Business Owners, Women-owned Firms; 1997 Survey of Women-owned Business Enterprises.

with receipts of $1 million or more, accounting for 1.8 percent of the total number of women-owned businesses and 66.6 percent of their total receipts. The receipts size of women-owned businesses may not be an accurate measure over time as inflationary adjustments were not made in the data between 1997 and 2002.

Of all women-owned employer firms, 82.5 percent made at least $50,000 in total receipts in 2002, slightly less than in 1997 (Table 4.11). Receipts in firms earning $50,000 or more amounted to more than 99.5 percent of total women-owned employer business receipts. These firms employed 97.7 percent of the workers in women-owned employer businesses.

Examining firms by employment size provides another perspective (Table 4.12). In 2002, 84 percent of women-owned employer firms had fewer than 10 employees. They accounted for 29 percent of women employer business receipts, employed nearly 27 percent of these firms' workers, and paid more than 26 percent of their payroll. The 7,240 firms with 100 employees or more accounted for $275.0 billion or 34.2 percent of total gross receipts of women-owned employer firms in 2002. The number of middle-sized firms with 10 to 499 employees increased, while the number, employment, and payroll of large women-owned firms with 500 or more employees decreased compared with 1997.

Industries

Most women-owned businesses (55 percent) were in the service sector as classified in the 1997 Survey of Women-owned Business Enterprises (Table 4.13). These service businesses accounted for 23 percent of all women-owned business receipts. In the 2002 Survey of Business Owners, (Women-owned Firms), the service sector was further classified into several divisions. Sixteen percent of women-owned firms were in health care and social assistance, the largest division among women-owned businesses, which, however, produced only 7 percent of total women-owned business receipts in 2002. Another large division was professional, scientific, and technical services, 14 percent of total women-owned firms, with 8 percent of total women-owned business receipts. Women-owned businesses in wholesale and retail trade constituted about 17 percent of the number of businesses but accounted for 38 percent of women-owned business revenue, slightly down from 1997.

Geographic Characteristics

By state, California had the largest number of women-owned firms in 2002 at 870,612 (13.4 percent), with receipts of $138.0 billion (14.7 percent) (Table 4.14). New York was second with 505,134 (7.8 percent) and receipts of more than $71.4 billion (7.6 percent). Texas was third in number of firms with 468,705 (7.2 percent) and receipts of $65.8 billion (7.0 percent).

Table 4.11 Receipts Sizes of All Women-owned Employer Businesses, 1997 and 2002

Receipts size of firms	2002			1997		
	Employer Firms (number)	Receipts (thousands of dollars)	Employees (number)	Employer Firms (number)	Receipts (thousands of dollars)	Employees (number)
All women-owned employer firms	**916,768**	**804,097,284**	**7,146,229**	**846,780**	**717,763,965**	**7,076,081**
Less than $5,000	12,521	32,385	30,666	5,023	14,650	3,342
$5,000–$9,999	16,051	112,358	6,387	12,029	85,546	7,218
$10,000–$24,999	51,272	875,739	33,520	45,746	794,243	42,884
$25,000–$49,999	80,462	2,953,485	85,623	80,084	2,973,390	105,475
$50,000–$99,999	141,482	10,329,863	237,803	141,045	10,296,605	272,881
$100,000–$249,999	240,476	39,210,007	709,719	234,764	38,065,828	782,966
$250,000–$499,999	154,468	54,466,842	838,322	142,057	49,937,956	854,692
$500,000–$999,999	105,623	73,703,228	986,290	89,836	62,089,343	893,969
$1,000,000 or more	114,414	622,413,377	4,217,898	96,195	553,506,404	4,112,652
Percent of all women-owned employer firms						
Less than $5,000	1.4	0.0	0.4	0.6	0.0	0.1
$5,000–$9,999	1.8	0.0	0.1	1.4	0.0	0.1
$10,000–$24,999	5.6	0.1	0.5	5.4	0.1	0.6
$25,000–$49,999	8.8	0.4	1.2	9.5	0.4	1.5
$50,000–$99,999	15.4	1.3	3.3	16.7	1.4	3.9
$100,000–$249,999	26.2	4.9	9.9	27.7	5.3	11.1
$250,000–$499,999	16.9	6.8	11.7	16.8	7.0	12.1
$500,000–$999,999	11.5	9.2	13.8	10.6	8.7	12.6
$1,000,000 or more	12.5	77.4	59.0	11.4	77.1	58.1

All dollar amounts are in current rather than constant values that can be used for comparison.

Data Sources: 2002 Survey of Business Owners, Women-owned Firms; 1997 Survey of Women-owned Business Enterprises.

Table 4.12 Employment Size of Women-owned Firms, 1997 and 2002

Firm employment size	2002				1997			
	Employer firms (number)	Receipts (thousands of dollars)	Employees (number)	Annual payroll (thousands of dollars)	Employer firms (number)	Receipts (thousands of dollars)	Employees (number)	Annual payroll (thousands of dollars)
All women-owned employer firms	916,768	804,097,284	7,146,229	173,709,355	846,780	717,763,965	7,076,081	149,115,699
0*	161,310	23,566,372	—	3,955,935	115,281	14,538,408	—	2,649,394
1 to 4	461,896	113,455,460	939,479	20,485,194	444,121	103,567,582	923,514	17,055,243
5 to 9	149,063	96,553,311	970,986	21,366,953	150,300	84,335,319	974,625	17,712,160
10 to 19	82,942	103,155,850	1,105,339	25,943,298	79,327	91,167,777	1,046,787	20,594,115
20 to 49	43,244	118,005,642	1,269,752	31,603,163	39,987	104,393,025	1,167,829	25,029,270
50 to 99	11,072	74,405,956	750,562	19,337,750	10,325	71,473,096	693,586	16,109,917
100 to 499	6,578	114,737,129	1,195,043	30,060,267	6,566	113,055,559	1,213,289	25,908,642
500 +	662	160,217,565	915,068	20,956,794	873	135,233,199	1,056,451	24,056,959
Percent of women-owned employer firms								
0*	17.6	2.9	—	2.3	13.6	2.0	—	1.8
1 to 4	50.4	14.1	13.1	11.8	52.4	14.4	13.1	11.4
5 to 9	16.3	12.0	13.6	12.3	17.7	11.7	13.8	11.9
10 to 19	9.0	12.8	15.5	14.9	9.4	12.7	14.8	13.8
20 to 49	4.7	14.7	17.8	18.2	4.7	14.5	16.5	16.8
50 to 99	1.2	9.3	10.5	11.1	1.2	10.0	9.8	10.8
100 to 499	0.7	14.3	16.7	17.3	0.8	15.8	17.1	17.4
500 +	0.1	19.9	12.8	12.1	0.1	18.8	14.9	16.1

* Firms reported annual payroll, but did not report any employees on their payroll during the specified period of the year.

Data Sources: 2002 Survey of Business Owners, Women-owned Firms; 1997 Survey of Women-owned Business Enterprises.

Table 4.13 Industries Accounting for the Most Receipts of Women-owned Firms, 1997 and 2002

	2002				1997			
	Firms		Receipts[1]		Firms		Receipts[1]	
Kind of Business	Number	Percent	Millions of dollars	Percent	Number	Percent	Millions of dollars	Percent
All Industries	6,492,795	100	940,775	100	5,417,034	100	818,669	100
Wholesale trade	121,421	2	210,802	22	125,645	2	188,489	23
Retail trade	944,682	15	149,231	16	919,990	17	152,041	19
Manufacturing	110,348	2	93,312	10	121,108	2	113,722	14
Professional, scientific, and technical services	934,851	14	79,247	8	NA	NA	NA	NA
Health care and social assistance	1,035,834	16	68,458	7	NA	NA	NA	NA
Services[2]	NA	NA	NA	NA	2,981,266	55	186,161	23

NA = Not available.

[1] Receipts in current values are for firms with and without paid employees.

[2] As classified in the 1997 Survey of Women-owned Business Enterprises, "services" include North American Industry Classification System (NAICS) codes: Other Services (NAICS 81); Rental and Leasing Services (NAICS 532); Administrative and Support and Waste Management and Remediation Services (NAICS 56); Arts, Entertainment, and Recreation Services (NAICS 71); Professional, Scientific, and Technical Services (NAICS 54).

Data Sources: 2002 Survey of Business Owners, Women-owned Firms; 1997 Survey of Women-owned Business Enterprises.

Table 4.14 Number and Receipts of Women-owned Firms by State, 1997 and 2002

| Geographic area | 2002 | | 1997 | | Rate of growth in number (percent) | Ranking by growth in number | Real receipts growth rate (percent) | Ranking by receipts growth rate |
	Firm number	Sales and receipts (millions of dollars)	Firm number	Sales and receipts (millions of dollars)				
United States	6,489,483	940,775	5,417,034	818,669	19.8		5.2	
Alabama	81,820	11,426	69,515	10,230	17.7	19	2.3	32
Alaska	16,309	2,422	16,633	1,942	-1.9	51	14.2	14
Arizona	109,749	15,762	88,780	11,305	23.6	7	27.7	4
Arkansas	49,614	6,338	42,581	6,490	16.5	23	-10.6	49
California	870,612	138,003	700,513	121,191	24.3	6	4.3	28
Colorado	135,220	16,363	114,807	13,763	17.8	18	8.9	21
Connecticut	82,119	12,219	72,393	9,276	13.4	32	20.6	9
Delaware	15,344	2,021	13,662	1,831	12.3	33	1.1	36
District of Columbia	15,675	2,403	13,979	1,813	12.1	35	21.3	8
Florida	437,415	61,327	337,811	48,261	29.5	3	16.3	12
Georgia	196,195	30,029	145,576	25,267	34.8	2	8.8	22
Hawaii	29,897	4,562	25,807	3,253	15.8	26	28.4	3
Idaho	28,824	3,216	25,763	2,405	11.9	37	22.4	7
Illinois	284,950	46,860	239,725	44,273	18.9	13	-3.1	38
Indiana	118,857	16,481	107,082	13,578	11.0	41	11.1	16
Iowa	63,821	7,399	57,527	8,093	10.9	42	-16.3	51
Kansas	59,635	6,949	54,638	6,928	9.1	47	-8.2	47

State							
Kentucky	77,159	9,451	65,965	9,877	17.0	20	-12.4	50
Louisiana	86,876	12,253	70,550	11,463	23.1	8	-2.1	37
Maine	32,512	3,282	30,598	3,212	6.3	49	-6.5	45
Maryland	137,410	17,333	115,801	14,657	18.7	15	8.3	24
Massachusetts	161,919	23,138	142,661	16,753	13.5	31	26.4	5
Michigan	217,674	29,287	184,590	26,499	17.9	17	1.2	35
Minnesota	123,905	16,252	108,417	13,458	14.3	29	10.6	18
Mississippi	47,102	6,728	38,321	5,995	22.9	9	2.7	31
Missouri	120,438	18,596	103,626	15,003	16.2	24	13.5	15
Montana	24,519	2,139	22,404	2,048	9.4	45	-4.4	41
Nebraska	38,681	5,793	33,469	4,537	15.6	27	16.9	11
Nevada	47,674	8,639	33,311	5,972	43.1	1	32.4	2
New Hampshire	31,024	4,665	27,265	3,113	13.8	30	37.2	1
New Jersey	185,197	35,583	155,345	30,001	19.2	12	8.6	23
New Mexico	42,252	4,710	38,706	4,450	9.2	46	-3.1	39
New York	505,134	71,414	394,014	59,497	28.2	4	9.9	19
North Carolina	173,874	26,743	139,900	24,166	24.3	5	1.3	34
North Dakota	13,203	1,318	12,417	1,167	6.3	48	3.4	29
Ohio	229,973	32,324	205,044	30,597	12.2	34	-3.3	40
Oklahoma	75,029	9,255	67,481	8,912	11.2	40	-4.9	42
Oregon	88,318	10,618	80,543	10,335	9.7	44	-5.9	43
Pennsylvania	227,119	39,085	202,990	34,043	11.9	36	5.1	27
Rhode Island	23,195	3,641	19,886	2,684	16.6	22	24.2	6

Table 4.14 Number and Receipts of Women-owned Firms by State, 1997 and 2002—continued

Geographic area	2002 Firm number	2002 Sales and receipts (millions of dollars)	1997 Firm number	1997 Sales and receipts (millions of dollars)	Rate of growth in number (percent)	Ranking by growth in number	Real receipts growth rate (percent)	Ranking by receipts growth rate
South Carolina	76,831	10,891	64,232	10,634	19.6	11	-6.2	44
South Dakota	15,573	1,547	14,121	1,202	10.3	43	17.8	10
Tennessee	117,934	17,640	99,772	14,538	18.2	16	11.1	17
Texas	468,705	65,819	381,453	65,065	22.9	10	-7.4	46
Utah	48,474	5,920	41,991	5,096	15.4	28	6.4	25
Vermont	18,989	1,454	17,030	1,313	11.5	39	1.4	33
Virginia	157,076	22,139	132,219	17,486	18.8	14	15.9	13
Washington	137,396	17,375	123,042	15,099	11.7	38	5.4	26
West Virginia	31,301	3,252	30,231	3,299	3.5	50	-9.7	48
Wisconsin	104,170	17,582	89,284	15,654	16.7	21	2.8	30
Wyoming	12,945	1,130	11,148	945	16.1	25	9.5	20

Notes: Detail may not add to total because firms with more than one domestic establishment are counted in each state in which they operate, but only once at the U.S. total. Real growth rates of receipts were calculated with price level adjustment so that the monetary value of 1997 and 2002 receipts can be compared. Data include firms with paid employees and firms with no paid employees.

Data Sources: 2002 Survey of Business Owners, Women-owned Firms; 1997 Survey of Women-owned Business Enterprises.

Other geographic characteristics of women-owned businesses can be seen in Tables 4.15 through 4.17, namely the 10 combined statistical areas, 12 counties, and 12 cities with the largest number of women-owned firms.[4]

To exhibit women-owned business growth in those geographic regions, the tables include both 2002 and 1997 information. All geographic definitions are subject to changes made by the U.S. Bureau of the Census between data years 1997 and 2002; therefore, the data may not be comparable.

The New York, Los Angeles-Long Beach, Chicago, and Washington metropolitan areas had the largest numbers of women-owned businesses in both 1997 and 2002 (Table 4.15). Counties with the largest numbers of women-owned businesses in both years were Los Angeles County, California; Cook County, Illinois; Miami-Dade County, Florida; and New York County, New York (Table 4.16).

Table 4.17 illustrates the importance of large cities for women-owned businesses in their states. For instance, New York City had 251,057 women-owned businesses in 2002—50 percent of the total New York state firm number and 49 percent of total state women-owned business receipts. The 28,460 women-owned firms in San Francisco, with more than $5 million in receipts, represented just 3 percent of the total number of women-owned businesses in the state and 3 percent of total state women-owned business receipts.

---

4   Metropolitan Statistical Areas (metro areas), by Census definition, are metropolitan areas with at least one urbanized area of 50,000 or more population, plus adjacent territory that has a high degree of social and economic integration with the core as measured by commuting ties. Micropolitan Statistical Areas (micro areas) have at least one urban cluster of at least 10,000, but less than 50,000 population, plus adjacent territory with a high degree of social and economic integration with the core as measured by commuting ties. Metropolitan Divisions (metro divisions): if specified criteria are met, a metro area containing a single core with a population of 2.5 million or more may be subdivided to form smaller groupings of counties referred to as Metropolitan Divisions. Combined Statistical Areas (combined areas): if specified criteria are met, adjacent metro and micro areas, in various combinations, may become the components of a new set of areas called Combined Statistical Areas. The areas that combine retain their own designations as metro or micro areas within the larger combined area.

Table 4.15 Ten Areas with the Largest Number of Women-owned Firms, 1997 and 2002

2002 Combined Statistical Area	2002 All women-owned firms		1997 Primary Metropolitan Statistical Area	1997 All women-owned firms	
	Firms (number)	Receipts (millions of dollars)		Firms (number)	Receipts (millions of dollars)
New York-Newark-Bridgeport, NY-NJ-CT-PA	586,362	92,808	New York, NY PMSA	201,016	34,213
Los Angeles-Long Beach-Riverside,CA	435,135	72,504	Los Angeles-Long Beach, CA PMSA	200,793	32,300
Chicago-Naperville-Michigan City, IL–IN–WI	218,670	37,884	Chicago, IL PMSA	161,252	33,426
Washington-Baltimore-Northern Virginia, DC-MD-VA-WV	205,090	28,228	Washington, DC-MD-VA-WV PMSA	117,713	15,685
San Jose-San Francisco-Oakland, CA	199,565	33,376	Atlanta, GA PMSA	87,098	16,897
Boston-Worcester-Manchester,MA–NH	145,907	21,881	Philadelphia, PA-NJ PMSA	84,100	14,865
Dallas-Fort Worth, TX	131,230	20,311	Boston, MA-NH PMSA	83,366	10,570
Atlanta-Sandy Springs-Gainesville, GA-AL	129,240	22,177	Houston, TX PMSA	79,026	17,011
Houston-Baytown-Huntsville, TX	118,929	18,431	Detroit, MI PMSA	77,494	14,465
Detroit-Warren-Flint, MI	117,933	18,326	Dallas, TX PMSA	76,399	12,267

Note: 2002 Combined Statistical Areas and 1997 Primary Metropolitan Statistical Areas (PMSAs) are not comparable. For maps of the areas covered see http:// www.census.gov/population/www/estimates/metroarea.html. See footnote 4 for definitions of the 2002 metropolitan areas. Women-owned firms include firms with paid employees and firms with no paid employees. Firms with more than one domestic establishment are counted in each geographic area in which they operate, but only once in the U.S. total.

Data Sources: U.S. Bureau of Census, 2002 Survey of Business Owners, Women-owned Firms, and 1997 Survey of Women-owned Business Enterprises.

Table 4.16 Twelve Counties with the Largest Number of Women-owned Firms in 2002 (data for 1997 and 2002)

County	2002 All women-owned firms[1]		1997 All women-owned firms[1]		Growth rates (percent)	
	Firms (number)	Receipts (millions of dollars)	Firms (number)	Receipts (millions of dollars)	Firms	Receipts[2]
Los Angeles, CA	265,919	41,816	200,793	32,300	32.4	29.5
Cook, IL	130,418	22,452	99,604	20,485	30.9	9.6
Miami-Dade, FL	88,173	8,660	56,234	8,135	56.8	6.5
New York, NY	86,364	21,840	70,042	18,495	23.3	18.1
Harris, TX	86,042	14,904	65,372	13,687	31.6	8.9
Orange, CA	79,634	17,960	65,136	12,646	22.3	42.0
San Diego, CA	73,475	10,561	60,867	8,024	20.7	31.6
Maricopa, AZ	67,892	11,255	54,182	8,087	25.3	39.2
Kings, NY	62,500	5,113	38,286	5,405	63.2	-5.4
Broward, FL	54,889	7,397	37,416	4,026	46.7	83.7
Queens, NY	53,550	4,877	38,090	3,258	40.6	49.7
Dallas, TX	52,539	10,731	49,526	9,968	6.1	7.7

[1] Includes firms with paid employees and firms with no paid employees. Firms with more than one domestic establishment are counted in each county in which they operate, but only once in the state total.

[2] Growth rates of receipts were calculated with price level adjustments to make monetary values of 1997 and 2002 receipts comparable.

Data Sources: U.S. Bureau of Census, 2002 Survey of Business Owners, Women-owned Firms, and 1997 Survey of Women-owned Business Enterprises.

Table 4.17 Twelve Cities with the Largest Number of Women-owned Firms Compared with Women-owned Firms in the State, 2002

City	All women-owned firms[1]		State	All women-owned firms[1]		Percent city to state	
	Firms (number)	Receipts (millions of dollars)		Firms (number)	Receipts (millions of dollars)	Firms	Receipts
New York, NY	251,057	34,722	New York	505,134	71,414	50	49
Los Angeles, CA	117,713	15,701	California	870,612	138,003	14	11
Chicago, IL	68,581	9,266	Illinois	284,950	46,860	24	20
Houston, TX	51,564	10,632	Texas	468,705	65,819	11	16
San Diego, CA	32,513	5,057	California	870,612	138,003	4	4
San Francisco, CA	28,460	4,688	California	870,612	138,003	3	3
Dallas, TX	26,959	5,940	Texas	468,705	65,819	6	9
Phoenix, AZ	25,212	4,866	Arizona	109,749	15,762	23	31
San Antonio, TX	22,073	4,508	Texas	468,705	65,819	5	7
Seattle, WA	19,945	3,106	Washington	137,396	17,375	15	18
Miami, FL	19,127	1,894	Florida	437,415	61,327	4	3
Philadelphia, PA	18,977	2,381	Pennsylvania	227,119	39,085	8	6

[1] Includes firms with paid employees and firms with no paid employees. Firms with more than one domestic establishment are counted in each city in which they operate, but only once in the state total.

Data Sources: U.S. Bureau of Census, 2002 Survey of Business Owners, Women-owned Firms.

The Dynamics of Women-owned Businesses

Growth

The number of women-owned businesses grew at a faster rate than the number of U.S. businesses overall in the 1997 to 2002 period (Table 4.8). Women-owned firms increased by 19.8 percent, women-owned employer firms by 8.3 percent—both higher than the overall growth rates for U.S. firms. Firms owned by women increased employment by 70,000; those owned by men lost 1 million employees; those owned jointly by men and women lost 2.6 million; and publicly held and other firms not classifiable by gender increased employment by 10.9 million between 1997 and 2002. Total receipts and annual payroll grew significantly for all U.S. firms; much of the growth was in publicly held and other firms not classifiable by gender.

By state, the largest increases in the number of women-owned firms were in Nevada (43 percent), Georgia (35 percent), Florida (29 percent), New York (28 percent), and, in two sets of ties, North Carolina, California, and Arizona (all 24 percent), and Louisiana, Mississippi, and Texas (all 23 percent) (Table 4.14). States with the least growth in these businesses were Alaska (-2 percent), West Virginia (4 percent), Maine and North Dakota (both 6 percent), Kansas, New Mexico, and Montana (all 9 percent), Oregon and South Dakota (both 10 percent), and Iowa (11 percent). The top five states in real growth of women-owned business receipts were New Hampshire (37.2 percent), Nevada (32.4 percent), Hawaii (28.4 percent), Arizona (27.7 percent) and Massachusetts (26.4 percent) (Table 4.14). States that lost the most ground in receipts were Iowa (-16.3 percent), Kentucky (-12.4 percent), Arkansas (-10.6 percent), West Virginia (-9.7 percent), and Kansas (-8.2 percent).

The 1997–2002 growth in women-owned businesses occurred across all receipts sizes of firms at an average rate of 19.8 percent (Table 4.18). The strongest increases occurred in the number of the smallest employer firms with less than $5,000 in receipts; their number increased by 149.3 percent. The number of employer firms with between $5,000 and $10,000 in receipts grew by 33.4 percent. Total receipts and employment also increased most in small employer firms with less than $5,000 in receipts; their total employment increased by 817.6 percent, while most other sizes of employer firms lost employment, except firms with receipts of $500,000 or more.

Table 4.18 Rates of Growth in Women-owned Firms by Receipts Size of Firm, 1997 to 2002 (percent)

	All women-owned firms		Women-owned employer firms		
	Number of firms	Receipts*	Number of firms	Receipts*	Employment
All women-owned firms	19.8	5.2	8.3	2.6	1.0
Less than $5,000	12.3	4.0	149.3	102.4	817.6
$5,000–$9,999	19.7	10.0	33.4	20.2	-11.5
$10,000–$24,999	26.0	15.1	12.1	0.9	-21.8
$25,000–$49,999	28.1	17.3	0.5	-9.1	-18.8
$50,000–$99,999	24.1	13.3	0.3	-8.1	-12.9
$100,000–$249,999	18.8	9.2	2.4	-5.7	-9.4
$250,000–$499,999	16.5	6.8	8.7	-0.1	-1.9
$500,000–$999,999	21.2	11.7	17.6	8.7	10.3
$1,000,000 or more	18.4	2.6	18.9	3.0	2.6

* The growth rates of receipts were calculated with price level adjustments so that the monetary values of 1997 and 2002 receipts could be compared.

Data Sources: U.S. Bureau of Census, 2002 Survey of Business Owners, Women-owned Firms, and 1997 Survey of Women-owned Business Enterprises.

While the number of "no year-round employee" employer firms grew almost 40 percent between 1997 and 2002, the number of the largest firms with 500 or more employees declined by 24.2 percent (Table 4.19). The smallest employer firms with no year-round employees had increases of 48.4 percent in business receipts and 36.7 percent in payroll. While all small employer firms increased their payroll between 1997 and 2002, large firms with 500 or more employees actually reduced payroll by 20.2 percent and employment by 13.4 percent, while also increasing receipts.

Survival, Expansion, and Contraction of Women-owned Establishments

What were the dynamics—business survival rates, expansions, and contractions—over the 1997–2000 period of the minority women-owned employer establishments that were in operation in 1997? Data limitations because of small sample sizes mean that only the four largest racial/ethnic women-owned business groups can be discussed here: African Americans, Asians and Pacific

Table 4.19 Rates of Growth in Women-owned Employer Firms by Employment Size of Firm, 1997 to 2002 (percent)

Employment size of firm	Number of firms	Receipts[1]	Employment	Annual payroll[1]
All women-owned firms	8.3	2.6	1.0	6.7
No employees[2]	39.9	48.4	—	36.7
1 to 4 employees	4.0	0.3	1.7	10.0
5 to 9 employees	-0.8	4.8	-0.4	10.4
10 to 19 employees	4.6	3.6	5.6	15.3
20 to 49 employees	8.1	3.5	8.7	15.6
50 to 99 employees	7.2	-4.7	8.2	9.9
100 to 499 employees	0.2	-7.1	-1.5	6.2
500 employees or more	-24.2	8.5	-13.4	-20.2

[1] The growth rates of receipts were calculated with price level adjustments so that the monetary values of 1997 and 2002 receipts and payroll could be compared.

[2] Firms reported annual payroll, but did not report any employees on their payroll during the specified period of the year.

Data Sources: U.S. Bureau of Census, 2002 Survey of Business Owners, Women-owned Firms, and 1997 Survey of Women-owned Business Enterprises.

Islanders, American Indians and Alaska Natives, and Hispanic women. Non-Hispanic Whites constitute nearly 86 percent of the category, "all women" in Tables 4.20 and 4.21.

Asian women employer establishments had the highest survival rate: 77 percent of their businesses in operation in 1997 remained in business in 2000. Significant numbers of women-owned firms expanded—more than 31 percent—and more than 20 percent contracted over the 1997–2000 period (Table 4.20).

By 2000, 31 percent of the employment of establishments existing in 1997 that were owned by African American women had been shed because of business closings, as well as 19 percent of that in Hispanic women-owned businesses, 16 percent in businesses owned by Asian and Pacific Islander women, and 11 percent in American Indian and Alaska Native women-owned businesses (Table 4.21). Employment in women-owned establishments increased significantly because of business expansions. By 2000, all but one group of women-owned businesses had net losses in employment because of business closings, expansions, and contractions. Only American Indian or Alaska

Table 4.20 Survival, Expansion, and Contraction Rates of Women-owned Employer Businesses by Race or Ethnicity of Owner, 1997–1998, 1997–1999, and 1997–2000 (percent of firms in operation in 1997)

Change period*	All women			African American			Asian and Pacific Islander			American Indian and Alaska Native			Hispanic		
	A	B	C	A	B	C	A	B	C	A	B	C	A	B	C
Survival rate	91	83	75	88	77	68	92	85	77	92	85	75	91	82	73
Expansion rate	33	33	31	34	30	29	36	35	34	40	36	29	33	32	31
Contraction rate	23	24	22	23	24	21	22	26	22	25	23	21	21	22	20

* Change period: A=1997–1998, B=1997–1999, and C=1997–2000.

Data Source: Special tabulation prepared by the U.S. Census Bureau for the National Women's Business Council. See Table 4A.3 in Appendix 4A.

Table 4.21 Change in Women-owned Business Employment Because of Business Death, Expansion, or Contraction, by Race or Ethnicity of Firm Owner, 1997–1998, 1997–1999, and 1997–2000 (percent change in employment)

Change period*	All women			African American			Asian and Pacific Islander			American Indian and Alaska Native			Hispanic		
	A	B	C	A	B	C	A	B	C	A	B	C	A	B	C
Business death	-5	-10	-16	-4	-23	-31	-4	-10	-16	-4	-7	-11	-4	-10	-19
Business expansion	19	22	25	21	24	25	23	25	29	36	37	58	54	41	27
Business contraction	-11	-13	-14	-16	-18	-16	-13	-16	-15	-9	-10	-11	-12	-14	-13

* Change period: A=1997–1998, B=1997–1999 and C=1997–2000.

Data Source: Special tabulation prepared by the U.S. Census Bureau for the National Women's Business Council. See Table 4A.3 in Appendix 4A.

Native women-owned businesses had a net gain—of 23,460—in employment (Appendix Table 4A.3). (Gains because of startups are not included here.)

Conclusion: Women's Business Ownership and Economic Well-being

This chapter shows the dramatic growth in women-owned businesses over the 1997 to 2002 time period across all business size categories and demographic groups. Data here further explore correlations between women's business ownership and their economic well-being.

Four variables in Table 4.22 are used to illustrate the intensity of business ownership: women-owned firm density is the number of 2002 women-owned firms per 10,000 women in the population; women-owned employer density is the number of 2002 women-owned employer firms per 10,000 women; all firm density is the total number of firms per 10,000 population; and all employer firm density is the total number of employer firms per 10,000 population. A simple correlation analysis illustrates relationships between business ownership and economic well-being as reflected in average income per capita, average household income, and poverty. This analysis suggests: 1) business ownership is related positively to income and negatively to poverty;[5] and 2) these correlations are stronger for women-owned firms than for all firms.[6]

---

5   Because of the complexity of the economy, it is impossible to find an economic variable that perfectly explains another economic variable. For example, well-educated women may be less likely to have a large number of children; therefore, they may be less likely to be in poverty.

6   Using data for the 50 United States and the District of Columbia, simple correlation analysis results are provided in the table below. Each number is a correlation coefficient of two corresponding variables. For instance, the correlation coefficient of women-owned firm density and average income per capita is 0.4341 and that of women-owned employer density and poverty rate A is -0.3704. The larger the number is, the closer the relationship of the two variables would be. A coefficient of "1" implies a perfect relationship between two variables. A negative sign implies the two variables are negatively correlated.

	Women-owned firm density	Women-owned employer density	All firm density	All employer density
Average income per capita	0.4341	0.3211	0.1364	0.0786
Average household income	0.4581	0.3371	0.0994	0.0860
Poverty rate A	-0.4102	-0.3704	-0.2490	-0.3017
Poverty rate B	-0.3275	-0.2827	-0.2966	-0.3122

Table 4.22 Women-owned Business Density and Economic Well-being by State

	Women-owned firm density[1]	Women-owned employer density[2]	All firm density[3]	All employer density[4]	Average income per capita	Average household income	Poverty rate A[5]	Poverty rate B[6]
United States	445	63	804	193	22,759	51,742	9.9	9.2
Alabama	357	52	697	169	18,938	35,412	15.5	12.5
Alaska	522	94	979	245	24,830	56,536	6.8	6.7
Arizona	404	58	700	174	20,663	41,172	8.4	9.9
Arkansas	362	54	776	186	18,048	34,402	13.8	12.0
California	492	65	827	192	24,026	49,738	8.1	10.6
Colorado	605	96	1,039	262	24,819	48,282	7.4	6.2
Connecticut	465	63	892	223	30,187	56,543	7.0	5.6
Delaware	374	71	797	245	24,930	50,025	7.9	6.5
District of Columbia	517	80	825	236	34,212	43,681	16.4	16.7
Florida	518	77	937	219	22,175	39,265	9.1	9.0
Georgia	454	63	801	188	21,964	42,069	13.5	9.9
Hawaii	485	74	811	192	22,579	50,565	7.4	7.6
Idaho	434	68	935	255	18,388	37,261	8.3	8.3
Illinois	444	63	766	195	24,356	46,528	8.3	7.8
Indiana	382	52	711	180	20,758	41,906	7.7	6.7
Iowa	432	59	815	215	20,032	39,288	7.7	6.0
Kansas	438	68	817	219	21,045	40,051	8.1	6.7
Kentucky	374	50	743	170	19,395	34,973	14.2	12.7
Louisiana	379	53	739	176	18,114	33,311	16.7	15.8

State							
Maine	497	77	1,067	265	21,150	39,990	10.2	7.8
Maryland	490	64	813	191	27,863	55,650	8.5	6.1
Massachusetts	489	68	871	220	28,956	55,266	8.9	6.7
Michigan	427	57	742	187	22,228	43,795	8.2	7.4
Minnesota	492	67	878	225	24,848	49,352	8.2	5.1
Mississippi	321	49	673	164	16,398	31,690	18.8	16
Missouri	419	67	787	206	21,132	40,198	9.9	8.6
Montana	544	103	1,108	312	18,932	35,257	9.1	10.5
Nebraska	445	69	854	236	20,484	39,904	8.0	6.7
Nevada	452	62	799	199	22,419	43,928	7.1	7.5
New Hampshire	484	78	991	251	27,129	54,225	7.2	4.3
New Jersey	420	70	824	232	29,198	58,759	7.8	6.3
New Mexico	449	68	743	188	19,230	36,019	12.8	14.5
New York	509	66	885	215	25,037	44,923	11.3	11.5
North Carolina	415	61	787	194	20,626	38,204	13.2	9.0
North Dakota	421	63	897	263	19,849	36,237	11.1	8.3
Ohio	395	52	725	179	21,658	40,697	8.1	7.8
Oklahoma	425	61	954	237	18,636	35,568	11.1	11.2
Oregon	500	77	871	270	21,412	40,378	7.6	7.9
Pennsylvania	362	55	917	257	22,197	41,171	9.1	7.8
Rhode Island	424	65	1,014	305	24,484	45,634	10.6	8.9
South Carolina	368	56	925	260	20,870	37,936	13.9	10.7
South Dakota	411	72	1,039	322	19,454	37,252	11.1	9.3
Tennessee	401	48	1,000	230	20,337	37,281	13.5	10.3

Table 4.22 Women-owned Business Density and Economic Well-being by State—continued

	Women-owned firm density[1]	Women-owned employer density[2]	All firm density[3]	All employer density[4]	Average income per capita	Average household income	Poverty rate A[5]	Poverty rate B[6]
Texas	429	58	961	217	20,808	41,376	12.8	12.0
Utah	416	54	962	276	18,735	46,443	5.8	6.5
Vermont	611	80	1,282	335	22,371	43,914	8.5	6.3
Virginia	427	64	876	250	25,689	48,986	9.5	7.0
Washington	453	72	803	261	23,830	46,041	7.5	7.3
West Virginia	344	50	760	233	17,423	30,982	11.9	13.9
Wisconsin	382	62	809	253	22,061	43,617	7.4	5.6
Wyoming	528	103	1,131	363	22,096	41,099	8.9	8.0

Notes:

[1] Women-owned firm density=number of 2002 women-owned firms per 10,000 women in the population.

[2] Women-owned employer density=number of 2002 women-owned employer firms per 10,000 women in the population.

[3] All firm density=total number of firms per 10,000 in the population.

[4] All employer firm density=total number of employer firms per 10,000 in the population.

[5] Poverty rate A=income in 1999 below poverty level; percent of population for whom poverty status is determined; 65 years and over.

[6] Poverty rate B=income in 1999 below poverty level; percent of families.

Data Sources:

• Appendix Tables 4A.1 and 4A.2.

• 2002 Survey of Business Owners. Data include firms with paid employees and firms with no paid employees.

• Population data are from the data set: Census 2000 Summary File 3 (SF 3) - Sample Data.

• Detail may not add to total because firms with more than one domestic establishment are counted in each state in which they operate, but only once at the U.S. total.

• Poverty data: 2000 U.S. Census.

Further data, especially microdata, are needed to further explore the trends in women's business ownership discussed here. The Office of Advocacy will continue to provide updated data and analysis of the role and status of women-owned businesses in the U.S. economy.

APPENDIX 4A
Tables

Table 4A.1 Women's Population and Women-owned Firms, 2002

	Women's Population	Women's share of total population (percent)	Number of firms	Total receipts (millions of dollars)	Total number of employer firms	Total employer receipts (thousands of dollars)	Total employment	Annual payroll (thousands of dollars)	A	B	C
United States	146,057,108	51.1	6,489,483	940,775	917,946	813,188,494	7,224,246	175,863,498	14.1	445	63
Alabama	2,296,823	51.7	81,820	11,426	11,848	10,140,274	98,175	2,080,302	14.5	357	52
Alaska	312,349	49.2	16,309	2,422	2,940	2,118,282	18,395	475,931	18.0	522	94
Arizona	2,716,606	49.9	109,749	15,762	15,729	13,725,486	130,403	2,993,858	14.3	404	58
Arkansas	1,372,257	51.0	49,614	6,338	7,459	5,635,014	55,635	1,124,142	15.0	362	54
California	17,710,084	50.4	870,612	138,003	115,944	116,967,186	959,490	25,789,755	13.3	492	65
Colorado	2,236,127	50.0	135,220	16,363	21,498	13,700,750	128,810	3,118,693	15.9	605	96
Connecticut	1,764,766	52.2	82,119	12,219	11,053	10,145,323	88,626	2,412,811	13.5	465	63
Delaware	411,074	51.5	15,344	2,021	2,917	1,663,911	19,637	461,701	19.0	374	71
District of Columbia	303,300	53.0	15,675	2,403	2,430	2,036,699	18,881	639,765	15.5	517	80
Florida	8,440,209	51.4	437,415	61,327	65,155	51,416,434	435,674	9,882,669	14.9	518	77
Georgia	4,323,412	51.3	196,195	30,029	27,044	25,974,739	197,699	5,054,579	13.8	454	63
Hawaii	616,540	50.4	29,897	4,562	4,550	3,956,230	38,963	825,921	15.2	485	74
Idaho	664,640	51.1	28,824	3,216	4,542	2,746,527	26,637	535,685	15.7	434	68
Illinois	6,422,287	51.4	284,950	46,860	40,426	41,724,201	354,826	9,618,587	14.2	444	63
Indiana	3,110,855	51.0	118,857	16,481	16,300	14,594,978	139,239	3,050,964	13.7	382	52
Iowa	1,477,191	50.9	63,821	7,399	8,755	6,530,101	63,338	1,230,837	13.7	432	59

State										
Kansas	1,361,843	50.7	59,635	6,949	9,285	6,030,182	61,877	1,343,386	15.6	438	68
Kentucky	2,065,781	51.1	77,159	9,451	10,338	8,144,367	84,976	1,764,354	13.4	374	50
Louisiana	2,291,100	51.5	86,876	12,253	12,210	10,676,352	116,495	2,307,589	14.1	379	53
Maine	653,939	51.5	32,512	3,282	5,025	2,719,729	26,592	571,282	15.4	497	77
Maryland	2,803,157	51.4	137,410	17,333	17,971	14,881,734	144,702	4,055,663	13.1	490	64
Massachusetts	3,313,063	51.2	161,919	23,138	22,660	19,466,271	176,495	4,742,289	14.0	489	68
Michigan	5,105,008	51.5	217,674	29,287	29,029	25,779,818	232,539	5,588,851	13.3	427	57
Minnesota	2,517,652	49.8	123,905	16,252	16,754	14,145,002	123,315	2,878,581	13.5	492	67
Mississippi	1,468,031	52.7	47,102	6,728	7,170	5,755,441	54,230	1,009,017	15.2	321	49
Missouri	2,873,839	51.5	120,438	18,596	19,225	17,074,112	152,121	3,743,391	16.0	419	67
Montana	451,156	49.8	24,519	2,139	4,635	1,754,392	21,238	363,137	18.9	544	103
Nebraska	868,936	51.0	38,681	5,793	6,027	5,310,819	47,056	1,069,142	15.6	445	69
Nevada	1,055,407	49.8	47,674	8,639	6,493	7,517,590	57,306	1,434,262	13.6	452	62
New Hampshire	640,536	50.6	31,024	4,665	5,020	4,133,964	38,293	879,134	16.2	484	78
New Jersey	4,416,810	51.3	185,197	35,583	30,914	31,490,748	245,599	7,150,816	16.7	420	70
New Mexico	941,824	51.2	42,252	4,710	6,397	3,998,143	42,053	853,978	15.1	449	68
New York	9,933,979	51.5	505,134	71,414	65,322	60,002,742	473,186	12,912,886	12.9	509	66
North Carolina	4,194,994	51.4	173,874	26,743	25,539	23,553,478	225,439	4,935,537	14.7	415	61
North Dakota	313,818	49.6	13,203	1,318	1,976	1,121,870	11,651	203,276	15.0	421	63
Ohio	5,825,793	51.6	229,973	32,324	30,486	28,434,347	265,752	6,370,146	13.2	395	52
Oklahoma	1,764,528	50.7	75,029	9,255	10,775	8,041,622	92,945	1,837,615	14.4	425	61
Oregon	1,765,190	50.3	88,318	10,618	13,572	8,969,573	86,195	1,934,836	15.4	500	77

Table 4A.1 Women's Population and Women-owned Firms, 2002—continued

	Women's Population	Women's share of total population (percent)	Number of firms	Total receipts (millions of dollars)	Total number of employer firms	Total employer receipts (thousands of dollars)	Total employment	Annual payroll (thousands of dollars)	A	B	C
Pennsylvania	6,282,915	51.5	227,119	39,085	34,753	35,204,818	283,056	6,512,881	15.3	362	55
Rhode Island	547,235	51.8	23,195	3,641	3,581	3,279,013	26,871	694,821	15.4	424	65
South Carolina	2,088,575	52.3	76,831	10,891	11,764	9,456,770	93,101	1,927,919	15.3	368	56
South Dakota	378,881	50.9	15,573	1,547	2,746	1,348,026	14,772	249,061	17.6	411	72
Tennessee	2,939,254	51.8	117,934	17,640	14,232	15,402,420	117,742	2,672,453	12.1	401	48
Texas	10,932,093	50.8	468,705	65,819	63,388	56,398,782	559,479	13,057,355	13.5	429	58
Utah	1,165,712	50.5	48,474	5,920	6,243	5,122,040	53,739	1,130,842	12.9	416	54
Vermont	311,100	50.3	18,989	1,454	2,481	1,143,401	14,996	284,612	13.1	611	80
Virginia	3,682,480	51.7	157,076	22,139	23,630	19,090,373	183,813	4,733,322	15.0	427	64
Washington	3,037,495	50.6	137,396	17,375	22,007	14,907,196	127,053	3,210,600	16.0	453	72
West Virginia	911,021	52.0	31,301	3,252	4,544	2,793,024	31,806	629,978	14.5	344	50
Wisconsin	2,730,446	49.9	104,170	17,582	16,910	16,020,074	150,666	3,283,831	16.2	382	62
Wyoming	244,998	50.2	12,945	1,130	2,524	944,127	12,670	230,452	19.5	528	103

A=Employer firm ratio: Number of employer firms as a percentage of number of all firms.

B=Firm density: All firm number per 10,000 persons in the population.

C=Employer density: Employer firm number per 10,000 persons in the population.

Data Sources: Population data are from the Census 2000 Summary File 3 (SF 3) - Sample Data; 2002 Survey of Business Owners.

Table 4A.2 Men's Population and Men-owned Firms, 2002

	Men's Population	Men's share of total population (percent)	Number of firms	Total receipts (millions of dollars)	Total number of employer firms	Total employer receipts (thousands of dollars)	Total employment	Annual payroll (thousands of dollars)	A	B	C
United States	139,876,302	48.9	13,185,703	7,096,465,049	3,525,524	6,598,978,228	42,677,931	1,327,515,579	26.7	943	252
Alabama	2,142,971	48.3	188,416	100,780,380	49,707	93,879,453	657,503	18,024,905	26.4	879	232
Alaska	322,692	50.8	32,106	13,070,959	8,598	12,016,366	77,540	2,649,000	26.8	995	266
Arizona	2,725,827	50.1	199,554	105,121,690	52,116	97,408,498	679,581	19,505,893	26.1	732	191
Arkansas	1,319,908	49.0	118,803	52,696,242	29,596	48,717,164	338,558	8,197,764	24.9	900	224
California	17,448,821	49.6	1,625,687	882,472,936	421,047	810,914,060	5,174,007	174,203,975	25.9	932	241
Colorado	2,240,489	50.0	253,302	116,196,268	69,709	106,626,276	697,055	22,565,935	27.5	1131	311
Connecticut	1,617,466	47.8	181,366	100,994,183	49,871	92,579,829	527,582	20,156,924	27.5	1121	308
Delaware	387,109	48.5	34,533	20,549,442	10,940	19,103,965	132,468	3,988,531	31.7	892	283
District of Columbia	268,964	47.0	24,615	14,167,822	7,301	13,197,688	100,019	4,302,090	29.7	915	271
Florida	7,988,698	48.6	885,343	374,091,890	221,734	338,676,307	2,251,725	66,453,351	25.0	1108	278
Georgia	4,102,162	48.7	395,180	211,629,666	102,669	196,075,907	1,216,828	36,847,383	26.0	963	250
Hawaii	607,735	49.6	51,077	22,143,949	12,994	20,183,769	150,887	4,432,423	25.4	840	214
Idaho	635,126	48.9	62,416	27,722,906	18,875	25,822,525	189,615	4,998,529	30.2	983	297
Illinois	6,082,171	48.6	540,417	344,746,946	155,873	326,012,188	1,974,016	66,005,392	28.8	889	256
Indiana	2,989,608	49.0	244,182	152,135,541	69,314	144,436,626	962,088	27,720,033	28.4	817	232
Iowa	1,425,659	49.1	127,749	65,758,653	38,015	62,135,212	424,526	11,289,462	29.8	896	267

Table 4A.2 Men's Population and Men-owned Firms, 2002—continued

	Men's Population	Men's share of total population (percent)	Number of firms	Total receipts (millions of dollars)	Total number of employer firms	Total employer receipts (thousands of dollars)	Total employment	Annual payroll (thousands of dollars)	A	B	C
Kansas	1,322,904	49.3	116,131	77,776,570	34,839	74,357,742	403,835	11,548,169	30.0	878	263
Kentucky	1,980,208	48.9	174,984	84,647,270	43,167	78,861,846	527,937	14,131,726	24.7	884	218
Louisiana	2,155,858	48.5	186,916	94,953,286	48,496	88,655,371	643,876	17,581,852	25.9	867	225
Maine	615,179	48.5	79,648	29,274,020	20,405	26,561,959	204,412	5,396,550	25.6	1295	332
Maryland	2,654,476	48.6	248,111	123,776,719	66,225	114,909,590	783,564	26,164,501	26.7	935	249
Massachusetts	3,157,424	48.8	338,764	203,393,508	93,789	189,007,629	1,085,538	40,590,222	27.7	1073	297
Michigan	4,805,325	48.5	415,659	260,300,613	122,677	245,484,207	1,573,645	50,696,958	29.5	865	255
Minnesota	2,536,078	50.2	249,887	151,888,199	71,156	143,475,803	865,573	27,517,148	28.5	985	281
Mississippi	1,319,047	47.3	109,857	53,357,154	28,592	49,576,395	360,168	8,602,614	26.0	833	217
Missouri	2,711,658	48.5	236,856	144,155,847	67,732	136,834,192	864,824	25,002,040	28.6	873	250
Montana	454,990	50.2	53,220	18,003,439	15,631	16,580,395	127,057	2,978,749	29.4	1170	344
Nebraska	834,591	49.0	75,340	45,383,557	22,882	43,247,924	287,677	8,080,634	30.4	903	274
Nevada	1,065,834	50.2	90,756	53,521,023	25,193	49,415,233	367,785	11,387,020	27.8	852	236
New Hampshire	625,098	49.4	75,719	35,390,604	19,940	31,947,068	210,123	6,932,312	26.3	1211	319
New Jersey	4,187,588	48.7	435,653	271,730,202	135,696	253,723,585	1,431,550	52,061,380	31.1	1040	324
New Mexico	897,921	48.8	67,806	28,621,714	18,558	26,662,217	216,169	5,427,694	27.4	755	207
New York	9,348,555	48.5	1,024,227	535,198,207	282,248	496,927,363	2,758,075	101,168,732	27.6	1096	302

North Carolina	3,966,941	48.6	377,313	189,425,908	100,064	177,233,943	1,222,486	33,913,099	26.5	951	252
North Dakota	319,093	50.4	31,068	16,532,780	10,231	15,734,526	110,624	2,746,281	32.9	974	321
Ohio	5,456,573	48.4	482,637	287,906,828	133,880	271,584,567	1,852,211	54,319,327	27.7	885	245
Oklahoma	1,712,406	49.3	163,313	71,559,114	40,628	65,831,383	453,637	11,826,671	24.9	954	237
Oregon	1,744,840	49.7	152,029	82,348,607	47,111	76,929,691	495,893	15,070,446	31.0	871	270
Pennsylvania	5,906,611	48.5	541,574	310,182,963	151,962	290,144,436	1,900,465	58,240,113	28.1	917	257
Rhode Island	509,106	48.2	51,647	27,430,138	15,543	25,690,433	159,223	4,991,885	30.1	1014	305
South Carolina	1,908,327	47.7	176,501	83,665,241	49,564	77,217,857	592,458	15,058,126	28.1	925	260
South Dakota	365,981	49.1	38,042	19,346,104	11,772	18,257,270	120,077	2,945,449	30.9	1039	322
Tennessee	2,732,498	48.2	273,183	131,285,210	62,805	121,174,791	809,607	23,467,382	23.0	1000	230
Texas	10,596,434	49.2	1,018,495	508,639,150	229,782	466,016,330	3,115,345	91,135,442	22.6	961	217
Utah	1,144,210	49.5	110,079	50,419,338	31,621	46,456,607	360,573	9,605,246	28.7	962	276
Vermont	307,892	49.7	39,466	15,986,508	10,325	14,754,046	101,299	2,736,392	26.2	1282	335
Virginia	3,435,508	48.3	300,891	156,725,670	85,716	146,457,585	1,097,200	33,829,138	28.5	876	250
Washington	2,963,152	49.4	238,041	135,673,789	77,392	127,268,529	794,455	25,654,953	32.5	803	261
West Virginia	840,249	48.0	63,895	28,306,012	19,538	26,695,210	204,504	4,986,088	30.6	760	233
Wisconsin	2,744,977	50.1	222,124	152,491,694	69,558	145,422,663	947,572	28,413,184	31.3	809	253
Wyoming	243,364	49.8	27,513	12,814,779	8,836	12,020,204	73,794	1,954,741	32.1	1131	363

A=Employer firm ratio: Number of employer firms as a percentage of number of all firms.

B=Firm density: All firm number per 10,000 persons in the population.

C=Employer density: Employer firm number per 10,000 persons in the population.

Data Sources: Population data are from the Census 2000 Summary File 3 (SF 3) - Sample Data; 2002 Survey of Business Owners.

Table 4A.3 Change in the Number of Establishments and Employment of Minority Women-owned Firms Resulting from Closure, Expansion, and Contraction, 1997–2000

Women-owned establishments	1997 Total	Establishment / employment change		
		1997–1998	1997–1999	1997–2000
All women-owned establishments	**890,266**			
Deaths		81,683	153,130	221,915
Expansions		294,856	290,860	279,980
Contractions		203,823	211,603	196,981
Employment in all women-owned establishments	**6,674,589**			
Net change resulting from deaths		-316,071	-667,293	-1,046,902
Net change resulting from expansions		1,272,380	1,475,196	1,679,607
Net change resulting from contractions		-736,814	-883,760	-911,236
Total net change in employment		219,495	-75,857	-278,531
African American women-owned establishments	**21,286**			
Deaths		2,650	4,922	6,790
Expansions		7,188	6,354	6,137
Contractions		4,841	5,022	4,444
Employment in African American women-owned establishments	**166,091**			
Net change resulting from deaths		-7,008	-37,603	-51,663
Net change resulting from expansions		35,049	39,279	41,540
Net change resulting from contractions		-26,441	-30,602	-26,145
Total net change in employment		1,600	-28,926	-36,268
Asian / Pacific Islander women-owned establishments	**54,364**			
Deaths		4,238	8,357	12,489
Expansions		19,715	18,916	18,660
Contractions		12,210	14,048	12,222
Employment in Asian / Pacific Islander women-owned establishments	**284,501**			
Net change resulting from deaths		-10,790	-29,597	-44,761

Table 4A.3 Change in the Number of Establishments and Employment of Minority Women-owned Firms Resulting from Closure, Expansion, and Contraction, 1997–2000—continued

Women-owned establishments	1997 Total	Establishment / employment change		
		1997–1998	1997–1999	1997–2000
Net change resulting from expansions		64,107	70,010	81,671
Net change resulting from contractions		-35,790	-44,900	-41,683
Total net change in employment		17,527	-4,487	-4,773
American Indian / Alaska Native women-owned establishments	**8,190**			
Deaths		665	1,231	2,043
Expansions		3,270	2,940	2,355
Contractions		2,016	1,873	1,759
Employment in American Indian/ Alaska Native women-owned establishments	**65,105**			
Net change resulting from deaths		-2,588	-4,551	-7,018
Net change resulting from expansions		23,698	24,035	37,407
Net change resulting from contractions		-6,074	-6,741	-6,929
Total net change in employment		15,036	12,743	23,460
Hispanic women-owned establishments	**34,377**			
Deaths		3,192	6,197	9,241
Expansions		11,410	11,130	10,655
Contractions		7,192	7,539	6,748
Employment in Hispanic women-owned establishments	**225,240**			
Net change resulting from deaths		-9,863	-23,349	-41,586
Net change resulting from expansions		122,349	91,448	60,053
Net change resulting from contractions		-26,778	-30,717	-28,754
Total net change in employment		85,708	37,382	-10,287

Data Source: Special tabulations from the U.S. Census Bureau for the National Women's Business Council.

APPENDIX 4B
Data Comparability to Prior Surveys

The data for 2002 are not directly comparable to data from previous survey years for variables constituting the U.S. total because of several significant changes to the survey methodology. [7] The most significant change occurred in data presentation by kind of business with the transition from the 1987 Standard Industrial Classification (SIC) system to the 2002 North American Industry Classification System (NAICS).

Comparability of the 1997 SWOBE and 2002 SBO Data by Industry

The data presented in the 2002 SBO are based on the 2002 NAICS. Previous data were presented according to the SIC system developed in the 1930s. Because of this change, comparability between census years is limited (see Relationship to Historical Industry Classifications section).

The 2002 SBO covers more of the economy than any previous survey. New for 2002 are data on information, finance and insurance, real estate, and health-care industries. The scope of the census includes virtually all sectors of the economy.

Additional information about NAICS is available from the Census Bureau Internet site at www.census.gov/naics.

The Status of the Economic Census

The economic census is the major source of facts about the structure and functioning of the nation's economy. It provides essential information for government, business, industry, and the general public. Title 13 of the United States Code (Sections 131, 191, and 224) directs the Census Bureau to take the economic census every 5 years, covering years ending in 2 and 7.

---

7   Based on information provided at http://www.census.gov/econ/census02/text/sbo/sbomethodology. htm.

The economic census furnishes an important part of the framework for such composite measures as the gross domestic product estimates, input/output measures, production and price indexes, and other statistical series that measure short-term changes in economic conditions. Specific uses of economic census data are the following:

- Policymaking agencies of the federal government use the data to monitor economic activity and to assess the effectiveness of policies.

- State and local governments use the data to assess business activities and tax bases within their jurisdictions and to develop programs to attract business.

- Trade associations study trends in their own and competing industries, which allows them to keep their members informed of market changes.

- Individual businesses use the data to locate potential markets and to analyze their own production and sales performance relative to industry or area averages.

Basis of Reporting

The economic census is conducted on an establishment basis. A company operating at more than one location is required to file a separate report for each store, factory, shop, or other location.

Each establishment is assigned a separate industry classification based on its primary activity and not that of its parent company. (For selected industries, only payroll, employment, and classification are collected for individual establishments, while other data are collected on a consolidated basis.)

The Survey of Business Owners (SBO) is conducted on a company or firm basis rather than an establishment basis. A company or firm is a business consisting of one or more domestic establishments that the reporting firm specified under its ownership or control at the end of 2002.

Industry Classifications

Data from the 2002 SBO are summarized by kind of business based on the 2002 North American Industry Classification System (NAICS). The 2002

SBO includes all firms operating during 2002 with receipts of $1,000 or more which are classified in one or more of the following NAICS sectors:

11	Forestry, fishing and hunting, and agricultural support services (NAICS 113-115)
21	Mining
22	Utilities
23	Construction
31–33	Manufacturing
42	Wholesale trade
44–45	Retail trade
48–49	Transportation and warehousing
51	Information
52	Finance and insurance
53	Real estate and rental and leasing
54	Professional, scientific, and technical services
55	Management of companies and enterprises
56	Administrative and support and waste management and remediation services
61	Educational services
62	Health care and social assistance
71	Arts, entertainment, and recreation
72	Accommodation and food services
81	Other services (except public administration)
99	Industries not classified

The 20 NAICS sectors are subdivided into 96 subsectors (three-digit codes) and 317 industry groups (four-digit codes).

The following NAICS industries are not covered in the 2002 SBO:

- Crop and animal production (NAICS 111, 112)
- Scheduled air transportation (NAICS 4811, part)
- Rail transportation (NAICS 482)
- Postal service (NAICS 491)
- Funds, trusts, and other financial vehicles (NAICS 525), except real estate investment trusts (NAICS 525930)

- Religious, grantmaking, civic, professional, and similar organizations (NAICS 813)
- Private households (NAICS 814), and
- Public administration (NAICS 92).

Relationship to Historical Industry Classifications

Prior to the 2002 SBO, data were published according to the Standard Industrial Classification (SIC) system. NAICS identifies new industries, redefines concepts, and develops classifications to reflect changes in the economy. While many of the individual NAICS industries correspond directly to industries as defined under the SIC system, most of the higher level groupings do not. Particular care should be taken in comparing data for construction, manufacturing, retail trade, and wholesale trade, which are sector titles used in both the NAICS and SIC systems, but cover somewhat different groups of industries.[8]

Geographic Area Coding

Accurate and complete information on the physical location of each establishment is required to tabulate the economic census data for states, metropolitan and micropolitan statistical areas, counties, and corporate municipalities (places) including cities, towns, townships, villages, and boroughs. Respondents were required to report their physical location (street address, municipality, county, and state) if it differed from their mailing address. For establishments not surveyed by mail (and those single-establishment companies that did not provide acceptable information on physical location), location information from administrative sources is used as a basis for coding.

The 2002 SBO data are presented for the United States, each state and the District of Columbia; metropolitan and micropolitan statistical areas; counties; and corporate municipalities (places) including cities, towns, townships, villages, and boroughs with 100 or more minority- or women-owned firms. Although collected on a company basis, data are published such that firms with more than one domestic establishment are counted in each geographic area in which they operate. The employment, payroll, and receipts reflect the sum of their locations within the specified geographic area and are, therefore,

---

8 A description and comparison of the NAICS and SIC systems can be found in the 2002 NAICS and 1987 Correspondence Tables on the Internet at www.census.gov/epcd/naics02/N02TOS87.HTM.

additive to higher levels. The sum of firms, however, reflects all firms in a given tabulation level and is not additive. For example, a firm with operating locations in two counties will be counted in both counties, but only once in the state total.

Historical Information of the Economic Census

The economic census has been taken as an integrated program at 5-year intervals since 1967 and before that for 1954, 1958, and 1963. Prior to that time, individual components of the economic census were taken separately at varying intervals.

The economic census traces its beginnings to the 1810 Decennial Census, when questions on manufacturing were included with those for population. Coverage of economic activities was expanded for the 1840 Decennial Census and subsequent censuses to include mining and some commercial activities. The 1905 Manufactures Census was the first time a census was taken apart from the regular decennial population census. Censuses covering retail and wholesale trade and construction industries were added in 1930, as were some service trades in 1933. Censuses of construction, manufacturing, and the other business censuses were suspended during World War II.

The 1954 Economic Census was the first to be fully integrated, providing comparable census data across economic sectors and using consistent time periods, concepts, definitions, classifications, and reporting units. It was the first census to be taken by mail, using lists of firms provided by the administrative records of other federal agencies. Since 1963, administrative records also have been used to provide basic statistics for very small firms, reducing or eliminating the need to send them census report forms.

The range of industries covered in the economic census expanded between 1967 and 2002. The census of construction industries began on a regular basis in 1967, and the scope of service industries, introduced in 1933, was broadened in 1967, 1977, and 1987. While a few transportation industries were covered as early as 1963, it was not until 1992 that the census broadened to include all of transportation, communications, and utilities. Also new for 1992 was coverage of financial, insurance, and real estate industries. With these additions, the economic census and the separate census of governments and census of agriculture collectively covered roughly 98 percent of all economic activity.

New for 2002 is coverage of four industries classified in the agriculture, forestry, and fishing sector under the SIC system: landscape architectural services, landscaping services, veterinary services, and pet care services.

The Survey of Business Owners, formerly known as the Survey of Minority-owned Business Enterprises, was first conducted as a special project in 1969 and was incorporated into the economic census in 1972 along with the Survey of Women-owned Businesses.

An economic census has also been taken in Puerto Rico since 1909, in the Virgin Islands of the United States and Guam since 1958, in the Commonwealth of the Northern Mariana Islands since 1982, and in American Samoa for the first time as part of the 2002 Economic Census.

Printed statistical reports from the 1992 and earlier censuses provide historical figures for the study of long-term time series and are available in some large libraries. Reports for 1997 were published primarily on the Internet and copies of 1992 reports are also available there. CD–ROMs issued from the 1987, 1992, and 1997 Economic Censuses contain databases that include nearly all data published in print, plus additional statistics, such as ZIP Code statistics, published only on CD–ROM.

Sources for More Information

More information about the scope, coverage, classification system, data items, and publications for the 2002 Economic Census and related surveys is published in the Guide to the 2002 Economic Census at www.census.gov/econ/census02/guide. More information on the methodology, procedures, and history of the census will be published in the *History of the 2002 Economic Census* at www.census.gov/econ/www/history.html.

Comparability of the 2002 and 1997 SBO Data by Gender, Race, and Ethnicity

The following changes were made in survey methodology in 2002 which affect comparability with past reports:[9]

---

9   See http://www.census.gov/econ/census02/text/sbo/sbomethodology.htm#comparability for more information

The 1997 Surveys of Minority- and Women-Owned Business Enterprises (SMOBE/SWOBE) form that was mailed to sole proprietors or self-employed individuals who were single filers or who filed joint tax returns instructed the respondent to mark one box that best described the gender, Spanish/Hispanic/Latino origin, and race of the primary owner(s). The gender question included an equal male/female ownership option.

The 2002 SBO form that was mailed to sole proprietors or self-employed individuals who were single filers or who filed a joint tax return instructed the respondent to provide the percentage of ownership for each owner and the gender of the owner(s). The equal male/female ownership option was eliminated.

The form that corporations/partnerships received in 1997 requested the percentage of ownership by gender of the owners. In 2002, a business was asked to report the percentage of ownership and gender for each of the three largest percentage owners.

Male/female ownership of a business in both 1997 and 2002 was based on the gender of the person(s) owning the majority interest in the business. However, in 2002, equally male/female ownership was based on equal shares of interest reported for businesses with male and female owners. Businesses equally male-/female-owned were tabulated and published as a separate entity in both 1997 and 2002.

The 1997 SWOBE/SMOBE forms may be viewed at www.census.gov/epcd/www/pdf/97cs/mb1.pdf (corporations/partnerships) or at www.census.gov/epcd/www/pdf/97cs/mb2.pdf (sole proprietors or self-employed individuals).

The 2002 SBO forms may be viewed at www.census.gov/csd/sbo/sbo1.pdf (corporations/partnerships) or at www.census.gov/csd/sbo/sbo2.pdf (sole proprietors or self-employed individuals).

The Hispanic or Latino origin and racial response categories were updated in 2002 to meet the latest Office of Management and Budget guidelines. There were nineteen check-box response categories and four write-in areas on the 2002 SBO questionnaire, compared to the twenty check-box response categories and five write-in areas on the 1997 SMOBE/SWOBE.

The Hispanic or Latino origin of business ownership was defined as two groups:

- Hispanic or Latino
- Not Hispanic or Latino

Four Hispanic subgroups were used on the survey questionnaires: Mexican, Mexican American, Chicano; Puerto Rican; Cuban; and Other Spanish/Hispanic/Latino.

The 2002 SBO question on race included fourteen separate response categories and two areas where respondents could write in a more specific race. The response categories and write-in answers were combined to create the following five standard OMB race categories:

- American Indian and Alaska Native
- Asian
- Black or African American
- Native Hawaiian and Other Pacific Islander
- White

Response check boxes were added for "Samoan" and "Guamanian or Chamorro."

The check box for "Some Other Race" and the corresponding write-in area provided in 1997 were deleted.

If the "American Indian and Alaska Native" race category was selected, the respondent was instructed to print the name of the enrolled or principal tribe.

In 1997, sole proprietors or self-employed individuals who were single filers or who filed a joint tax return were asked to mark a box to indicate the Spanish/Hispanic/Latino origin of the primary owner(s) and to mark the one box that best described the race of the primary owner(s). In 2002, they were asked to provide the percentage of ownership for the primary owner(s), his/her Spanish/Hispanic/Latino origin, and to select one or more race categories to indicate what the owner considers himself/herself to be.

The form that corporations/partnerships received in 1997 requested the percentage of ownership by Spanish/Hispanic/Latino origin and race of the owners. In 2002, a business was asked to report the percentage of ownership, Spanish/Hispanic/Latino origin, and race for each of the three largest owners, allowing them to mark one or more races to indicate what the owner considers himself/herself to be. The 2002 SBO was the first economic census in which each owner could self-identify with more than one racial group, so it was possible for a business to be classified and tabulated in more than one racial group.

Business ownership in both 1997 and 2002 was based on the Hispanic or Latino origin and race of the person(s) owning majority interest in the business; however, in 2002, multiple-race reporting by the owner(s) could affect where a business was classified. Note: In the 2000 population census, 2.4 percent of the population reported more than one race.

The *Survey of Business Owners: Native Hawaiian- and Other Pacific Islander-Owned Firms* report is new for 2002. Previously, estimates for this group of business owners were included in the *Asian- and Pacific Islander-Owned Businesses* report for some tables (at the U.S., state, and metropolitan area by kind of business level). However, estimates at the county, place, and size of firm (employment, receipts) levels provided only the total number of businesses classified as Asian- and Pacific Islander-owned, with no detailed estimates by subgroup. Therefore, particular care should be taken in comparing the estimates for Asian-owned firms and/or Native Hawaiian- and Pacific Islander-owned firms from 1997 to 2002.

5 Entrepreneurship *and* Education: What *is* Known *and* Not Known *about the* Links Between Education *and* Entrepreneurial Activity

Synopsis

The importance of individual entrepreneurial activity to economic growth and well-being at the national level for both industrialized and developing countries is well established.[1] Research has suggested important links between education and venture creation and entrepreneurial performance. To the extent that education can provide both a greater supply of entrepreneurs and higher levels of entrepreneurial performance, appropriate investments are justified. Thus the question of the significance of the impact of education on selection into entrepreneurship and entrepreneurial performance is an important one. This paper provides a review of research that examines the relationship between both general education and education specific to entrepreneurship, and entrepreneurship and entrepreneurial performance.

A review of recent research measuring the impact of general education on entrepreneurship and entrepreneurial performance suggests three key generalizations. First, the evidence suggesting a positive link between education and entrepreneurial performance is robust. Second, although the link between education and selection into entrepreneurship is somewhat ambiguous, evidence suggests that when "necessity entrepreneurship" and "opportunity entrepreneurship" are considered separately, and when country differences are considered, the link is less ambiguous. Finally, the relationship between education and selection into entrepreneurship is not linear in nature. The highest levels of entrepreneurship are linked to individuals with at least some college education. Education beyond a baccalaureate degree has generally not been found to be positively linked to entrepreneurship.

---

1 This chapter was prepared under contract with the U.S. Small Business Administration, Office of Advocacy, by Mark Weaver, professor of entrepreneurship, Louisiana State University; Pat Dickson, associate professor, Wake Forest University; and George Solomon, associate professor, George Washington University.

The findings of the review of research specific to entrepreneurship education indicate that although existing research does not provide definitive evidence of direct economic impacts from entrepreneurship education, the research does provide evidence suggesting such links. The review acknowledges the limitations, both methodologically and theoretically, of current entrepreneurship education research, but also reveals the growing understanding of how the precursors of entrepreneurial activity can be important and measurable outcomes for entrepreneurship education. Finally, based on what is learned about the state of entrepreneurship education in this review, this chapter discusses a number of important policy implications for organizations supporting entrepreneurship education.

Introduction

The primary purpose of this research is to evaluate the impact of education on entrepreneurial activity. Four key research questions are posed. First, as an individual's level of general education increases, does the probability of selection into entrepreneurship increase?[2] Second, is the level of education linked to entrepreneurial performance? Third, does education specific to entrepreneurship lead to higher rates of selection into entrepreneurship? Finally, is education specific to entrepreneurship linked to entrepreneurial performance? The acknowledged importance of entrepreneurship to the economic well-being of a nation and the role of education in encouraging and supporting entrepreneurial activity make these important research questions. The following sections will provide a review of recent research that empirically measures the relationship between general education and entrepreneurship education and entrepreneurial activity.

A Review of Research Linking General Education and Entrepreneurial Activity

Study Purpose

The significant impact of entrepreneurship on the economy of the United States, as well as the economic well-being of both industrialized and develop-

---

2 "Selection into entrepreneurship" means the choice of an individual to forego employment with an existing business in order to pursue some form of self-employment.

ing countries, is well established. Research specific to entrepreneurial activity is both widespread and multidisciplinary in nature. A fundamental assumption that seems to permeate much of the research on entrepreneurship is the positive relationship between education and entrepreneurial activity. In recent years, several international studies have called into question this general assumption. The authors of the Global Entrepreneurship Monitor (GEM) research program, one of the first multi-country studies focusing on a wide range of entrepreneurial issues, suggest from their findings that when viewed across a wide range of countries (34 in 2004) the relationship between the average level of general education and the rate of venture formation is ambiguous and differs greatly across countries.[3] Van der Sluis and colleagues, in two of the most comprehensive meta-analyses of existing research, reach a similar conclusion regarding the relationship between general education and new venture formation, but conclude that the evidence is quite strong indicating a positive relationship between education and entrepreneurial performance.[4] Both of these studies appear to somewhat contradict a wide range of studies reporting positive relationships between education and entrepreneurial activity. The following section will provide a brief review of some of the most recently published research studies and the explanations the studies' authors have offered for the sometimes contradictory findings.

Study Methodology

The following review of the literature has a specific focus on empirical research linking general education to entrepreneurial activity and entrepreneurial firm success and survival, and draws specifically on research published in the past 10 years. Articles for inclusion in this overview were obtained from a wide range of published sources by a thorough database search utilizing ABI/Inform Complete, the Social Sciences Research Network (SSRN) electronic library, the Journal Storage Project (JSTOR) electronic library, the Organisation for Economic Cooperation and Development (OECD) publication archive, and an iterative process utilizing citations provided by recently published research. Because research relating to the economic returns for education is of such great interest, studies span a wide range of academic disciplines including econom-

---

3 Acs, Arenius, Hay, and Minniti, 2004; Autio, 2005; Minniti and Bygrave, 2003; Neck, Zacharakis, Bygrave, and Reynolds, 2003.

4 Van der Sluis, van Praag, and Vijverberg, 2004; 2005.

ics, sociology, and management, among others. Additionally, the published proceedings of three entrepreneurship-focused organizations, the United States Association for Small Business and Entrepreneurship (USASBE), the International Council of Small Business (ICSB), and the Babson-Kauffman Entrepreneurship Conference were reviewed.

Defining Education and Entrepreneurial Outcomes

One difficulty in aggregating research across disciplines, national settings, and time is the wide range of definitions operationalized by researchers relating to both education and entrepreneurship.[5] Education level has alternately been measured in terms of "total years of education," or operationalizated as a dummy variable denoting "secondary school graduate," or "college graduate." In some studies, the acquiring of an advanced graduate degree is the key variable studied. A wide range of measures have also been employed for entrepreneurship and entrepreneurial performance. In some cases, entry into self-employment is the operative measure of entrepreneurship, while in others it is the formation of a new venture. Entrepreneurial performance has been operationalized in such measures at the firm level as "growth in sales," "growth in profits," and "innovation." At the level of the entrepreneur it is measured primarily in terms of "growth in personal income," or "income in comparison to wage earners." Table 5A.1 in the appendix to this chapter provides a brief description of the studies included in this review and how each has operationalized measures of education, entrepreneurship, and entrepreneurial performance. These definitional differences have been offered as explanation by some studies for the contradictory findings sometimes evidenced.

Findings

The literature search yielded 30 studies that explicitly measure the relationship between education and entrepreneurship or education and entrepreneurial performance. Of these studies, twelve were U.S.-based, ten were drawn from Europe, one from Asia, three from Africa, and four included data drawn from multiple countries. Additionally, two meta-analyses drawing on both published and unpublished research going back as far as the early 1980s were identified and are included in this review.

---

5   Ibid.

The most definitive studies aimed at aggregating research measuring general education and entrepreneurship and entrepreneurial performance are those by van der Sluis, van Praag and Vijverberg.[6] The 2004 meta-analysis had as its focus research done in industrialized countries and drew on 94 published and unpublished studies dating to as early as the 1980s. The 2005 meta-analysis focused on research done in developing countries and drew on 60 published and unpublished studies from the same time period. The primary conclusions drawn by the researchers in both studies were similar. First, even given the definitional and measurement difficulties discussed earlier, the researchers conclude that the preponderance of the evidence, in both developing and industrialized nations, supports a positive and significant relationship between the level of education of the entrepreneur and entrepreneurial performance. They conclude that the higher the level of education of the entrepreneur, the higher the level of performance of the venture—whether measured as growth, profits, or earnings power of the entrepreneur. Second, the researchers conclude that the evidence linking general education and selection into entrepreneurship, however measured, is ambiguous and cannot be classified as either positive or negative. These findings are not dissimilar to those expressed by the GEM researchers, who conclude that evidence linking education to entrepreneurial performance is strong, while that linking education to entrepreneurial activity is ambiguous when viewed across national boundaries.[7]

Somewhat different conclusions from those drawn by van der Sluis et al. are suggested by a brief review of 30 published articles describing research done since 1995 (Table 5A.1); for example, the latter finds:

- An individual's educational level is positively associated with the probability of selection into entrepreneurship (or self-employment);
- The higher the average education level in a country, the higher the rates of venture formation;
- Education beyond a baccalaureate degree has generally not been found to be positively linked to selection into entrepreneurship;
- In studies including a broad range of socioeconomic and institutional variables as predictors of selection into entrepreneurship, education is generally the strongest predictor;

---

6   Ibid.

7   Acs, Arenius, Hay, and Minniti, 2004.

- Significant differences in the impact of education on entrepreneurial activity are seen based on ethnicity, but not on gender;
- A significant and positive relationship is observed between the educational level of the entrepreneur (or entrepreneurial team) and various venture performance measures including profitability, growth, and innovation;
- The educational attainment of the entrepreneur (or entrepreneurial team) has not been shown to significantly affect firm survival.

Although these generalizations are consistent with those expressed by both van der Sluis, et al., and other studies regarding the relationship between education and entrepreneurial performance, they do diverge with respect to the relationship between education and selection into entrepreneurship. Three additional conclusions drawn from the research presented in Table 5A.1 may help in providing an explanation. First, the findings of those studies utilizing data drawn from multiple countries suggest important differences across countries in the impact of education on selection into entrepreneurship.[8] Second, when venture type—that is, "necessity" versus "opportunity" entrepreneurship—is considered, significant differences exist.[9] Finally, a number of studies seem to suggest that the relationship between education and selection into entrepreneurship is not linear in nature, with both the lowest and highest levels of education having little impact on selection into entrepreneurship.[10] All three conclusions would appear to be linked. In countries where necessity entrepreneurship is most prevalent, educational attainment would have little impact on selection into entrepreneurship. Van der Sluis et al. offer an economic explanation as to why higher levels of education might in fact have an inverse relationship to selection into entrepreneurship in countries with strong economic opportunities.[11] They cite Le's argument that higher levels of education might offer greater opportunities for high-paid wage employment, making selection into

---

8 Arenius and DeClercq, 2005; Delmar and Davidsson, 2000; McManus, 2000; Uhlaner, Thurik, and Hutjes, 2002.

9 Block and Wagner, 2006; Lofstrom and Wang, 2006; McManus, 2000. Necessity entrepreneurship is entrepreneurial behavior typically driven by the lack of job alternatives, while opportunity entrepreneurship is entrepreneurial behavior that is in response to the recognition of a previously unexploited business opportunity (Reynolds et al., 2005).

10 Minniti and Bygrave, 2004; Neck, Zacharakis, Bygrave, and Reynolds, 2003.

11 Van der Sluis et al., 2004.

entrepreneurship a more difficult choice.[12] The studies conducted by van der Sluis et al., while controlling for country of origin, are unable to control for differences in the types of entrepreneurship—necessity or opportunity—since few of the studies included in their analyses do so.

In brief, it would appear that there is sufficient evidence to suggest that the level of educational attainment by entrepreneurs is significantly and positively associated with entrepreneurial performance. The evidence linking education to selection into entrepreneurship is more ambiguous and differs in important ways across countries. When individual countries are considered, particularly developed economies, a positive relationship does appear to exist between the level of education of an individual and the probability of selection into entrepreneurship, but this relationship is not linear in nature. Individuals with at least some college education appear to be the most likely to select into entrepreneurship, while more highly educated individuals are not.

A Review of Research Linking Entrepreneurship Education and Entrepreneurial Activity

Growth in Entrepreneurship Education

Scholars and researchers in entrepreneurship education in the United States have reported that small business management and entrepreneurship courses at both the two- and four-year college and university levels have grown in both the number and diversity of course offerings from 1990 to 2005. The current number of colleges and universities offering small business management and entrepreneurship education programs has grown to 1,600 (Chart 5.1).[13]

Recent studies indicate that the real total may be far greater and that the course offerings represent a broader range of topics. This expansion of educational offerings has been fueled in part by dissatisfaction with the traditional Fortune 500 focus of business education—dissatisfaction voiced by students and accreditation bodies.[14] The dilemma is not that demand is high but that

---

12 Le, 1999.

13 Solomon et al., 2002; Solomon et al., 1994; Solomon and Fernald, 1991; Solomon, 1979; and Solomon and Sollosy, 1977.

14 Solomon and Fernald, 1991.

Chart 5.1. Number of Schools Offering Courses in Small Business Management and Entrepreneurship, 1947–2004

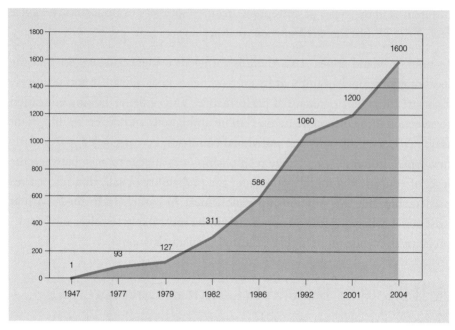

Sources: Solomon, et al., 2002; Solomon et al., 1994; Solomon and Fernald, 1991; Solomon, 1979; and Solomon and Sollosy, 1977

the pedagogy selected meets the new and innovative and creative mindset of students. Plaschka and Welsch recommend an increased focus on entrepreneurial education and more reality- and experientially-based pedagogies such as those recommended by Porter and McKibbin.[15]

The challenge to educators has been to craft courses, programs and major fields of study that meet the rigors of academia while keeping a reality-based focus and entrepreneurial climate in the learning experience environment. If entrepreneurship education is to produce entrepreneurial founders capable of generating real enterprise growth and wealth, the challenge to educators will be to craft courses, programs, and major fields of study that meet the rigors of academia while keeping a reality-based focus and an entrepreneurial climate in the learning experience environment. In addition, the need for new ways of

---

15   Plaschka and Welsch, 1990; Porter and McKibbin, 1988.

thinking to remain competitive has led to entrepreneurship education being applied outside of higher education.

The entrepreneurial experience can be characterized as being chaotic and ill-defined, and entrepreneurship education pedagogies appear to reflect this characterization. In addition, the assumption is often made that it is relatively easy for entrepreneurship students to develop new ideas for their business start-ups. Quite a number of researchers have written about entrepreneurial competencies; however, the competencies that are required for new business start-ups are often addressed by educators in an ad hoc manner. There is little consensus on just what exactly entrepreneurship students should be taught. For entrepreneurship educators, the challenge is to provide the subject matter, resources, and experiences that will prepare entrepreneurship students to cope with the myriad expectations and demands they will face as they start their new ventures. More important, administrators and funders now have added to the discussion by requiring outcome measures—specifically, the number of new business starts as a result of students taking entrepreneurship education courses and programs. Recently *Entrepreneur* magazine joined *The Princeton Review* in ranking entrepreneurship programs. Among the criteria for judging the importance of the entrepreneurial program was the number of business starts generated by students and alumni.

Equally impressive in terms of growth are endowed positions at U.S. colleges and universities. The number of chairs and professorships in entrepreneurship and related fields grew 71 percent, from 237 in 1999 to 406 in 2003 (Chart 5.2). Economists talk about "dollar votes" or voting with one's checkbook, and if that is truly possible, then the popular and government evaluation of endowed positions in entrepreneurship is highly positive, with over a quarter of a billion dollars being spent on newly endowed positions in the past four years. The situation in the United States parallels the situation worldwide, with 563 endowed positions around the world, up from 271 in 1999.[16]

Based on the 1999 survey, the growth in the number of positions in the United States (237 to 406) resulted in a new endowed position every eight days.[17] The rate of growth has been accelerating, as can be seen by the increasingly steep

---

16   Katz, 2004.

17   Ibid.

Chart 5.2 Number of Endowed Positions in the United States, 1962–2003

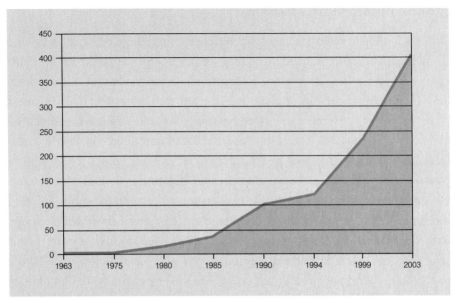

Source: Katz, 2004.

line in Chart 5.2. The earlier growth rates since 1995 were a new endowed position every:

- 8 days (1995–2003);
- 11 days (1995–1999, 112 to 234 positions);
- 66 days (1991–1994, 97 to 112 positions);
- 46 days (1980–1990, 18 to 97 positions); and
- 343 days (1963–1980, 1 to 18 positions).[18]

This growth in endowed chairs is directly correlated to the growth of entrepreneurial activity in the United States. Many successful entrepreneurs are "giving back" to their alma maters in hopes of creating the next generation of entrepreneurs. Colleges and universities see the acquisition of endowed chairs and centers as an opportunity to integrate the theory and concepts in the classroom with the practical reality of starting, managing, and growing new ventures. The significant growth in funding support and educational programs unique

18   Ibid.

to entrepreneurship education leads to the question, "Does education that is uniquely designed to train entrepreneurs lead to entrepreneurial activity?"

Relationship of Entrepreneurial Education and Entrepreneurship: Study Purpose

The purpose of the following section is to review existing research linking various forms of entrepreneurial education to entrepreneurial activity, specifically, those empirical studies linking education both to the act of venture creation and to those antecedents that have been proposed as directly linked to entrepreneurial activity. The overview of research is limited to research published in peer-reviewed outlets between 1995 and 2005. Gorman, Hanlon, and King provide a review of such research for the period between 1985 and 1994, and Dainow provides a review of research prior to 1985.[19] Both reviews look at a wide range of entrepreneurial education issues, and each provides an overview of research linking such education to entrepreneurial outcomes. The findings of these and other earlier studies will be briefly summarized as part of this review. Although a relatively broad body of research focuses on entrepreneurial education and its relationship to the ongoing management of entrepreneurial firms and small- to medium-sized enterprises, this overview is limited to research specifically focusing on new venture creation.

Overview of Theoretical Frameworks Linking Education and Entrepreneurial Activity

A brief review of some theoretical frameworks historically utilized in developing and understanding entrepreneurship education may be of some value. Béchard and Grégoire report, based on their review of entrepreneurship education research, that such research is principally underpinned by academic theories (62.5 percent of the research they reviewed) and less often by social and technical theories (21.2 and 10.6 percent of the research they reviewed).[20] Two of the most often utilized theories are Bandura's "social learning theory" and "action learning theory."[21] Bandura's theory provides a framework involving five steps necessary for learning:

---

19 Gorman, Hanlon, and King, 1997; Dainow, 1986.

20 Béchard and Grégoire, 2005.

21 "Social learning theory," Human, Clark, and Baucus, 2005; "action learning theory," Leitch and Harrison, 1999.

1) skill and attitude assessment, 2) skill and attitude learning, 3) behavioral guidelines and action steps, 4) skill and attitude analysis, and 5) skill practice.[22] The model of action learning was first proposed by Revans and focuses on learning through reflection on actions being taken in solving real organizational problems.[23] While these are only two of many theoretical frameworks utilized, they suggest that a primary focus for entrepreneurial education is the impact of such education on attitudes, skill development, and entrepreneurial actions.

Defining Entrepreneurial Education and Activity

A number of preevious writers have pointed out the significant definitional weaknesses that exist in entrepreneurship education research.[24] As noted by Sexton and Bowman, the most fundamental problem is the definition of entrepreneurial activity—whether it is the founding of a new venture, the acquisition of an existing business, or the management of an ongoing small- to medium-sized firm.[25] De Faoite, Henry, Johnson, and van der Sijde suggest that the activity of interest is most often categorized as either the implementation of a venture or the raising of entrepreneurial awareness, that entrepreneurial education should be considered distinctly different from management training and business skill development, and that it should be specific to a unique stage of the business life cycle.[26]

Entrepreneurship education is often delineated based on the educational source—higher education, vocational training programs, continuing education, or secondary school programs[27]—or the structure of the education—didactic, skill-building or inductive.[28] Unfortunately many entrepreneurship education studies do not provide the underlying theories or strategies employed in the educational intervention. Since most do provide the source of the educational program, this paper uses the organizational framework based on the categori-

---

22   Human, Clark, and Baucus, 2005.

23   Revans, 1971; Leitch and Harrison, 1999.

24   Matlay, 2005.

25   Sexton and Bowman, 1984.

26   De Faoite, Henry, Johnson, and van der Sijde, 2003.

27   Béchard and Grégoire, 2005; Gartner and Vesper, 1994; Raffo, Lovatt, Banks, and O'Connor, 2000; Sexton and Bowman, 1984.

28   Garavan and O'Cinneide, 1994.

zation scheme employed by Raffo, Lovatt, Banks, and O'Connor.[29] They categorize the source of the entrepreneurial training and education as "higher education" (HE), "further education" (FE), and other "vocational education training" (VET). This categorization unfortunately does not clearly delineate education at the secondary level, and it will be noted here when the education course or training offering is at that level.

Following the suggestion of De Faoite and colleagues, attention is focused here on research specific to either the founding of an entrepreneurial venture or the "raising of awareness" associated with the act of entrepreneurship.[30] In specific, as it relates to entrepreneurial awareness, a review of recent research suggests five antecedents for venture creation. These include "entrepreneurial intentions," "opportunity recognition," "entrepreneurial self-efficacy," certain psychological characteristics, and "entrepreneurial knowledge."[31]

General Findings of Earlier Research

Gorman, Hanlon, and King conducted a survey of entrepreneurship education research published between 1985 and 1994.[32] Although their focus was relatively broad (both theoretical and empirical research), they provided a detailed review of empirical research published in leading academic journals that focused on the antecedents of venture creation and the ongoing management of entrepreneurial firms. Their review located 63 articles divided between those focusing on venture creation and those focusing on the management of small- to medium-sized firms. They suggested that the central theme in the research they reviewed is the extent to which formal education can contribute to entrepreneurship. The authors noted that most of the research they reviewed consisted of specific program descriptions and evaluations of those programs. They argued that the existing empirical research published during the time period of their review seems to suggest a consensus among researchers that entrepreneurship can be taught and that entrepreneurial attributes can

---

29   Raffo, Lovatt, Banks, and O'Connor, 2000.

30   De Faoite, Henry, Johnson, and van der Sijde, 2003.

31   "Entrepreneurial intentions," Autio, Keelyey, Klofsten, and Ulfstedt, 1997, Krueger and Carsrud, 1993; "opportunity recognition," DeTienne and Chandler, 2004, Dimov, 2003; "entrepreneurial self-efficacy," Alvarez and Jung, 2003; psychological characteristics, Hansemark, 1998; "entrepreneurial knowledge," Kourilsky and Esfandiari, 1997.

32   Gorman, Hanlon, and King, 1997.

be positively influenced by educational programs. The authors conclude that research on education for entrepreneurship, as of 1994, was still in the exploratory stages, with most studies utilizing cross-sectional survey designs and self-reports, with few basic experimental controls employed.

In one of the earliest studies of entrepreneurship education, Dainow reviewed entrepreneurship education literature for a ten-year period prior to 1984.[33] In his findings, Dainow noted a limited number of empirical studies focusing on entrepreneurship education. He concluded that there was a significant need for a more systematic collection of data and a more varied methodological framework to move research in the area forward.

Study Methodology

The following review of the literature builds upon the Gorman, Hanlon, and King, and the Dainow studies, but with a specific focus on empirical research linking entrepreneurship education and entrepreneurial action. Accordingly, published articles for inclusion in this overview of entrepreneurship education research were obtained by a thorough database search utilizing ABI/ Inform Complete with a broad array of search terms related to entrepreneurship education. The articles are drawn from a wide range of peer-reviewed journals. Additionally, the published proceedings of three entrepreneurship-focused organizations—the United States Association for Small Business and Entrepreneurship (USASBE), the International Council of Small Business (ICSB), and the Babson-Kauffman Entrepreneurship Conference—were reviewed for the study period of 1995–2005. These organizations in particular have a stated purpose of supporting the dissemination of research relating specifically to entrepreneurship education. Articles were categorized as empirical, theoretical, or descriptive, and based on the type of education program studied. Only those empirical articles that reported specific findings related to entrepreneurship education and the links of such education to entrepreneurial antecedents and outcomes associated with new venture formation were included in the overview (Table 5A.2). Although the studies included are not the full range of studies done during the study period, they provide a good representation. Undoubtedly, additional reports relating to specific and unique programs exist that may not be published in either peer-reviewed journals or

---

33   Dainow, 1986.

peer-reviewed conference proceedings, but may appear as narrowly published program reports.

Findings

Of the empirical research articles included in this review. seven were located that attempted to measure the impact of some form of education specifically on the act of venture creation (Table 5A.2). All but one of the studies focused on the outcomes of a specific educational program. Most of the studies were located at the university level, but two reported the results of vocational education programs and one reported the results of a continuing education program. In general, the study authors concluded that there was a significant and positive correlation between participation in the educational programs and venture creation. In those that compared program participants and nonprogram participants, higher rates of venture creation were reported for program participants.

Entrepreneurial intention—the expressed intention to start a venture at some point in the future—is the most often studied antecedent of venture creation. This research draws on a well-established body of literature linking intentions to subsequent actions[34] and has been proposed for some time as the best predictor of entrepreneurial behavior.[35] Six studies testing the relationship between entrepreneurial education and entrepreneurial intentions were located: five were conducted at the university level and one was a vocational training program at the secondary school level. In general, the studies found a positive correlation between entrepreneurial education and the expressed "intent" to form a venture at some point in time. Interestingly, one study noted that a majority of those students expressing an intention to found a venture indicated that they planned to start the venture only after an extended period of 10 years or more. Studies noted that prior work experience affected both participation in the training programs and subsequent intentions to start a venture.

A second antecedent of venture creation measured as an outcome of entrepreneurial education is that of "opportunity recognition." The implicit assumption of these studies is that the ability to recognize venture opportunities will be positively linked to the subsequent creation of ventures, although there is

---

34 Ajzen, 1987; Ajzen and Fishbein, 1980.

35 Honig, 2004; Krueger and Carsrud, 1993; Shapero 1975, 1982.

limited evidence of this linkage. Three studies were located that measured the impact of education on opportunity recognition. In one study, a link was shown between entrepreneurial education, recognition of entrepreneurship as personally desirable, and the level of opportunity recognition. A second study linked specific skill training with opportunity recognition, and a third found a negative correlation between prior industry-specific knowledge and opportunity recognition.

Four studies tested the link between entrepreneurial education and entrepreneurial self-efficacy—an individual's belief that he or she is capable of entrepreneurial behavior. Three of the studies were conducted at the university level and one at the secondary school level. In general the studies conclude that entrepreneurial training positively affects an individual's perception of their ability to start a new venture.

In addition to these three proposed antecedents to venture creation, one study sought to measure the relationship between an entrepreneurial vocational training program and the participants' "need for achievement" and "locus of control." The implied assumption was that those individuals scoring higher on these traits might be more likely to engage in entrepreneurial behavior. A positive relationship between training and changes in these two psychological traits was noted. Also, an entrepreneurial vocational training program at the secondary school level sought to measure the relationship between entrepreneurial education and specific entrepreneurial knowledge proposed as necessary for venture creation. The results of the study indicated that the program did increase the levels of specific entrepreneurial knowledge in participants.

In brief, the following conclusions can be drawn from a review of this literature. First, although the volume of empirical research has increased since Dainow's review in 1986 and has stayed relatively constant with that reviewed by Gorman, Hanlon, and King in 1997, many of the limitations noted by both still seem to persist. Most studies focus on the outcomes of specific educational programs, are exploratory in nature, and employ cross-sectional surveys with few experimental controls. Second, there has been a notable increase in the number of studies focusing on entrepreneurial intentions as a precursor of entrepreneurial behavior following on the broad foundation of research suggesting intentions as the best predictor of subsequent behavior. Third, while the most direct measure of venture creation is the act itself, researchers have come to understand that there may be long time periods between the educational experience and subsequent behavior. Therefore, the focus on proposed antecedents to entrepreneurial behavior has in general gained momentum. Finally, even though the vast majority of research still has as its focus specific and often unique educational programs, the general consensus seems to be that there is a positive correlation between entrepreneurial education and entrepreneurial activity.

Research Implications: What Is Known and Not Yet Known

General Education and Entrepreneurship

The apparent country differences and differences in the types of entrepreneurial opportunities pursued suggest a starting point for understanding why the result of past research measuring the link between general education and selection into entrepreneurship is ambiguous. These findings suggest the importance of considering both the type of entrepreneurship selected by the entrepreneur and the opportunities afforded both by the level of education of the entrepreneur and the economic conditions of the entrepreneur's environment. While the evidence for selection into entrepreneurship may be ambiguous, a strong consensus appears to exist across research studies regarding the significant link between education and entrepreneurial performance. Ultimately, if definitive answers are to be found, a general consensus must be reached regarding how the level of education, selection into entrepreneurship, and entrepreneurial performance are to be operationalized and measured.

Entrepreneurship Education and Entrepreneurship

Given the state of entrepreneurship education research, the strongest conclusion that can be drawn at this point is that there are indications of a positive link between entrepreneurial education and subsequent entrepreneurial activity. The key dilemma facing most researchers is that the evidence also seems to suggest that there might be a lengthy time period between the education experience and subsequent action. This suggests both a need for more long-term longitudinal studies and an increased focus on the antecedents of venture creation. Of equal importance is the need to definitively link any proposed precursors of behavior to the actual behavior both through strong theoretical foundations and empirical research.

Several limitations in the current body of entrepreneurial education research must also be noted. The overreliance on post hoc survey methodologies, the limited focus on specific, unique, and sometimes nontransferable educational programs, and the probability that only the results of successful programs end up being published, are all critical limitations. Additionally, one of the fundamental difficulties in linking entrepreneurship education to entrepreneurial behavior in general through post hoc analysis or even through experimental analysis of existing educational programs is the concern that there is a selection bias at the outset for students choosing to engage in entrepreneurial education. The work of Sagie and Elizur, for example, highlights that psychological differences exist between students enrolled in entrepreneurship courses and those enrolled in general business and economics.[36] These psychological differences are the same as those often measured as antecedents of entrepreneurial behavior.

In spite of these and other measurement difficulties, numerous opportunities exist for future research. First, given the growing empirical research focused on entrepreneurship education, even though the educational programs reviewed are often very different, it may now be possible through meta-analytic techniques to combine existing research with specific outcome measures—particularly venture founding, intentions, and opportunity recognition—to provide a more rigorous test of the impact of entrepreneurial education. Second, the international nature of entrepreneurship education is evident from the research cited here. Interestingly, while there has been much work across countries, little has been done across differing cultures and regions within countries. For example, Audretsch and Lehmann find important differences in the relationship between knowledge spillovers from universities and levels of entrepreneurial activity across regions within the United States.[37] Given the seemingly important relationship between education and entrepreneurial knowledge, there may well also be interesting and important differences in how that relationship leads to venture creation across regions. Finally, such studies as the one completed by Sørensen and Chang and the GEM report have suggested a strong relationship

---

36 Sagie and Elizur, 1999.

37 Audretsch and Lehmann, 2005.

between general education and levels of entrepreneurial activity at the country level.[38] For researchers interested in the relationship between entrepreneurial education and venture creation, separating the effects of education in general at the macro level from entrepreneurial education specifically at the program and individual level is both a challenge and a future opportunity.

Policy Implications

Since education has been shown in multiple situations to have a positive impact on formation and venture success measures, ongoing questions include who is going to pay for these educational efforts, why they are going to pay, and what outcomes the funding source should expect. The most common forms of education specific to entrepreneurship are the short courses and seminars run by chambers of commerce, the U.S. Small Business Administration-supported small business development centers (SBDCs), SCORE, women's business centers, trade/professional associations, and university continuing education centers. Rapid increases in academic institutions and courses at the university level show a significant impact in this area. A key question that needs to be answered here is what all of this means from a public policy and support perspective. Research by Autio et al. showed that entrepreneurial intentions can be changed; others showed the impact of education on starts and success.[39] If education can influence attitudes, intentions, and start-ups, who should be involved and what should be done to further develop these educational resources?

Entrepreneurial Education Policy in the United States

Johnson and Sheehy of the Heritage Foundation offer an illustration of de facto small business policy in the United States vis-à-vis small business policy in other parts of the world (Chart 5.3).[40] The typology presented contains two axes: the horizontal axis represents government intervention, and the vertical axis represents the extent of assistance available to entrepreneurs from government programs. The model also classifies the level of intervention and assistance as "high," meaning governments are greatly involved in the operations of

---

38   Sørensen and Chang, 2006; Neck, Zacharakis, Bygrave, and Reynolds, 2003.

39   Autio et al., 1997.

40   Johnson and Sheehy, 1995.

Chart 5.3 Typology of Public Policy Toward Small Business and Entrepreneurship Education

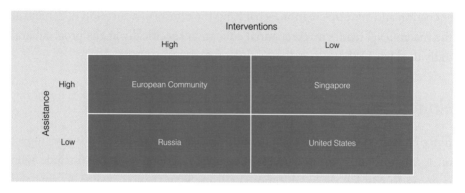

Source: Johnson, B. T., and Sheehy, T. P., *The Index of Economic Freedom*, Heritage Foundation: Washington, D.C., 1995.

a small business and provide an extensive amount of assistance, or "low," meaning that governments basically leave small businesses alone and allow them to survive on their own abilities and resources, and provide minimal assistance programs. In Chart 5.3, the United States falls in the quadrant of low direct intervention and low assistance. Compared with most other parts of the world, the United States adopts a laissez faire policy toward its education and training of small businesses. It is important to examine closely what Chart 5.3 means by low intervention to better understand whether the United States pursues a consistent entrepreneurial education policy.

Johnson and Sheehy's four-tier classification system rates the world's nations (101 of them) in terms of economic freedom. The classification system is based on such issues as property rights, regulation, tax policy, free trade, and other such factors. The levels of intervention and assistance are the key factors they consider. The United States and six other countries fall into the highest category, i.e., economically "free." Hong Kong and Singapore have the highest ratings. Most industrialized countries are classified "mostly free." (A similar work conducted for the Fraser Institute yielded similar ratings.[41]) Even if one does not subscribe to Johnson and Sheehy's subjective rating system, their description of the regulatory environment has face validity and appears to be essentially correct. The conclusion is that free market systems by their

---

41   See Gwartney et al., 1996.

very design are supportive of entrepreneurial ventures and basically allow the market itself to determine who survives. This approach could help explain how the growth in the number of educational programs and professorships has evolved. Without government paying for and controlling everything, educational institutions and entrepreneurs have teamed up to create a broad range of educational efforts.

Role of the States as a Broker to Deliver Support for Entrepreneurs

At the state level, a significant report from the National Governors Association (NGA) found clear and convincing best practices in strengthening state economic policies to create more and more successful entrepreneurial endeavors.[42] One finding they cited to support the need for some level of intervention was that the National Commission on Entrepreneurship had reported that the Inc. 500 firms grew at an average rate of 1,312 percent over the last five years and that to prosper, states needed to try to create the conditions to make this possible for more firms. Of particular interest here is the need the governors saw to leverage state resources to promote growth. States such as Oklahoma, Kansas, Michigan, Louisiana, and Maine were recognized for their efforts in developing technology centers to turn innovations into opportunities, leveraging existing SBDCs to develop training focusing on networks, development of a community of mentors and service providers for entrepreneurs, and ways to nurture entrepreneurs in rural or disadvantaged areas.

A second major effort cited in the NGA report was to "bolster entrepreneurial, capital, and research networks." Nevada worked to increase efforts with angel networks; Washington added a policy representative to its technology council; and Michigan and Maryland helped integrate resources, including education, university researchers, and funders.

A third major area of interest was termed "deploy the workforce, unemployment, and community development systems to support entrepreneurs and promote entrepreneurship." Several examples of education-related efforts were included: Maine lets the unemployed attend start-up seminars and develop business plans while collecting unemployment; Missouri and Illinois offer entrepreneurship workshops to dislocated and disadvantaged workers to

---

42   National Governors Association, 2004.

promote self-employment; and Nebraska uses subsidies to community colleges to teach and coordinate ongoing efforts to educate entrepreneurs.

Within this "bolstering" effort the governors also proposed nurturing entrepreneurs through the K-12 system to create a pipeline of future entrepreneurs and assist with curriculum design. The logic was that attitude and beliefs can be influenced long before the technical skills need to be developed. This result is consistent with the research reported here. In addition, it was stated that the public universities should provide entrepreneurship education in curricular and noncurricular areas to develop new skill sets and career alternatives. The report from the National Governors Association begins the process of assuring all states that this is a legitimate and necessary field of study and should be encouraged.

A Solomon report cited earlier suggests that individual universities may be ahead of the governors, but the support at the state level is great to see.[43] An excellent summary statement excerpted from a report by the Kauffman Foundation stated that states have to become as "entrepreneurial as the clients they serve."[44]

This focus on entrepreneurship, as well as the recognized need for entrepreneurship training and for academic education efforts in many disciplines associated with entrepreneurship, is an indication that more education for entrepreneurship is coming. Ongoing evaluation of the impacts and best practices is critical to retaining the innovation and flexibility learned from entrepreneurs.[45] Moreover, attention to best practices keeps the focus on the need to stay innovative and use the passion and support that exist in the field of entrepreneurship education.

Several of the questions Kuratko posed have some policy as well as educational implications. For example, the fact that the use of technology by entrepreneurs and entrepreneurial educators is limited is often an access issue: entrepreneurs are often in areas that do not have high-speed Internet access, and educators do not have "smart" classrooms. Public support of education budgets is one solution, of course, but access is a state and local issue for

---

43 Solomon, Duffy, and Tarabishy, 2002.

44 Excerpted in National Governors Association, 2004.

45 Kuratko, 2005.

which regulatory concerns will need to be addressed. Pointing policymakers to the topics Kuratko identifies—the ongoing need for vision, willingness to change, and rethinking risk—may be a way to help them stay focused on supporting entrepreneurial efforts rather than creating new programs.

Evidence that both general and entrepreneurial education influence entrepreneurial activity provides even more reasons to support opportunities for people of all ages, ethnicities, and genders to take part in education efforts. These efforts can serve as a source for new ideas, help in identification of gaps in niche markets, and provide the knowledge needed to succeed in new ventures. Evidence in current research of the positive relationship between educational attainment and profitability, growth, and innovation would suggest that traditional educational institutions are a valuable tool in advancing the goals of venture formation and success. Support in the form of, for example, a self-rejuvenating loan fund that encourages people to seek additional educational opportunities, could increase the potential for new ventures.

Chambers of commerce and trade associations could be a significant private sector force by using their contacts and resources to offer educational opportunities to nonmembers at differential and affordable fees, thereby helping raise the overall educational level of the community. This support could mean more and stronger ventures in the future.

Foundations also have a role to play in finding ways to support educational efforts and help keep students in school longer. Computer training, minority- and ethnic-based support systems, training for people transitioning to teaching from other professions, and similar efforts could be enhanced to produce a local and national good.

Universities may need to rededicate themselves to providing scholarship and financial aid to underserved populations to help increase the general educational level of the nation and of regions within it. The consistent evidence that education is linked to higher entrepreneurial performance and productivity is supported by the economic evidence provided by the OECD suggesting significant productivity increases for each year of added education.[46]

---

46   Englander and Gurney, 1994.

At the federal level, expansion of the tax savings plans that currently exist, income tax credits for tuition and fees, and other tax incentives seem appropriate given the evidence of the returns in entrepreneurial performance afforded by education. Research should also be encouraged at the national level to more clearly define the impact on entrepreneurial starts and performance for each measurable increase in the average national and regional levels of educational attainment, and what these increased starts and performance mean for national and regional productivity.

Conclusions

The primary purpose of this study has been to provide a review of relevant research related to what is known and not known about the links between general education, selection into entrepreneurship, and entrepreneurial performance, and between entrepreneurial education and entrepreneurial activity. A further purpose is to provide suggestions for both future research and future policy decisions. With respect to general education, the general consensus across research from multiple countries is that there is a significant and positive relationship between education and entrepreneurial performance. The findings regarding the link between education and selection into entrepreneurship are ambiguous: several possible explanations for this ambiguity exist. In research published in recent years—in particular, research that considers the necessity or opportunity types of entrepreneurship—the relationship between education and selection into entrepreneurship seems to be less ambiguous and in general positive.

This report also highlights the significant increase in entrepreneurship education programs. While these programs have been growing at all levels, significant growth has occurred in particular at the university level, in programs, course offerings, and endowed professorships. In part because of the rapid growth of entrepreneurial programs and in part because of a limited understanding of the effectiveness of specific forms of entrepreneurial education, this growth has often been chaotic and ill-defined. Underlying the growth is the implicit assumption that entrepreneurship can be taught and that entrepreneurial education can have a measurable impact on entrepreneurial activity. A review of research published between 1995 and 2005 linking entrepreneurship education with entrepreneurial activities highlights both the current state of knowledge and several important questions regarding future research. The most fundamental difficulty, and therefore a future opportunity for entrepreneurship education research, is developing a consensus regarding both the definitions of entrepreneurial education and what the focus should be regarding appropriate and measurable outcomes for such education. The authors of this report have chosen to focus on research relating to new venture creation rather than on the link between education and the managing of ongoing small to medium-sized enterprises. For this purpose, it would seem that the most appropriate and measurable outcome for entrepreneurship education would be the formation of a new venture; however, research strongly suggests that such outcomes may often be many years after the educational experience. Therefore, it is not surprising that many researchers have chosen to focus on a range of precursors of venture creation.

The most often studied antecedents are "entrepreneurial intentions" and "opportunity recognition." A review of this research provides indications of a positive link between entrepreneurial education and subsequent entrepreneurial activity. It also suggests that a study of the precursors of entrepreneurial activity or venture founding can provide relevant measures of educational impact. The limitations of the existing research do not allow more definitive conclusions at this time. This overview of existing research suggests, in order to overcome these limitations, a need for more longitudinal studies as well as research aimed specifically at linking the proposed antecedents of entrepreneurial activity to the act of venture founding.

The growth of entrepreneurship education and the associated research regarding the impact of such education present several important policy questions both for the institutions and academicians delivering entrepreneurship education and for support organizations providing funding for entrepreneurship education. Although the findings regarding the link between entrepreneurial education and entrepreneurial activity are not definitive, there is significant research suggesting such a linkage. Reports of the positive impact of specific programs have led a number of government and private sector support organizations to call for increasing support for entrepreneurship education. The future challenge for support organizations will be to encourage entrepreneurship education providers to clearly delineate the theoretical foundations of their course and program offerings and to both track and adequately measure the impact of the programs they provide over time. Second, support organizations should encourage the frequent consolidation of research findings in order to assess the cumulative evidence provided by these reports regarding the link between entrepreneurial education and entrepreneurial activity. Finally, based on what is learned through this research as well as ongoing "best practices," support organizations should encourage entrepreneurial education providers to adopt, when merited, innovations and processes known to provide outcomes linked to entrepreneurial activity.

References

Acs, Z.J., Arenius, P., Hay, M., and Minniti, M. (2004). *Global entrepreneurship monitor: 2004 executive report.* Babson, MA: Babson College.

Acs, Z.C., and Armington, C. (2005). *Using census BITS to explore entrepreneurship, geography and economic growth.* Small Business Research Summary no. 248, Washington, D.C.: U.S. Small Business Administration, Office of Advocacy.

Aidis, R., and Mickiewicz, T. (2004). *Which entrepreneurs expect to expand their businesses? Evidence from survey data in Lithuania.* William Davidson Institute Working Paper no. 723, William Davidson Institute, University of Michigan.

Ajzen, I. (1987). Attitudes, traits, and actions: Dispositional prediction of behavior in personality and social psychology. *Advances in Experimental Social Psychology,* 20, 1–63.

Ajzen, I., and Fishbein, M. (1980). *Understanding attitudes and predicting social behavior.* Englewood Cliffs, NJ : Prentice-Hall.

Almus, M., and Nerlinger, E.A. (1999). Growth of new technology based firms: Which factors matter? *Small Business Economics,* 13(2), 141–154.

Alvarez, R.D., and Jung, D. (2003). Educational curricula and self-efficacy: Entrepreneurial orientation and new venture intentions among university students in Mexico. *Frontiers of Entrepreneurship Research,* Babson-Kauffman Research Conference Proceedings.

Arenius, P., and DeClercq, D. (2005). A network-based approach to opportunity recognition. *Small Business Economics,* 24(3), 249–265.

Audretsch, D.B., and Lehmann, E.E. (2005). Does the knowledge spillover theory of entrepreneurship hold for regions? *Research Policy* 34(8), 1191–1202.

Autio, E. (2005). *Global entrepreneurship monitor: 2005 report on high-expectation entrepreneurship.* Babson, MA: Babson College.

Autio, E., Keelyey, R., Klofsten, M., and Ulfstedt, T. (1997). Entrepreneurial intent among students: Testing an intent model in Asia, Scandinavia and the United States. *Frontiers of Entrepreneurship Research*, Wellesley, MA: Babson College.

Basu, A., and Goswami, A. (1999). Determinants of South Asian entrepreneurial growth in Britain: A multivariate analysis. *Small Business Economics*, 13, 57–70.

Béchard, J., and Grégoire, D. (2005). Entrepreneurship education revisited: The case of higher education. *Academy of Management Learning and Education*, 4(1): 22–43.

Block, J., and Wagner, M. (2006). *Necessity and opportunity entrepreneurs in Germany: Characteristics and earnings differentials*. Working Paper Series, Munich, Germany: Munich University of Technology.

Bosma, N., van Praag, M., Thurik, R., and de Wit, G. (2004). The value of human and social capital investments for the business performance of startups. *Small Business Economics*, 23, 227–236.

Brännback, M., Heinonen, J., Hudd, I., and Paasio, K. (2005). A comparative study on entrepreneurial opportunity recognition and the role of education among Finnish business school students, Presented at the Annual ICSB Conference, Washington D.C.

Camp, S.M. (2005). *The innovation-entrepreneurship NEXUS: A national assessment of entrepreneurship and regional economic growth and development*. Small Business Research Summary no. 256, Washington, D.C.: U.S. Small Business Administration, Office of Advocacy.

Charney, A.H., and Libecap, G. (2000). *The impact of entrepreneurship education: An evaluation of the Berger entrepreneurship program at the University of Arizona, 1985–1999*. Kauffman Research Series. Kansas City, MO: Ewing Marion Kauffman Foundation.

Chrisman, J.J., McMullan, E., and Hall, J. (2005). The influence of guided preparation on the long-term performance of new ventures. *Journal of Business Venturing*, 20: 769–791.

Chrisman, J.J., and McMullan, W.E. (2004). Outsider assistance as a knowledge resource for new venture survival. *Journal of Small Business Management*, 42(3), 229–244.

Dainow, R. (1986). Training and education of entrepreneurs: The current state of the literature. *Journal of Small Business and Entrepreneurship*, 3(4): 10–23.

De Faoite, D., Henry, C., Johnston, K., and van der Sijde, P. (2004). Entrepreneurs' attitudes to training and support initiatives: Evidence from Ireland and the Netherlands. *Journal of Small Business and Enterprise Development*, 11(4), 440–448.

De Faoite, D., Henry, C., Johnston, K., and van der Sijde, P. (2003). Education and training for entrepreneurs: A consideration of initiative in Ireland and the Netherlands. *Education & Training*, 45(8/9), 430–437.

Delmar, F., and Davidsson, P. (2000). Where do they come from? Prevalence and characteristics of nascent entrepreneurs. *Entrepreneurship and Regional Development*, 12, 1–23.

DeTienne, D.R. and Chandler, G.N. (2004). Opportunity identification and its role in the entrepreneurial classroom: A pedagogical approach and empirical test. *Academy of Management Learning and Education*, 3(3): 242–257.

Dimov, D.P. (2003). The nexus of individual and opportunity: Opportunity recognition as a learning process. *Frontiers of Entrepreneurship Research*, Babson-Kauffman Research Conference Proceedings.

Dumas, C. (2001). Evaluating the outcomes of microenterprise training for low income women: A case study. *Journal of Developmental Entrepreneurship*, 6(2), 97–128.

Dunn, T., and Holtz-Eakin, D. (2000). Financial capital, human capital, and the transition to self-employment: Evidence from intergenerational links. *Journal of Labor Economics*, 18(2), 282–305.

Ehrlich, S.B., De Noble, A.F., Jung, D.I., and Pearson, D. (2000). The impact of entrepreneurship training programs on an individual's entrepreneurial self-efficacy. *Frontiers of Entrepreneurship Research*, Babson-Kauffman Research Conference Proceedings.

Englander, A.S., and Gurney, A. (1994). Medium-term determinants of OECD productivity. *OECD Economic Studies*, 22, 49–109.

Fairlie, R.W. (1999). The absence of the African-American owned business: An analysis of the dynamics of self-employment. *Journal of Labor Economics*, 17(1), 80–108.

Frank, H., Korunka, C., Lueger, M., and Mugler, J. (2005). Entrepreneurial orientation and education in Austrian secondary schools. *Journal of Small Business and Enterprise Development*, 12(2), 259–273.

Galloway, L., Anderson, M., Brown, W., and Wilson, L. (2005). Enterprise skills for the economy. *Education & Training*, 47(1), 7–17.

Galloway, L., and Brown, W. (2002). Entrepreneurship education at university: A driver in the creation of high growth firms? *Education & Training*, 44(8/9), 398–404.

Garavan, T.N., and O'Cinneide, B. (1994). Entrepreneurship education and training programs: A review and evaluation—Part 2. *Journal of European Industrial Training*, 18(11), 13–22.

Gartner, W.B., and Vesper, K.H. (1997). Measuring progress in entrepreneurship education. *Journal of Business Venturing*, 12(5), 403–421.

Gartner, W.B.,and Vesper, K.H. (1994). Experiments in entrepreneurship education: Successes and failures. *Journal of Business Venturing*, 9: 179–187.

Gimeno, J., Folta, T.B., Cooper, A.C., and Woo, C.Y. (1997). Survival of the fittest? Entrepreneurial human capital and the persistence of underperforming firms. *Administrative Science Quarterly*, 42(4), 750–783.

Goedhuys, M., and Sieuwaegen, L. (2000). Entrepreneurship and growth of entrepreneurial firms in Côte d'Ivoire. *The Journal of Development Studies*, 36(3), 122–145.

Gorman, G., Hanlon, D., and King, W. (1997). Some research perspectives on entrepreneurship education, enterprise education and education for small business management: A ten-year literature review. *International Small Business Journal*, 15(3), 56–78.

Greene, P.G., Katz, J., and Johannisson, B. (2004). Entrepreneurship education. *Academy of Management Learning and Education*, 3(3): 238–241.

Gwartney, J., Lawson, R., and Block, W. (1996). *Economic freedom of the world: 1975–1995*, Fraser Institute: Vancouver, BC.

Hansen, O.C. (1998). The effects of an entrepreneurship program on need for achievement and locus of control of reinforcement. *International Journal of Entrepreneurial Behavior & Research*, 4(1), 28–44.

Honig, B. (2004). Entrepreneurship education: Toward a model of contingency-based business planning. *Academy of Management Learning and Education*, 3(3): 258–273.

Human, S.E., Clark, T., and Baucus, M.S. (2005). Student self-assessment: Structuring individual-level learning in a new venture creation course. *Journal of Management Education*, 29(1), 111–134.

Jo, H., and Lee, J. (1996). The relationship between an entrepreneur's background and performance in a new venture. *Technovation*, 16(4), 161–171.

Johnson, B.T., and Sheehy, T. P. (1995). *The index of economic freedom*, Washington, D.C.: Heritage Foundation.

Jones-Evans, D., Williams, W., and Deacon, J. (2000). Developing entrepreneurial graduates: An action-learning approach. *Education & Training*, 42(4/5), 282–288.

Katz, J. (2004). *Survey of endowed positions in entrepreneurship and related fields in the United States*, Kansas City, MO: Ewing Marion Kauffman Foundation, 2004.

Katz, J. A. (2003). The chronology and intellectual trajectory of American entrepreneurship education, 1876–1999. *The Journal of Business Venturing*. 18(2), 283–300.

Kirchoff, B., and Armington, C. (2002). *The influence of R&D expenditures on new firm formation and economic growth*. White Paper Series, Washington, D.C.: U.S. Small Business Administration, Office of Advocacy.

Klapper, R. (2004). Government goals and entrepreneurship education—an investigation at a grande ecole in France. *Education + Training*, 46(3), 127–137.

Kolvereid, L., and Moen, O. (1997). Entrepreneurship among business graduates: Does a major in entrepreneurship make a difference? *Journal of European Industrial Training*, 21(4), 154–160.

Kourilsky, M.L., and Esfandiari, M. (1997). Entrepreneurship education and lower socioeconomic black youth: An empirical investigation. *Urban Review*, 29(3), 205–215.

Krueger, N.F., Reilly, M.D., and Carsrud, A.L. (2000). Competing models of entrepreneurial intentions. *Journal of Business Venturing*, 15: 411–432.

Krueger, N.F., and Carsrud, A. (1993). Entrepreneurial intentions: Applying the theory of planned behavior. *Entrepreneurship and Regional Development*, 5: 316–323.

Kuratko, D.F. (2005). The emergence of entrepreneurship education: Development, trends, and challenges. *Entrepreneurship Theory and Practice*, 29(5): 577–598.

Le, A.T. (1999). Empirical studies of self-employment. *Journal of Economic Surveys*, 13(4): 381–416.

Leitch, C.M. and Harrison, R.T. (1999). A process model for entrepreneurship education and development. *International Journal of Entrepreneurial Behavior & Research*, 5(3), 83–102.

Lofstrom, M., and Wang, C. (2006). *Hispanic self-employment: A dynamic analysis of business ownership.* IZA Discussion Paper no. 2101, Bonn, Germany: Magnus Lofstrom Institute for the Study of Labor.

Lüthje, C., and Franke, N. (2002). *Fostering entrepreneurship through university education and training: Lessons from Massachusetts Institute of Technology.* 2nd Annual Conference on Innovative Research in Management, Stockholm, Sweden.

Maes, J., Sels, L., and de Winne, S. (2005). *Innovation as a corporate entrepreneurial outcome in newly established firms: A human resource-based view.* Working Paper Series. Leuven, Belgium: Catholic University of Leuven.

Matlay, H. (2005). *Business school graduates as nascent entrepreneurs: Some policy considerations.* National Council for Graduate Entrepreneurship Policy Paper #006. Birmingham: UK: National Council for Graduate Entrepreneurship..

Matlay, H. (2005) Researching entrepreneurship and education, Part 1: What is entrepreneurship and does it matter? *Education + Training.* 47(8/9), 665–677.

McLarty, R. (2005). Entrepreneurship among graduates: Towards a measured response. *The Journal of Management Development*, 24(3), 223–238.

McManus, P.A. (2000). Market, state, and the quality of new self-employment jobs among men in the United States and Western Germany. *Social Forces*, 78(3), 865–905.

Minniti, M., and Bygrave, W.D. (2003). *Global entrepreneurship monitor: National entrepreneurship assessment, United States of America: 2003 executive report.* Babson MA: Babson College.

Monroe, S.R., Allen, K.R., and Price, C. (1995). The impact of entrepreneurial training programs on transitioning workers: The public policy implications. *Frontiers of Entrepreneurship Research*, Babson-Kauffman Research Conference Proceedings.

Morris, M. H., and Pitt, L.F. (1995). Informal sector activity as entrepreneurship: Insights from a South African township. *Journal of Small Business Management*, 33(1), 78–86.

National Governors Association (1994). *A governor's guide to strengthening state entrepreneurship policy.*

Neck, H.M., Zacharakis, A.L., Bygrave, W.D., and Reynolds, P.D. (2003). *Global entrepreneurship monitor: 2002 executive report.* Babson MA: Babson College.

Nicholas, T. (1999). Clogs to clogs in three generations? Explaining entrepreneurial performance in Britain since 1850. *The Journal of Economic History*, 59(3), 688–713.

Noel, T.W. (2000). Effects of entrepreneurial education on intent to open a business. *Frontiers of Entrepreneurship Research*, Babson-Kauffman Research Conference Proceedings.

Osborne, S.W., Falcone, T.W., and Nagendra, P.B. (2000). From unemployed to entrepreneur: A case study in intervention. *Journal of Development Entrepreneurship*, 5(2), 115–136.

Peña, I. (2002). Intellectual capital and business start-up success. *Journal of Intellectual Capital*, 3(2), 180–198.

Peterman, N.E., and Kennedy, J. (2003). Enterprise education: Influencing students' perceptions of entrepreneurship. *Entrepreneurship Theory and Practice*, 28(2): 129–145.

Plaschka, G.R., and Welsch, H. P. (1990). Emerging structures in entrepreneurship education: Curricula designs and strategies. *Entrepreneurship Theory and Practice*, 14(3), 55–71.

Porter, L. W., and McKibbin, L. E. (1988). *Management education: Drift or thrust into the 21st century?* New York: McGraw-Hill.

Raffo, C., Lovatt, A., Banks, M., and O'Connor, J. (2000). Teaching and learning entrepreneurship for micro and small businesses in the cultural industries sector. *Education & Training*, 42(6), 356–365.

Revans, R. (1971). *Developing effective managers*. Longman, UK: Harlow.

Reynolds, P.D., Carter, N.M., Gartner, W.B., and Greene, P.G. (2004). The prevalence of nascent entrepreneurs in the United States: Evidence from the Panel Study of Entrepeneurial Dynamics. *Small Business Economics*, 23, 263–284.

Reynolds, P.D., Bosma, N., Autio, E., Hunt, S., De Bono, N., Servais, I., Lopez-Garcia, P., and Chin, N. (2005). Global entrepreneurship monitor: Data collection design and implementation, 1998–2003. *Small Business Economics*, 24(3): 205–231.

Sagie, A., and Elizur, D. (1999). Achievement motive and entrepreneurial orientation: A structural analysis. *Journal of Organizational Behavior*, 20(3), 375–388.

Sexton, D.L., and Bowman, N.B. (1984). Entrepreneurship education: Suggestions for increasing effectiveness. *Journal of Small Business Management*, 22: 18–25.

Shapero, A. (1982). Social dimension of entrepreneurship. In C. Kent, D. Sexton., and K. Vesper (eds.), *The Encyclopedia of Entrepreneurship*. Englewood Cliffs, NJ: Prentice-Hall.

Shapero, A. 1975. The displaced, uncomfortable entrepreneur. *Psychology Today*, November: 83–86.

Solomon, G.G., Duffy, S., and Tarabishy, A. (2002). The state of entrepreneurship education in the United States: A nationwide survey and analysis. *International Journal of Entrepreneurship Education*, 1(1), 65–86.

Solomon, G.T. (2002). Entrepreneurship education and training in the United States: Policy, strategy or disjointed incrementalism. in *The Dynamics of Entrepreneurship*, Tan Wee Liang, ed. Singapore: Prentice Hall .

Solomon, G.T., Weaver, K.M., and Fernald L.W., Jr. (1994). Pedagogical methods of teaching entrepreneurship: An historical perspective. *Gaming and Simulation*, 25 (3).

Solomon, G.T., and Fernald, L.W., Jr. (1991). Trends in small business management and entrepreneurship education in the United States. *Entrepreneurship Theory and Practice*, 15, 25–39.

Solomon, G.T. (1979). *Small business management resource guides*, vols. 1–6. Washington, D.C.: U.S. Small Business Administration.

Solomon, G.T., and Sollosy, M. (1977). *Nationwide survey in course offerings in small business management/entrepreneurship*. International Council for Small Business.

Sørensen, J.B., and Chang, P.M.Y. (2006). *Determinants of successful entrepreneurship: A review of the recent literature*. Kauffman Foundation Research. Kansas City, MO: Ewing Marion Kauffman Foundation.

Taylor, M.P. (1999). Survival of the fittest? An analysis of self-employment duration in Britain. *The Economic Journal*, 109(454), C104–C155.

Thurik, R., and Wennekers, S. (1999). Linking entrepreneurship and economic growth. *Small Business Economics*. 13(1), 27–53.

Uhlaner, L.M., Thurik, R., and Hutjes, J. (2002). *Post-materialism as a cultural factor influencing entrepreneurial activity across nations*. ERIM Report Series Research in Management no. ERS–2002–62–STR, Rotterdam: Erasmus Research Institute of Management.

van der Sluis, J., van Praag, M., and Vijverberg, W. (2005). Entrepreneurship selection and performance: A meta-analysis of the impact of education in developing economies. *The World Bank Economic Review*, 19(2), 225–261.

van der Sluis, J., van Praag, M., and Vijverberg, W. (2004). *Education and entrepreneurship in industrialized countries: A meta-analysis.* Tinbergen Institute Working Paper no. TI 03–046/3, Amsterdam: Tinbergen Institute.

Wagner, J., and Sternberg, R. (2004). Start-up activities, individual characteristics, and the regional milieu: Lessons for entrepreneurship support policies from German micro data. *The Annals of Regional Science*, 38, 219–240.

Wagner, J., and Sternberg, R. (2002). *The role of the regional milieu for the decision to start a new firm: Empirical evidence for Germany.* IZA Discussion Paper no. 494, Bonn, Germany: Magnus Lofstrom Institute for the Study of Labor.

APPENDIX 5A
Tables

Table 5A.1 Representative Sample of Evidence Linking General Education to New Venture Creation, Venture Success, and Venture Survival, 1995–2006

Study	Country	Sample Size[2]	Education Level[3]	+/- or n.s.[4]	Study description
General Education and Entrepreneurship[1]					
Acs and Armington (2005)	U.S.	394	HE	+	Regional level study with data aggregated into 394 regions. Human capital as measured by the percentage of college graduates was positively related to higher firm formation rates.
Arenius and DeClercq (2005)	Finland and Belgium	4,536	HE	+	Study finds individuals with higher educational levels more likely to perceive entrepreneurial opportunities.
Block and Wagner (2006)	Germany	1,109	YRS	+	The study separates necessity entrepreneurs and opportunity entrepreneurs. The level of overall education was significantly related to becoming an entrepreneur for the opportunity entrepreneurs but not the necessity entrepreneurs.
Camp (2005)	U.S.	394	HE	+	This study compares regional variations in entrepreneurship across 394 regions. Regions with higher percentages of college degree holders were found to have significantly higher levels of entrepreneurial activity.
Delmar and Davidsson (2000)	Sweden, Norway and U.S.	933	YRS	+	Higher levels of education were found to be associated with higher probabilities of becoming nascent entrepreneurs.
Dunn and Holtz-Eakin (2000)	U.S.	371	YRS	n.s.	The level of education was not found to be significant to the probability of self-employment when parent "variables" were considered.
Goedhuys and Sleuwaegen (2000)	Africa	141	SC, HE	+	Completion of secondary school and college were found to significantly impact an individual's propensity towards entrepreneurship.
Kirchoff and Armington (2002)	U.S.	3,152	SC, HE	+	Study concludes that there is a positive relationship between education levels and firm births, but study authors express strong concerns about collinearity among study variables.

Study	Location	N	Education Measure	Sign	Findings
Lofstrom and Wang (2006)	U.S.	19,271	YRS	+/-	Lower levels of education were associated with entry into low-barrier businesses, while higher education levels were associated with entry into medium- and high-barrier businesses. Significant differences were seen across cultural groups.
McManus (2000)	U.S. and Germany	7,342	YRS	+/n.s.	The study found that the level of education was positively linked to "high-quality" self-employment but not to "low-quality" self-employment.
Minniti, Bygrave, Zacharakis, and Cole (2004)	U.S. portion of GEM study	9,195	YRS	+	Drawing on the GEM project the study concludes that while higher education is linked to higher levels of entrepreneurship, the relationship is not linear. The highest level was found for individuals with some college but no degree. Authors concluded this is skewed by differences in necessity versus opportunity entrepreneurship.
Neck, Zacharakis, Bygrave, and Reynolds (2003)	U.S. portion of GEM study	7,059	YRS	+	Drawing on the 2002 GEM study, the authors conclude that in general the more education a person has, the more likely the person is to pursue entrepreneurship, although the relationship is found not to hold for the highest levels of educational attainment.
Renolds, Carter, Gartner, and Greene (2004)	U.S.	1,261	YRS	+	The level of education was significantly related to rates of nascent entrepreneurship, but significant cultural and gender differences were found with education having the greatest impact for minority groups.
Uhlaner, Thurik, and Hutjes (2002)	14 countries	14	YRS	+	The study is a country-level analysis with education as a predictor for levels of self-employment. The level of education is found to be significant and outweigh various country-level economic factors.
Wagner and Sternberg (2004)	Germany	7,802	SC, HE	+	Education positively linked to choice to become a nascent entrepreneur.
Wagner and Sternberg (2002)	Germany	1,000	SC, HE	+	Higher levels of education were found to raise the odds of an individual becoming an entrepreneur, but regional differences were noted.
General Education and Entrepreneurial Performance[5]					
Aidis and Mickiewicz (2004)	Lithuania	399	HE	+	Possession of an upper level degree was found to be positively and significantly related to growth expectations in entrepreneurial firms.

Table 5A.1 Representative Sample of Evidence Linking General Education to New Venture Creation, Venture Success, and Venture Survival, 1995–2006—continued

Study	Country	Sample Size[2]	Education Level[3]	+ / - or n.s.[4]	Study description
Almus and Nerlinger (1999)	Germany	20,602	HE	+	A positive correlation was found between technical degrees and the growth of technology-based ventures. Business-based degrees were found to have a positive correlation with growth in noninnovative firms. Individuals with a combination of technical and business degrees did not have a significant impact on firm growth.
Basu and Goswami (1999)	South Asia	118	HE	+	The entrepreneur holding a college degree was found to positively impact firm growth.
Bosma, van Praag, Thurik, and de Wit 2004	U.S.	896	HE	+/n.s.	Study results suggest a strong and positive relationship between level of education of the entrepreneur and venture profitability, although a nonsignificant relationship was found for firm survival.
Goedhuys and Sleuwaegen (2000)	Africa	141	SC, HE	+	Firms led by entrepreneurs with either secondary or college education were found to have higher growth in performance, with the largest effect for entrepreneurs with college degrees.
Jo and Lee (1996)	Korea	48	YRS	+	Researchers observe a positive and significant relationship between level of education and firm profits in a study of 48 Korean firms.
Maes, Sels, De Winne (2005)	Belgium	294	YRS	+	The level of education of the entrepreneurial team was measured based on years of education. A positive relationship was found between the level of education of the founding team and innovation within the entrepreneurial firm.
Morris and Pitt (1995)	Africa	30	YRS	+	A positive and significant relationship was reported in this study between the educational level of the entrepreneur and the operational sophistication of the venture.

	Country	Sample	Measure	Sign	
Nicholas (1999)	Britain	283	HE	-	A negative performance effect (based on wealth accumulation) was observed for entrepreneurs receiving high-status rather than lower-status education.
Peña (2002)	Spain	114	HE	+	Study concludes that the majority of companies experiencing sales growth were managed by entrepreneurs with college degrees.
General Education and Entrepreneurial Firm Survival					
Chrisman and McMullan (2004)	U.S.	159	YRS	n.s.	The level of education of the entrepreneur was not significant in predicting firm survival.
Fairlie	U.S.	6,417	HE	+/-	In a comparison of African-American-owned businesses and White-owned businesses, a mixed relationship between education and exit was found. Graduating from college decreases the probability of exit for both races. For Whites, graduating from college, in comparison with only high school, increased the probability of exit, while the effect was the opposite for African Americans.
Gimeno, Flota, Cooper, and Woo (1997)	U.S.	1,547	YRS	n.s./+	Education was measured based on the percentage of people in the sample with a lower level of education. Results suggest that higher levels of human capital, including education experience, did not necessarily predict higher survival rates, although more human capital was significantly related to better firm performance.
Taylor (1999)	Britain	10,000	YRS	n.s.	The exit rates of entrepreneurs with various levels of educational attainment were compared. No significant differences were observed based on educational level.

[1] Various measures are utilized including the choice of "self-employment," "firm formation," and "nascent entrepreneurs."

[2] In some studies the level of analysis is the individual entrepreneur, while in others it is the country or the region.

[3] "SC" = secondary school completion verses noncompletion; "HE" = higher education level completed versus no higher education completed; "GR" = graduate education completed versus no graduate education completed; "YRS" = overall years of education—secondary through graduate.

[4] +/- or n.s. = a positive, negative, or not significant relationship exists between the variables.

[5] Entrepreneurial performance is operationalized in various methods at the firm level including for example, "growth in sales," "overall growth," "meeting of expectations," and at the individual level as "wage/income growth."

Table 5A.2 Representative Sample of Evidence Linking Education with Entrepreneurial Activity, 1995–2005[2]

Study	Country	Educational Program[1]	Research Description and Findings
Entrepreneurial Education and Venture Creation			
Charney and Libecap (2000)	U.S.	HE	Study authors obtained completed surveys from 406 nonentrepreneurship graduates of the University of Arizona and 105 graduates of the Berger Entrepreneurship program at the university. Venture creation, along with a broader range of measures, was compared across groups. The study found that on average entrepreneurship graduates were three times more likely than nonentrepreneurship graduates to start new ventures: 17.4 percent of the nonentrepreneurship graduates had been involved in starting a new venture, while 54.0 percent of the entrepreneurship graduates had done so.
Dumas (2001)	U.S.	VET	This study provides a qualitative case analysis measuring the outcomes of a community-based entrepreneurship training program for low-income women. The program involved over 420 women in Boston's inner city neighborhood during the life of the program. The first group of 34 participants was followed during the study period. Nineteen businesses were created during the study period.
Kolvereid, L. and Moen, O. (1997)	Norway	HE	Study authors obtained completed surveys from 374 graduates from the Bodo Graduate School of Business. Students who had graduated with a major in entrepreneurial studies were compared with those majoring in other areas of study. Venture founding as well as the "intention" to found a venture were measured and a wide range of control variables was included. Results suggested a significant correlation between education in entrepreneurship and venture founding as well as between entrepreneurial education and the "intention" to found a venture in the future for those students who had not previously done so.
McLarty, R. (2005)	UK	HE	The study reports a qualitative research project involving 39 university graduates who had founded businesses and was focused on determining the relationship between their university preparation and their subsequent ability to found and successfully operate a new venture. The results indicated that 90 percent of the graduates had founded their businesses within two years of graduation, and most drew upon their degree area for their business idea. Additionally, results indicate that almost 75 percent of the business owners sought additional entrepreneurial training and a significant majority demonstrated critical skill deficiencies—particularly in the finance and marketing areas.

Study	Country	Type	Description
Monroe, Allen, and Price (1995)	U.S.	FE	The impact of the FastTrack entrepreneurship training program targeting four groups of displaced workers and welfare transitioning recipients who were graduates of entrepreneurial training programs was measured. Results indicated that of the 28 participants in a program in Rock Springs, WY, five businesses were founded, of which two survived; of the 34 displaced workers in a Kansas city study, 21 had founded businesses and another 11 were involved in business on a part-time basis; 41 welfare transitioning workers in Idaho created nine new ventures; and of the 23 welfare recipients participating in Kansas City, four had founded new businesses.
Osborne, Falcone, and Nagendra (2000)	U.S.	VET	This study assesses the relationship of entrepreneurship training delivered as part of the Self Employment Assistance Program (SEAP) instituted by the state of Pennsylvania. As part of this test program, participants were screened prior to the educational program with only those individuals more inclined towards entrepreneurial "personalities" accepted into the program. Following completion of the training program, 34 of the 51 individuals that completed the training had formed a business within one month of completion and exhibited signs of continuing operations.
Van der Sluis, van Praag, and Vijverberg (2005)	Wide range of developing economies	Other—general education	Study authors developed a meta-analytic review of 80 studies measuring the impact of general education on a number of entrepreneurial outcomes. Results suggest that a marginal year of schooling raised entrepreneurial income (activity) by 5.5 percent.

Entrepreneurial Education and Entrepreneurial Intentions

Study	Country	Type	Description
Autio, Keeley, Klofsten, and Ulfstedt (1997)	Finland, Sweden, Thailand, and the U.S.	HE	The study, in specific, tests a proposed model of entrepreneurial intent. General education is proposed as one predictor of intent. The study incorporated surveys of 1,956 university students in primarily technological programs. Results suggest education as one aspect of an individual's background is positively related to entrepreneurial intent.
Galloway and Brown (2002)	UK	HE	Completed surveys were obtained from 1,954 graduates of the University of Strathclyde. Results indicate that 78 percent of those students who had taken at least one entrepreneurship course indicated an "intention" to start a business at some point in their lives. Nineteen percent reported a desire to start a business within five years, while 43 percent indicated an expectation to start a business after a period exceeding 10 years.

Table 5A.2 Representative Sample of Evidence Linking Education with Entrepreneurial Activity, 1995–2005[2]—continued

Study	Country	Educational Program[1]	Research Description and Findings
Klapper (2004)	France	HE	In a study of 82 first- and 60 second-year students at a Grande Ecole in France, the researcher discovered a significant increase in the number of students that envisioned becoming an entrepreneur as opposed to working for a larger organization or a small to medium-sized enterprise (SME). It was hypothesized that this result was due in part to the participation of students, between the first and second years, in an entrepreneurship education program and project.
Lüthje and Franke (2002)	U.S. and Germany	HE	The study explored and compared the entrepreneurial intentions of business students at a major German university and the Massachusetts Institute of Technology (MIT). The study encompassed 312 surveys from German university students and 143 from MIT students. The study results indicated that a significantly higher number of the MIT students expressed the intention to start a venture than their German counterparts. Additionally, the U.S.-based education was seen as far more effective in instilling an entrepreneurial spirit among students and in providing activities supporting such endeavors. Those students in the United States with higher levels of risk propensity tended to rate the educational activities higher, while in Germany those students with higher levels of risk propensity tended to rate the educational activities lower.
Noel (2000)	U.S.	HE	Study encompassed 84 graduates with undergraduate degrees in entrepreneurship and comparison groups drawn from general business majors and nonbusiness majors. The study measured differences in business starts, entrepreneurial self-efficacy, and intentions to open a new business. Results suggested marginal support of the hypothesis that entrepreneurship graduates would create ventures at a greater rate, no support that they would have a higher entrepreneurial self-efficacy, and strong support that entrepreneurial intentions would be significantly greater in entrepreneurial graduates.
Peterman and Kennedy (2003)	Australia	VET (Secondary school students)	117 secondary school students completing an enterprise training program are compared with 119 students from the same school but not undergoing entrepreneurial training. Results indicated that students choosing to participate in the program had a significantly higher level of prior experience and prior positive experience than students not participating. The training program was also found to positively increase perceptions of desirability and feasibility.

Entrepreneurial Education and Opportunity Recognition

Brännback, Heinonen, Hudd, Paasio (2005)	Finland	HE	Study authors proposed to measure the link between entrepreneurial education, recognition of entrepreneurship as personally desirable and socially acceptable, and opportunity recognition. Completed surveys were obtained from 263 business school students at two universities. Study findings suggest a direct link between entrepreneurial intent and perceptions of entrepreneurship as personally desirable and feasible.
DeTienne and Chandler (2004)	U.S.	HE	The study focuses on the relationship between entrepreneurial education, specific skills training at the university level, and opportunity recognition. The experimentally designed study included 130 undergraduate students. The study had a range of control variables including prior involvement in venture creation. Study results suggest a positive relationship between skills training and students' ability to generate more venture ideas and ideas that had the characteristics of being innovative.
Dimov (2003)	U.S.	HE	The study involved 22 graduate students and measured the relationship between "prior knowledge" in general and opportunity recognition. Surprisingly, prior industry-specific knowledge was negatively correlated with opportunity recognition. Study author concludes that it is not prior knowledge in general, but how it is applied, that impacts opportunity recognition. The study also seems to establish a link between prior knowledge and entrepreneurial intentions.

Entrepreneurial Education, Entrepreneurial Self Efficacy, and Entrepreneurial Orientation

Alvarez and Jung (2003)	Mexico	HE	The study included 400 undergraduate students attending three universities in Mexico. The study suggests that the greater the exposure to entrepreneurial course work, the greater the students' perceived entrepreneurial self-efficacy and intention toward starting their own business.
Ehrlich, De Noble, Jung, Pearson (2000)	U.S.	HE	Twenty-four participants in two university-based entrepreneurial training courses were surveyed at the beginning and conclusion of the six-week program. The results of the study suggested that the entrepreneurial training significantly and positively impacted participants' perceptions of their ability to start and develop new ventures.
Frank, Korunka, Lueger, and Mugler (2005)	Austria	Other— secondary schools	Study authors surveyed 875 students of four different types of secondary schools (secondary schools, commercial academies, technical schools, and technical and business professional schools). The goal of the study was to determine if the type of education and/or other entrepreneurship-related activities impacted the students' preferences for an entrepreneurial career. The results of the study suggest a strong link between the type of education and orientation toward becoming an entrepreneur.

Table 5A.2 Representative Sample of Evidence Linking Education with Entrepreneurial Activity, 1995–2005[2]—continued

Study	Country	Educational Program[1]	Research Description and Findings
Galloway, Anderson, Brown, and Wilson (2005)	UK	HE	Drawing on a sample of 519 Scottish entrepreneurship students, study authors measure the perceptions of the students regarding entrepreneurial skill development. Study results suggest that the perception of the students regarding the impact of the program on developing their entrepreneurial skills varies based on the specific skill. Additionally, the results indicated that a higher percentage of students perceive that it will be a relatively long time (10 or more years) prior to their founding their first venture.
Entrepreneurial Education and Need for Achievement and Locus of Control			
Hansemark, O. (1998)	Sweden	VET	This study measured the impact of a 36-week training program carried out in a rural district. The program followed two models—problem-based learning and action learning. Outcomes measured were the individuals' "need for achievement" and "locus of control." The program included 70 participants and both an experimental and control group. Study results suggested a link between the training intervention and the development of a higher level of "n" achievement and a greater internal orientation of locus of control.
Entrepreneurial Education and Other—Entrepreneurial Knowledge			
Kourilsky and Esfandiari (1997)	U.S.	VET (High School)	The entrepreneurial knowledge and advance knowledge of a group of New York high school students was measured following the completion of an "entrepreneurship education intervention." The implicit assumption is that knowledge of entrepreneurship is linked to subsequent entrepreneurial activity. A total of 95 students (51 in a treatment group and 44 in a control group) were included in the study. Results indicate a significant relationship between entrepreneurial education and entrepreneurial knowledge. Treatment subjects were compared to both the control groups and a sample of general population high school students surveyed as part of a Gallup program.

[1] HE = Higher education both undergraduate and graduate, FE = Further education including continuing education, VET = Other vocational educational training programs. This is based on a framework suggested by Raffo, Lovatt, Banks, and O'Connor (2000).

[2] For reviews of research findings published prior to 1995, see Dainow (1986); Gorman, Hanlon, and King (1997).

6 Economic Gardening: Next Generation Applications *for a* Balanced Portfolio Approach *to* Economic Growth

Synopsis

Economic gardening is an innovative entrepreneur-centered economic growth strategy that offers balance to the traditional economic development practice of business recruitment.[1] It was developed in 1989 by the city of Littleton, Colorado, in conjunction with the Center for the New West. While it was introduced as a demonstration program to deal with the sudden erosion of economic conditions following the relocation of the largest employer in the city at that time, it has emerged as a prototype for a rapidly expanding movement of like-minded economic developers looking for additional methods to generate truly sustainable economic growth for their community, region, or state. The purpose of this article is to examine the history, context, and application of economic gardening principles and practices, as well as the evolving application of specific programs in cities, regions, and states beyond Littleton, Colorado. A basic tenet of the article is that smart civic leaders and decision-makers of the future will adopt a portfolio approach to economic development that balances "outside-in" with "inside-out" strategies, tailored to local conditions, assets, and leadership.

Economic gardening is finding application in a number of community settings, especially in the Western states. Next frontiers lie at the state level, where several states have adopted statewide economic gardening principles and practices. More than simply a metaphor for explaining evolving priorities

---

1 This chapter was prepared under contract with the U.S. Small Business Administration, Office of Advocacy, by Steve Quello and Graham Toft. As managing partner and principal of CCS Logic, Quello specializes in the development of custom programs designed to accelerate organizational growth by identifying and engaging solutions that encourage the release of "network effect" principles. Toft is the principal of Growth Economics and a strategic planner specializing in how the "idea economy" brings change to communities, regions, states, countries, industries, and educational institutions.

and practices in the field of economic development, economic gardening is emerging as a cohesive framework of proven techniques that both challenge and complement conventional wisdom in the field.

Background and Context

"Entrepreneurial innovation is the essence of capitalism."

—Joseph Schumpeter, 1934

The contemporary expression of economic gardening principles and practices has, at its core, elements common to longstanding tenets of free market economic theory. However, economic development as an art of public policy has evolved with changing economic conditions. Beginning in the 1930s, economic development focused on business recruitment ("outside-in") strategies.[2] After the early 1980s, entrepreneurship and small business policies and practices gained momentum. Now the focus is shifting to designing public policies to support various stages of business growth and growth companies, and fostering technology-based economic development (TBED). This evolution in economic development policy has its roots in the simple reality that state policymakers have a better understanding of the opportunity costs involved in incentive-based programs, and they recognize that the commitment of large businesses to a particular state, region, or community is more fluid than ever before.

This chapter is about the evolution of an experiment outside the mainstream of economic development that now offers insight and lessons learned, as economic development policy and practice adapts to what most agree is some form of "post-industrial economy."[3] This rapidly transforming U.S. economy is not about the demise of manufacturing but the emergence of advanced manufacturing methods,[4] advanced business and financial services, exploding leisure and recreation industries, biomedical technologies and services, the information technology industry, etc. It is also about the dramatically changing

---

2   W. Schwecke, Carl Rist, and Brian Dabson, *Bidding for Business: Are Cities and States Selling Themselves Short?* (Corporation for Enterprise Development, Washington, D.C, 1994).

3   Sharon Barrios and David Barrios, "Reconsidering Economic Development: The Prospects for Economic Gardening" (*Public Administration Quarterly* 28:1/2, Spring 2004), 70–101.

4   Glen Johnson, chairman of the Illinois Manufacturers' Association, dubbed such methods "intellifacturing;" see ima-net.org/library/tim/timsummer05.pdf.

proportions of firms in different size categories. The National Commission on Entrepreneurship noted in 1999: "In the late 1960s, one in four persons worked in a Fortune 500 firm; now 1 in 14 do."[5] In this context, constant innovation with commercialization becomes the hallmark of success, enabled by an entrepreneurial culture.

The economic gardening model developed in Littleton, Colorado, is instructive and timely, deserving wider consideration. What has evolved in Littleton, somewhat underreported in national and state economic development policy and practice, now deserves centerpiece consideration as state, regional, and local leaders play an increasingly competitive game in global economic redistribution. It is a game where reliance upon conventional recruitment and retention strategies is not as productive as in the past, and future success will require increasing innovation and adaptation from businesses and community leaders.

State / Local Economic Development Policy in Historical Context

The history of modern economic development policy and practice in the United States has its roots in Mississippi in the 1930s. At that time, the prospects for relocating manufacturing from the North to the South were becoming apparent. To make known its low-cost operating environment, Mississippi introduced direct marketing and incentives through the BAWI program (Balance Agriculture with Industry).[6] Mississippi's approach soon took root in the rest of the South, with land giveaways, financial incentives, and tax breaks offered in various forms. The southern states continue with this traditional "outside-in" approach, but the practice (with incentives) has become quite similar across most states. Some now believe that an "inside-out" approach adds needed differentiation to an overall growth strategy.

With the back-to-back harsh recessions of 1980 and 1982, much of the Northeast and Midwest were particularly hard hit. At this same time the first "tech fever" emerged in economic development. Virtually all states wanted to model their future growth after the success of Silicon Valley in California and

---

5   National Commission on Entrepreneurship, "Forging New Ideas for a New Economy" (Washington D.C. NCOE, 1999), 3.

6   Connie Lester, "Economic Development in the 1930s: Balance Agriculture with Industry," *Mississippi History Now*, May 2004, http://mshistory.k12.ms.us/features/feature52/economic.htm.

Route 128 in Massachusetts. This period was energized by the work of David Birch on the centrality of small companies and "gazelles" in job creation.[7] Quite fresh and innovative, Birch's insights influenced the development of new initiatives at the state level, including state-supported product development corporations, science and technology corporations, incubators, and early venture fund creation. By the end of the 1980s, some state and local policymakers were becoming concerned with the generous handouts for both business recruitment and new business creation. In particular, some realized they did not have the resources or organization to compete successfully in business recruitment. The Littleton experiment grew out of such modifications to conventional economic development practices.

As a result of the dot-com and technology boom of the 1990s, a second "tech fever" took hold. Its focus was even more technology- and venture capital-intense. Seeding university spin-offs and venture capital and angel networks, the trend especially targeted sectors believed to offer "winning technologies," such as the biosciences. Cluster theory, as conceived and advocated by Michael E. Porter, has influenced this second tech fever, leading to de facto industrial policy in some states and regions.[8]

While this second technology fever will inevitably play out in larger metropolitan areas and some college towns, it has eluded many small to mid-sized communities and rural regions. Some more fundamental rethinking is now under way: what are the essential engines of economic growth in a rapidly changing global economy? A small but growing community of advocates, representing cities and regions in every state of the country, has focused interest on the economic gardening approach of Littleton, Colorado, because it (1) is soundly based on economic growth principles, (2) requires fewer public resources than traditional recruitment initiatives, (3) is more focused on where rapid growth occurs—in second- and third-stage companies—and (4) does not require "picking winner industries," but rather recognizes the critical role played by growth companies of all sizes across diverse sectors.

---

7   David L. Birch, *Job Creation in America: How Our Smallest Companies Put the Most People to Work* (Free Press, 1987).

8   Michael E. Porter, "Clusters and the New Economics of Competition" (*Harvard Business Review* 76:6, Nov–Dec 1998), 78–79.

It is important to point out that business recruitment efforts remain very important to U.S. localities, regions, and states. In fact, with U.S. dollars accumulating in the hands of foreign investors because of large and continuing trade deficits, opportunities for foreign direct investment in the United States abound. In particular, it makes sense for states and large metro regions to be in the hunt for global capital on the move. Nevertheless, many localities and small regions, even small states, cannot afford to play this high-stakes game. What should they do? Reevaluate the dominance of their business recruitment efforts by adding a heavy dose of "growth from within."

Today's Economic Growth Focus: Second and Third Stage Growth, Growth Companies and Related Definitions

Stages of Growth

What counts for the future will be the number of growth companies or facilities located in a state, region, or locality. They can be locally owned, part of national chains, or foreign-owned. For example, the Denver Regional Council of Governments (DRCOG) reports for 2002–2005 that 81 percent of net new jobs in the Denver region were attributable to 21 percent of all firms. These firms can be of any size, but "second-stage" companies are particularly strategic.[9] The Edward Lowe Foundation describes the second stage of business development as a point in the business life cycle when the casual ad hoc methods of entrepreneurial ventures begin to fail. It is a stage when the complexity of employing an increasing number of workers and the related regulatory compliance issues begin to exceed the span of control of one owner or CEO. At this stage of business development, more formal systems and processes may be required to effectively manage the business if it is to sustain or accelerate its current rate of growth to the next stage of business. These companies have moved from where the founder is owner, operator, manager, innovator—all in one—to an operation organized around specialization and

---

9   Edward Lowe Foundation, "Second Stage Defined" (Edward Lowe Foundation, 2005, unpublished) 1–3.

Chart 6.1 Economic Development Policy—Business Distribution/Stage of Development

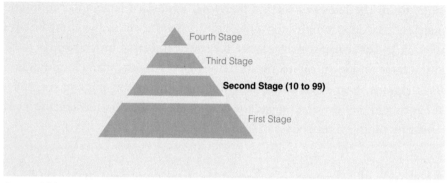

Source: CCS Logic.

more formal organizational structure.[10] While descriptive terms used to characterize this inherently fluid stage of business development can be helpful in providing a deeper understanding of second-stage businesses, a more precise definition that permits quantification is ultimately required to both identify and track this business segment. This report adopts a method advocated by the Edward Lowe Foundation in which employee count (10 to 99 employees) serves as a proxy for quickly and easily identifying this business segment (Chart 6.1). In 2003, 19.7 percent of all U.S. companies were second-stage, growing numerically at 1.23 percent per year (1993–2003), compared with all companies growing at 1.05 percent per year.[11] The only federal data of use at the subnational level to break business growth out by size of firm is County Business Patterns of the Statistics of U.S. Businesses, U.S. Bureau of the Census. A next data challenge is to identify the number and characteristics of growth companies within classes of firms by size. This is now possible with the National Establishment Time Series (NETS) database or similar datasets derived from Dun and Bradstreet sources.

A simple depiction of firm size by stage of development appears in Chart 6.1. Contemporary economic development policy and programs generally begin with the vertical cluster approach, shown as three vertical ellipses in Chart

---

10   Eric G. Flamholtz and Yvonne Randle, *Growing Pains: Transitioning from an Entrepreneurship to a Professionally Managed Firm* (San Francisco: Jossey-Bass, Inc., 2000), 28–30.

11   U.S. Department of Commerce, Bureau of the Census, Statistics of U.S. Businesses.

Chart 6.2 Economic Development Policy—"Horizontal" Entrepreneurship Cluster

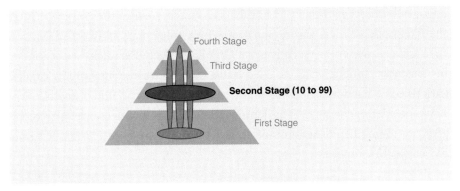

Source: CCS Logic.

6.2, and a related business creation or incubation strategy depicted as the small horizontal ellipse at the bottom of the chart. A balanced portfolio approach to economic development emphasizing economic gardening adds another element to that mix by elevating the importance of serving second-stage growth firms, represented by the large ellipse in the center of the pyramid. This "horizontal" entrepreneurship cluster, based on stage of development rather than vertical industry sector, highlights the stage-based threshold all growth firms pass through as they progress from being small enterprises to becoming large businesses. It is this orientation to understanding and serving local entrepreneurs, based on stage of development issues, that economic gardening programs seek to support and promote.

Growth Companies

Growth companies can be found in all firm size categories. They are important because evidence is mounting that they are strong job generators, offer better paying jobs than the average firm, provide more opportunities for advancement, do more research and development (R&D), and export more. Most important, because they are more agile, they are ideally suited to the fast-paced business environment of the 21st century.[12] Furthermore, since the late 1990s,

---

12   Ongoing research findings grounded on the empirical work of such early researchers as David Birch, Paul Reynolds, and John Jackson highlight the disproportionate share of economic growth attributable to growth companies. For a discussion of agility, see Edward Malecki, "Entrepreneurship in Regional and Local Development" (*International Regional Science Review*, vol 16, nos. 1 and 2), 1994.

research has revealed that growth companies frequently partner with other firms in creative ways—generating new ventures and deeper local supply-buy linkages with other firms.[13] The more growth companies there are, the more the likelihood of local and regional interfirm collaboration. Most important, their CEOs and senior executives network extensively. Peer networks connecting business owners, vendors, civic leaders and entrepreneur support organizations have been identified as a key accelerator of economic growth.[14] The network effect generated by a densely connected business community represents an intangible asset common to dynamic regions from Fairfax, Virginia, to Seattle, Washington.

Growth Strategy Portfolio

The growth strategy portfolio is that mix of new business formation, retention, expansion, and recruitment strategies that best capitalizes on assets and opportunities for economic growth (defined as wealth and job creation). Like any smart investor in a fast-paced and largely unpredictable marketplace, civic, business, and government leaders must pay attention to achieving balance in their economic development investment portfolio, then fine-tuning it regularly through an ongoing strategic planning process.

The Littleton, Colorado, Story

Conventional wisdom suggests that "necessity is the mother of invention." A public sector corollary to this notion would likely read "community crisis is the mother of innovative political policy."

In 1987 the state of Colorado was in the midst of a broad-based economic recession (see box).[15] The city of Littleton, a suburb of Denver, faced additional economic complications as it tried to recover from the layoffs of several thousand employees by the community's major employer. The magnitude of these challenging business conditions strained the resources of local residents

---

13   Ibid.

14   National Commission on Entrepreneurship, *Building Entrepreneurial Networks* (Washington D.C.: NCOE, 2001), 3–6.

15   City of Littleton web site, http://www.littletongov.org/bia/economicgardening/default.asp.

ECONOMIC GARDENING:
An Entrepreneurial Approach to Economic Development

On the website for the city of Littleton, Colorado, Littleton's director of business/ industry affairs, Christian Gibbons tells his own story about the genesis of economic gardening in Littleton. Following is a summary; to read more, see http:// www.littletongov.org/bia/economicgardening/default.asp.

Working in the economic development field after massive layoffs in Leadville, Colorado, in the 1980s, Chris Gibbons met two miners who had created an invention—a resin bolt to keep steel mats up overhead in the mine. It occurred to Chris that what Leadville needed in response to job losses in this remote location was not to attract more businesses from outside, but to take advantage of the ingenuity of those already there, who had created something that could be used in mines everywhere—and who had chosen to live in Leadville. Five years later, in 1987, he found himself in Littleton, Colorado, as director of economic development in another place that had lost a major employer.

Chris and others had noticed that the traditional approach to economic development—recruiting outside companies to establish a plant locally—had several downsides. The companies recruited often represented a minor part of job creation; they seemed to come to areas that were attracting new businesses anyway (not outlying areas like rural locations and small towns); and outlying areas competed primarily on low price and low-cost factors of production—cheap land, free buildings, tax abatements, low-cost labor. Companies attracted by low costs stayed in the community as long as costs stayed low; as living standards began to rise, they would again look elsewhere—often overseas—for low costs.

The Littleton situation offered a natural opportunity to try out Chris's insight from Leadville days. "For nearly two years Jim Woods . . . and I researched the best thinking we could find on the subject, talked to experts, (including the Center for the New West, a think tank in Denver), and fleshed out the concept. We kicked off the project in 1989 with the idea that 'economic gardening' was a better approach for Littleton (and perhaps many other communities) than 'economic hunting.' By this, we meant that we intended to grow our own jobs through entrepreneurial activity instead of recruiting them."

Almost immediately, Chris notes, it became clear that a few companies—dubbed "gazelles"—were responsible for creating most of the new jobs. The key factors driving the fast growth were more elusive than business size or any other single factor. It seemed there was a noticeable correlation between innovation and growth. "Ideas drive economies"—a lesson learned.

"Based on this we proceeded to develop a full blown 13-part seminar series to bring state-of-the art business practices to Littleton companies with a focus on innovation." They ran the seminars for four years, trying to increase revenues and employment in target companies, but found that despite all the effort to generate growing companies, "a few companies grew at sky rocket rates while most languished with low or no growth." A related insight from this period was the degree to which certain profiles of CEOs also tended to be more prominent within high-growth firms. Recognizing that simply training CEOs was not increasing the growth rates of Littleton companies, they went back to the drawing board.

By the mid-1990s another factor affecting high-growth companies began to be apparent: businesses are as much biological as mechanical. For centuries, human beings have invented one mechanical device after another with predictable outputs. This idea transferred to other disciplines: business managers and economists often talked as if businesses and economies were predictable mechanical machines. "The Santa Fe Institute, however, saw something different. They saw a biological world in which each living thing was constantly adapting to all of the other living things, all tied together by innumerable feedback loops. They saw a complex world in constant turmoil which was both unpredictable and uncontrollable. . . . It took Nobel Laureate scientists to show us that unpredictability in companies and economies is a deep law of living things." The science of "complexity" began to emerge.

Complexity science, although based on complex mathematical formulas using massive computer power, did produce some "handy rules of thumb," such as the "edge of chaos." The term refers to "the fine line between stability and chaos where innovation and survival are most likely to take place." In nature, Chris notes, ice is frozen, steam is highly chaotic, and water is stable. Organizations can be like that: frozen—a state in which nothing moves or adapts and no information is transferred; chaotic—where so much change occurs that the organization doesn't have an identity; or stable—where identity is retained, but adaptation is possible. The high growth companies in Littleton, Chris noticed, were those that could "ride the very edge of chaos like a seasoned surfer." They adapted through experimentation and by learning from many small mistakes, which helped them avoid the big fatal ones.

A related principle was self organization. A flock of geese retains its shape, identity, and function with no one in charge. Similarly, high-growth "gazelles" seem to "just do it" and it all comes together. In contrast, larger organizations, working on a command-and-control model "just order it" and set in motion meetings, committees, reports. The larger an organization gets, the less command and control works. Self organization as a strategy may seem more chaotic and redundant, but it is more adaptable, more nimble, and more likely to survive.

Another principle was increasing returns. Chris notes Economist Brian Arthur's contention that "winners continue to win because they have won in the past. His prime example is VHS vs. Beta tapes. Although Beta was generally acknowledged to be the better technology, a critical mass of people opted for VHS early on, which created a large installed base, and all of the supporting technology decided to move to where customers were concentrated."

The Littleton economic gardeners continued to work at the principles behind creating an environment in which entrepreneurs could flourish, and other communities began to take notice and experiment with the concept. "As new people added their insights and experiences to the cause, it became clear that we had only the most rudimentary understanding of entrepreneurial activity and were working with the simplest of frameworks (support entrepreneurs and things will get better)," Chris writes.

"Even though we knew the tools and techniques that helped make entrepreneurs successful, there was another intangible (but very real) factor keeping local economies from improving. For the lack of a better word, I initially called it the 'culture' of a community. By this, I meant the way that entrepreneurial activity and risk and innovation and even diversity and newness are viewed by local people."

He noticed that in resource production towns centered around farming, ranching, mining, timber, and fishing, the need to compete on price was paramount, and the smallest disturbance in price could mean that customers would look elsewhere for the commodity. These cultures tended to be very focused on stability, and risk-averse to the extent that they could become anti-entrepreneurial.

"This same anti-entrepreneur 'culture' also cropped up in areas where large corporations dominated the landscape. It seemed that in areas where big corporations employed a large percentage of the population, the typical employee saw wealth and job production as very distant from his or her realm of control. Any sense of self-reliance was bred out of the 'culture.'"

All of these realizations contributed to an understanding of the entrepreneurial culture as an entity as organic as any living creature. More attention needed to be paid to the "complex, biological, and interrelated factors of building an environment conducive to entrepreneurial activity: intellectual stimulation, openness to new ideas, the support infrastructure of venture capital and universities, information and community support."

"We by no means have solved the economic development riddle," Chris says. "We cannot patent it, put it in a jar and take it to any community and guarantee results. But we do think we are closing in on the answer. We think it involves slow, painstaking community development with an eye on the innovators."

and businesses and threatened to undermine the community's overall tax base. Unfortunately, near-term prospects for recovery were not favorable.

During this state of relative economic crisis, community leaders in Littleton chose a strategic path that diverged from conventional economic development wisdom. Rather than seek a quick fix to replace lost jobs by offering relocation incentives and tax breaks to firms outside the region—an approach city leaders came to refer to as "economic hunting"—they embraced an alternate, long-term entrepreneurial strategy designed to generate new jobs from the existing base of businesses in the community. This approach, which they termed "economic gardening," sought to cultivate an "inside-out" expansion strategy in contrast to conventional business recruitment efforts. This decision and the resulting policy implications proved to be significant for the city of Littleton and eventually for communities throughout the nation that have elected to follow a similar path.

Philosophy and Principles

The philosophical framework supporting Littleton's economic gardening program offers a compelling argument for elevating the importance of entrepreneurship in contemporary economic development policy. The framework is both innovative and intuitively simple, suggesting that sustainable economic development policy must strike a better balance of applying "outside-in" and "inside-out" growth strategies, subject to the unique attributes and resources of a given community. The economic gardening policy the city of Littleton crafted in 1989 was based on a simple belief: small local entrepreneurial firms would be the engine for the creation of sustainable wealth and new jobs, and the role of the city was to provide a nurturing environment within which these small firms could flourish.[16]

This shift in economic development policy away from the pursuit of and reliance upon large firms was fueled in part by the painful lessons learned, as city leaders saw how quickly out-of-market businesses could undermine the fabric of their local economy. Equally influential over time was the evolving research of David Birch, which confirmed that small businesses do, in fact, generate a majority of the net new jobs throughout most communities, particularly a select few high-growth firms he referred to as "gazelles." Today, experts in the field of economic development take the general insights and supporting data generated by David Birch as axiomatic. However, during the formative years of the economic gardening experiment in Littleton, the practical application of those themes by economic developers outside of Littleton remained the exception rather than the rule.

As with any truly entrepreneurial venture, the process of development is adaptive by nature. Over time, the original model of economic gardening in Littleton was refined and evolved to meet the needs of the intended market—small business owners, particularly growth-oriented entrepreneurs located in the city of Littleton. What has emerged is a powerful and effective set of tools ideally suited for a new brand of home-grown economic development practices.

Practices

The economic gardening best practices that evolved in Littleton, Colorado, were ultimately associated with one of three critical themes:

1. Infrastructure: building and supporting the development of community assets essential to commerce and overall quality of life (e.g. roads, education, and cultural amenities);

2. Connectivity: improving the interaction and exchange among business owners and critical resource providers (e.g. industry trade groups, public sector supporters, and academic institutions); and

---

16   Chris Gibbons, director, Business/Industry Affairs, City of Littleton, Colorado, interview, May 24, 2006.

3. Market information: access to competitive intelligence on markets, customers, and competitors comparable to the resources historically available only to large firms.

Of these three critical themes forged over time through an adaptive process tied to customer input and feedback, improved access to market information proved to be of greatest value to the owners and operators of small businesses in Littleton, Colorado.[17]

Affordable access to sophisticated market research tools, tools typically available only to large businesses, proved to be the centerpiece of Littleton's economic gardening program. The original suite of market research tools offered by the city expanded over time and eventually included database and data mining resources, supplemented by the enhanced display capabilities of geographic information systems (GIS). These business development services, partially underwritten by the city to provide both free and discounted fee-for-service solutions, offered a degree of competitive intelligence that local business owners came to see as both relevant and beneficial.

Widespread support for Littleton's economic gardening program among targeted business owners is understandable, given the degree to which the market research services offered by the city addressed stage-related issues faced by growth companies. Practically speaking, expansion-related challenges common to second-stage companies by definition involve the sales function and its relative impact on a company's capacity to fuel job growth and wealth creation for the firm. The targeted delivery of applied research and sales-support materials to these targeted firms resulted in an unusually productive alignment of public sector capabilities with private sector needs. The subsequent success of Littleton's economic gardening programs over time reflects the degree to which the city was able to deliver services to the growth companies most able to convert those services to the greatest number of net new jobs and related wealth creation.

Results

Since inception of the economic gardening program in 1989, the number of jobs in Littleton, Colorado, doubled from approximately 15,000 to over 35,000

---

17 Chris Gibbons, director, Business/Industry Affairs, City of Littleton, Colorado, interview, May 24, 2006.

during a period in which the city's general population grew at a more modest rate of only 30 percent.[18] Sales tax revenue during this same period tripled from $6.8 million to $19.6 million, in spite of two major recessions and the adoption of a policy that eliminated the use of all incentives and tax breaks in the business recruitment process. While tracking the growth paths of firms in Littleton is beyond the scope of this paper, the creative use of the NETS database now makes such analysis possible.

Lessons Learned

Development of the economic gardening program in Littleton, Colorado, according to those involved, has been a journey in the strictest sense of the word.[19] No roadmap or signpost existed to guide them through the process of designing and implementing their gardening programs. The journey has been anything but a straight and smooth path. While the Littleton, Colorado, development team acknowledges that the program remains a work in progress, they are also quick to point out that the lessons they have learned along the way can help others reduce the frustration associated with the inevitable wrong turns, potholes and dead-end paths associated with any journey into new and uncharted territory. The following "lessons learned" are presented as guidelines critical to designing effective and sustainable economic gardening programs. They are offered with the caveat that, ultimately, economic development is a "bottom up" phenomenon requiring the application of local knowledge and appropriate adaptation over time.

1. *Growth companies matter: clearly define and understand the needs of the target market.* Economic gardening programs cannot succeed without a clear understanding and commitment to meeting the needs of entrepreneurs—specifically, identifying and meeting the needs of growth-oriented entrepreneurs that generate a majority of the net new jobs and associated wealth at the core of any effective growth strategy. Commitment to this principle can be a politically sensitive issue, but it gets to the heart of what economic gardening is all about. Generally speaking, only a fraction of all entrepreneurs in a given community have the intent and capacity to

---

18 Christine Hamilton-Pennell, "CI for Small Business: The City of Littleton's Economic Gardening Program" (*Competitive Intelligence* Magazine, vol. 7, no. 6, December 2004), 13–14.

19 Chris Gibbons, director, Business/Industry Affairs, City of Littleton, Colorado, interview, May 24, 2006.

build growth-oriented businesses. The goal is to identify them and serve them well.

2. *Long-term commitment: seek to reconcile political and economic lead times.* Economic gardening is a long-term strategy. It represents a lifelong economic development "lifestyle" change rather than the short-term economic development "crash diet" so often associated with recruitment and incentive programs. Unfortunately, the development cycle of gardening programs is longer than typical political election cycles. As a result, few supporters of a balanced "portfolio approach" to economic development will be in a position to reap the political benefits generated by economic gardening programs. All stakeholders in economic gardening programs must appreciate the cyclical disconnect associated with a long-term economic development strategy and be prepared for the inevitable pressures that will emerge. Consequently, economic gardening programs depend on advocacy beyond city hall and mainstream economic development organizations. Successful and sustainable programs require a long-term commitment by private sector leaders in the community, including a commitment to measurement of results, now possible with real-time retention and expansion web surveys and secondary data sources such as NETS.

3. *Entrepreneurial climate: pay attention to the culture surrounding economic gardening programs.* Economic gardening programs do not exist in a vacuum. As with other economic development programs, a threshold level of resources must exist. Unlike other economic development initiatives, however, economic gardening is most effective in regions having sufficient entrepreneurial spirit or "entrepreneurial DNA" already in place. The entrepreneurial capacity of a region includes both resident entrepreneurs and the degree to which the prevailing business culture is inclined to support those entrepreneurs. Unfortunately, while it is generally recognized that entrepreneurs are spread widely across all regions throughout the nation,[20] the entrepreneurial culture required to effectively support growth-oriented entrepreneurs has been bred out of many communities through years of risk-avoidance or a misplaced confidence in the commitment

---

20 National Commission on Entrepreneurship, *High-Growth Companies: Mapping America's Entrepreneurial Landscape* (Washington D.C. NCOE 2001), 1.

large businesses hold toward assuring the long-term economic well-being of a given local community.

4. *Leadership: identify a "champion" for the long term.* Littleton has enjoyed the long tenure of key staff. As with anything new or unproven, the involvement and commitment of a recognized and respected local "champion" is critical to initial success. Often overlooked and unspoken in the process is the corresponding value of having management stability over time. Continuity of leadership at both levels both provides institutional memory and engenders the confidence of all stakeholders required to navigate the inevitable challenges that occur over time.

Does Littleton Owe Its Economic Progress to the Gardening Approach?

No definitive analysis has linked the economic gardening strategy of Littleton with its overall economic progress. Multiple factors contribute to a community's economic change, so only the most rigorous econometric methodology could single out primary causes. But overall evidence indicates that economic gardening has most likely been a positive force in Littleton, serving as an affirmative catalyst for economic growth and encouraging a culture that supports entrepeneurship.

While Colorado and the Denver region have underperformed the United States since the 2001 national recession, Littleton has performed remarkably well (Table 6.1).[21] And since its introduction of economic gardening principles in 1989, the number of net new jobs in Littleton has grown from 14,907 to 35,163, or 136 percent. (These numbers include wage-and-salary jobs plus self-employment.)[22] This growth is approximately twice the rate of the Denver region, three times that of Colorado, and six times that of the United States.[23] The growth can be partly explained by such factors as the general growth of suburban communities, Littleton's strong concentration in certain growth industries such as business services, and a vibrant Colorado economy in the

---

21 U.S. Department of Labor, Bureau of Labor Statistics, Quarterly Census of Employment and Wages, and Denver Regional Council of Governments.

22 Denver Regional Council of Governments.

23 National data from U.S. Department of Labor, Bureau of Labor Statistics, Quarterly Census of Employment and Wages.

Table 6.1 Change in Wage-and-Salary Employment, 1990–2005 (percent)

	Littleton	Denver Metro	Colorado	USA
1990–2005	135.3	64.2	47.2	21.4
2000–2005	35.0	-2.6	1.2	1.5

Source: U.S. Department of Labor, Bureau of Labor Statistics, Quarterly Census of Employment and Wages, and Denver Regional Council of Governments.

1990s. Nevertheless, communities with healthy growth conditions can still fail to flourish because of poor local economic development policies. Clearly this has not been the case in Littleton: economic gardening, consistently applied over more than a decade, appears to have had very favorable consequences.

Littleton's 35 percent job growth between 2000 and 2005 well exceeds that of comparable inner suburban Denver communities of similar size: Englewood (7.3 percent), Northglenn (6.2 percent), and Thornton (21.4 percent).

Insight

These figures confirm a strong employment track record in Littleton, now over one full business cycle from the 1991 to 2001 recessions and beyond into the current U.S. and global economic expansion. Littleton appears to perform well in both good and bad times, partly because of its diversified economy nurtured by the economic gardening approach. But probably the most compelling evidence that Littleton must have been doing something right is reflected in the ongoing support the Littleton business community has given to this initiative. Several times when the city has faced budget constraints, the economic gardening program has contronted possible cutback or elimination. In each instance, the testimony and support of the business community has sustained the program. Clearly, businesses see the benefit, even while the program is supported by an optional tax on business activity, the local sales tax.

Littleton's Broader Context—"Entrepreneurial Dynamism" in Colorado

The economic growth of localities and regions is notably enhanced or enabled by a conducive, multi-region, or statewide economic climate. Littleton's experiment has been aided by virtue of its location in a state that has been "on the move" over the past 15 years, notwithstanding a slowdown since 2001. Colorado, in economic development terms, can aptly be described as a "break-away state." Out of a troubling economic downturn in the mid-1980s, caused by a depressed energy and resources market, Colorado has found new vitality in technology-related and growth industries. The labor force has expanded with an influx of younger, well-educated workers, attracted, in part, by the state's natural amenities, beauty, and quality of life.

From 1990 to 2004, Colorado's per capita income increased 84.5 percent compared with 69.7 percent for the United States.[24] Per capita income is a preferred measure of overall wealth creation. Further, employment growth has been strong. Between 1990 and the third quarter of 2005, employment covered by unemployment insurance grew 47.2 percent, compared with 21.4 percent for the United States.[25] Since the 2001 national recession, Colorado's growth has been somewhat muted but is still quite healthy, with average annual growth rates in jobs and output a bit less then one-half percent below the U.S. average.

Most notably, Colorado presents conditions conducive for growth, especially entrepreneurial growth. One measure of the entrepreneurial environment of states is the Kauffman Index of Entrepreneurial Activity.[26] Using the Current Population Survey of the U.S. Bureau of the Census, the index measures the rate at which respondents in the sample shift from salaried or wage employment to starting a new business from one month to the next. The index is particularly good at sensing new business and sole proprietorship starts each month. Colorado presents very strong rates of such entrepreneurial activity, ranking second of all 50 states in 2005. It showed particularly strong improvement from a score of 0.35 percent (U.S. average 0.30 percent) in 2004 to 0.53 percent (U.S. average 0.29 percent) in 2005.

A second way of measuring a state's entrepreneurial environment is Entrepreneurial Dynamism as reported in the Entrepreneurship Score Card published by the Edward Lowe Foundation, with analysis and research from GrowthEconomics, Inc.[27] According to the Entrepreneurship Score Card,

---

24   U.S. Department of Commerce, Bureau of Economic Analysis.

25   U.S. Department of Labor, Bureau of Labor Statistics.

26   Robert Fairlie, *Kauffman Index of Entrepreneurial Activity* (Ewing Marion Kauffman Foundation, 2006).

27   Edward Lowe Foundation, Small Business Foundation of Michigan, and GrowthEconomics, " 2006 Entrepreneurship Score Card" (Edward Lowe Foundation, 2006).

states are showing marked differences in small business and entrepreneurial performance. (See the appendix for a brief description of the Score Card.) The top 10 states in Entrepreneurial Dynamism for 2005 were Massachusetts, California, New Mexico, Virginia, Maryland, Washington, Colorado, Utah, New York, and Rhode Island. Colorado scores in the top 10 on two of the three drivers that make up Entrepreneurial Dynamism: Entrepreneurial Vitality and Entrepreneurial Climate. In a third driver, Entrepreneurial Change, which measures recent growth in small business activity, Colorado rates in mid-range with a ranking of 26 out of 50.

Multiple factors can contribute to the changing entrepreneurial dynamics of a state or region, including many outside the direct control of the public sector or public-private partnerships. Rapidly changing local industry competitiveness, especially with respect to a changing global marketplace, can energize or enervate entrepreneurial response. Culture too, plays a big part. States with changing demographics experience different cultural dynamics regarding innovation, commercialization, and business creation. Notwithstanding these factors, it appears that those states experiencing high scores in Entrepreneurial Dynamism are well suited to local innovations that support small business and entrepreneurial development. In effect, the ambient state "entrepreneurial climate" sets the stage for creative local entrepreneurial development.

Colorado also performs well in the "Nexus" report.[28] In early 2005, the U.S. Small Business Administration's Office of Advocacy and the Edward Lowe Foundation cosponsored a significant study of *The Innovation-Entrepreneurship Nexus: A National Assessment of Entrepreneurship and Regional Economic Growth and Development.* Authored by Advanced Research Technologies of Ohio, the research is based on an analysis of the U.S. Census database, the Longitudinal Establishment and Enterprise Microdata (LEEM) file, which makes possible tracking firm performance by size over time. In the study, 394 regions in the United States were compared using three indexes: the Entrepreneurial Index, Innovation Index, and Economic Growth Index.

---

28 Advanced Research Technologies, *The Innovation-Entrepreneurship NEXUS: A National Assessment of Entrepreneurship and Regional Economic Growth and Development*, prepared for the U.S. Small Business Administration, Office of Advocacy, and the Edward Lowe Foundation, April 2005.

Of the top 30 ranked regions, six were located in Colorado. This distinction positioned Colorado as the state having the largest number of top-ranked regions. Key findings from the study are that:

- Regions with innovation capabilities may not necessarily exhibit high growth;
- High growth is related to the connection between innovation and entrepreneurship; and
- Entrepreneurial vitality is a critical component of economic prosperity.

While considerable attention has been given to building development capacity through both research and development and entrepreneurship, the Nexus study findings draw attention to linking the two themes. Such a linkage would result in more "deals" for venture investors, rapid transfer from discovery to application leading to higher productivity, and higher levels of worker knowledge and skills, resulting in higher pay and higher profits. Winning states and regions appear to be those where innovation and entrepreneurial activity synchronize in self-reinforcing ways.

Of particular note is Colorado's strong long-term showing in the growth of second-stage companies. Colorado's second-stage companies outperformed the United States throughout the 1990s in growth in number of firms, employment, and payroll (Charts 6.3–6.5).[29]

Since the recession of 2001, Colorado has underperformed the United States, likely because of the impact that recession had on Colorado's burgeoning technology companies.

The Evolving Application of Economic Gardening in Other Regions

The economic gardening practices forged in Littleton, Colorado, continue to evolve. Evidence of this evolution can be seen in how the sophisticated competitive intelligence services originally conceived in Littleton have been further refined by communities throughout the country as each community seeks to

---

29   U.S. Department of Commerce, Bureau of the Census, Statistics of U.S. Businesses.

Chart 6.3 Colorado Second-Stage Employment Growth, 10–99 Employees

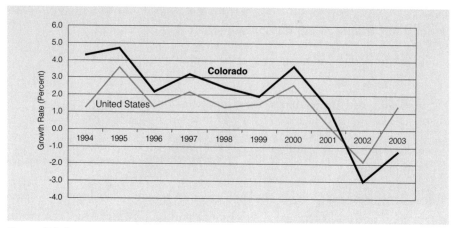

Source: U.S. Department of Commerce, Bureau of the Census, Statistics of U.S. Businesses.

Chart 6.4 Colorado Second-Stage Payroll Growth, 10–99 Employees

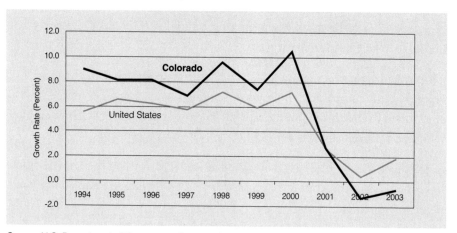

Source: U.S. Department of Commerce, Bureau of the Census, Statistics of U.S. Businesses.

customize its program to reflect local assets and needs. In each case, however, the guiding philosophy and principles of "inside-out" economic development remain central to all economic gardening initiatives. To demonstrate this evolution, the economic gardening programs of four communities other than Littleton have been selected as examples of emerging "best practices." The four programs and their host communities include search engine optimization (Oakland, California), cluster development (Santa Fe, New Mexico), connectivity (Madison, Wisconsin), and regional delivery (Cheyenne, Wyoming).

Chart 6.5 Colorado Second-Stage Firm Growth, 10–99 Employees

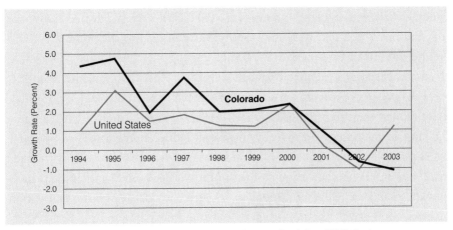

Source: U.S. Department of Commerce, Bureau of the Census, Statistics of U.S. Businesses.

Search Engine Optimization: Oakland, California

In 2004 the Oakland, California, Economic Development office launched an economic gardening pilot program.[30] The intent of the program was to encourage the use of business development principles that embraced the entrepreneurial themes common to the venture capital firms that proliferated in the region, rather than relying solely on conventional incentive-based practices.[31] The Oakland pilot program emphasized the use of information-related marketing resources similar to those found in Littleton, Colorado. The pilot program differed from the Littleton model, however, in offering consulting services related to search engine optimization, an expertise associated with that city's specialized technology talent pool. This particular web marketing expertise, a natural complement to other sales and market information services valued by second-stage companies, represents an important adaptation to the economic gardening program originated in Littleton. The search engine optimization program adds value to participating businesses by increasing the effectiveness of their Internet marketing efforts through more efficient use of website structure, file naming conventions, page titles, keyword meta tags, description meta tags, image tags and text links.

---

30   Ryan Tate, "Running After the Gazelles" (*San Francisco Business Times*, August 13, 2004).

31   Oakland, California, Community and Economic Development Agency, economic gardening website, www.oaklandeg.com.

Cluster Development: Santa Fe, New Mexico

Santa Fe Economic Development, Inc. (SFEDI), a New Mexico nonprofit corporation, is charged with the responsibility of leading economic development efforts in the region without compromising the community's distinctive character. Striking a balance between cultural preservation and the relentless forces of progress presents a true economic development challenge. To bridge these related but often opposing views, SFEDI chose economic gardening as the long-term strategy for diversifying Santa Fe's economy. It did so by crafting a plan that fused conventional industry cluster development techniques involving highly specialized economic inputs with economic gardening principles and practices.[32] The resulting plan, involving a four-step cluster cultivation process, emphasized the importance of entrepreneurship and its "inside-out" approach to development. At the same time, the SFEDI plan required the rigorous application of cluster development techniques by recognizing the importance of supporting those clusters that had developed naturally in the region rather than seeking to create or compete for clusters based on their relative potential or current popularity among other economic developers. The four-step process, designed for long-term effectiveness, included cluster identification, cluster activation, cluster support, and cluster expansion. The ultimate objective of the program is to create a competitive advantage for the region based on the existing local business environment.

Connectivity: Madison, Wisconsin

Connectivity among business owners and the broader business culture supporting entrepreneurs is an important but intangible component of all economic gardening programs. In 2004, the state of Wisconsin, at the direction of a newly elected governor, addressed this issue by establishing the Wisconsin Entrepreneurs' Network (WEN) and a related program called the Wisconsin PeerSpectives Network.[33] Both programs were designed to increase the density of connections and interaction among entrepreneurs and the broader community of organizations supporting entrepreneurship. The Wisconsin Entrepreneurs Network was designed to cast a wide net and improve referral links to information and service providers. The PeerSpectives program, a CEO

---

32 Santa Fe, New Mexico, economic development website, http://www.sfedi.org.

33 Wisconsin Small Business Development Center website, http://www.wisconsinsbdc.org/peerspectives.

peer-to-peer problem-solving resource, offered access to a narrow and highly targeted community of CEO peers. Taken together, the programs offered enhanced connectivity and exchange among a traditionally fragmented and isolated community of business owners and leaders.

Regional Delivery of Services: Cheyenne, Wyoming

The economic gardening program in Wyoming, a true statewide initiative, posed a set of challenges not faced in the entire history of the Littleton, Colorado, program.

The Littleton economic gardening program, for all its success in testing and delivering a suite of market information services, never dealt with the sheer scale of engaging and delivering that same service to such a large and geographically dispersed customer base. While the philosophy, principles, and proposed services of the Wyoming economic gardening initiative parallel that of Littleton, the greater challenge for the state had to do with logistics and customer service.

Responsibility for managing the 2003 implementation of the program was assigned to the Wyoming Market Research Center (WMRC).[34] WMRC, a co-venture involving the Wyoming Business Council and the University of Wyoming, modified program processes derived from Littleton by building a strategic distribution alliance with the Wyoming Small Business Development Center (SBDC) and its network of regional representatives. This distribution alliance effectively allowed WMRC to focus on its core competency of research and analysis and to outsource the sales and customer service aspects of the program.

The Georgia Story

The relatively rapid emergence, adaptation, and dissemination of economic gardening principles and related best practices throughout the country suggest a growing recognition among economic development leaders that entrepreneur-centered initiatives offer an important complement to conventional "outside-in" recruitment programs. Unfortunately, the adoption and implementation of

---

34 University of Wyoming website, http://uwadmnweb.uwyo.edu/wmrc/.

those programs has been so recent that very little data exist regarding overall program effectiveness.

Many communities, especially in rural regions and small urban markets, have become more receptive to economic gardening programs, given the degree of difficulty they have experienced in pursuing conventional business recruitment programs. In many cases, the price competition among communities involved in business recruitment has become so fierce that some practitioners argue that the eventual winners, in fact, become the real losers over the long term. In this context, recent changes in the economic policy for the state of Georgia offer a refreshing counterpoint to conventional wisdom.

The state of Georgia, like most states, has a long history of pursuing industrial recruitment as its primary strategy for economic development. In 2002, following the election of a new governor, a series of entrepreneur-centered programs was initiated to support the small businesses that constitute a majority of businesses in the state.[35] Those programs, administered by the Georgia Department of Economic Development's Entrepreneur and Small Business Office, eventually evolved to become a statewide demonstration of the economic gardening principles and practices created in Littleton, Colorado. In fact, the principles and practices conceived and tested in Littleton served as a model for the related programs proposed for Georgia. The key difference between the Littleton model and the programs designed for Georgia is the scale and operational complexity of administering a comparable program to a significantly larger set of stakeholders across a significantly larger geographical area.

In an effort to minimize the complications presented by these two substantial programmatic differences, the design and development of Georgia's economic gardening program draws upon the "lessons learned" in Littleton following more than a decade of experimentation and refinement, and specifically addresses the three critical themes that comprise Littleton's core principles.

Addressing the four lessons learned from the Littleton experience, the Georgia program:

---

35   Georgia Department of Economic Development website, gateway to assistance, http://www.georgia. org/Business/SmallBusiness/Governors+Welcome+Message.htm.

1. Specifically defines its primary target audience as business owners having no more than 19 employees and a demonstrated desire to grow their business;

2. Acknowledges the long-term strategic nature of the initiative;

3. Communicates an intended outcome of "changing the culture of entrepreneurship in the state;" and

4. Demonstrates political support at the highest level by virtue of the endorsement it has received from the governor.[36]

The Georgia program also has embraced each of the three core principles or themes identified by Littleton as essential for success by offering specific programs or resources; for example:

1. Infrastructure: Entrepreneur and Small Business Coordinating Network (ESBCN) and the "Entrepreneur Friendly" (EF) communities initiative;

2. Connectivity: Mentor-Protégé program; and

3. Access to market information: market research project.

Viewed together, the positioning and programmatic responses outlined in Georgia's economic gardening program clearly address the "lessons learned" and related critical themes advocated by Littleton. The comprehensive and integrated structure of these programs and related resources suggest that Georgia's economic gardening program is well positioned for success. Specific examples of each are outlined below.

Infrastructure

Infrastructure, from an economic gardening point of view, involves both conventional assets and services such as transportation and education, and related intangible assets and services such as financial resources and a business culture that supports entrepreneurship. While the state of Georgia is generally competitive in its delivery of conventional infrastructure, the intangible infrastructure it has developed to support entrepreneurship as a part of its economic gardening program shows great promise. Two specific examples include the

---

36 Greg Torre, Georgia Department of Economic Development, division director, Small Business and Innovation, interview, June 15, 2006.

Entrepreneur and Small Business Coordinating Network (ESBCN) and the Entrepreneur Friendly communities initiative.

The ESBCN is a multi-agency group involving state and federal agencies. The ESBCN is responsible, as its name suggests, for coordinating the state's entrepreneur and small business initiatives, including the Entrepreneur Friendly communities initiative. The ESBCN offers value to entrepreneurs by acting as an advocate for their interests and streamlining access to the vast and often complicated process of navigating bureaucratic channels.

The EF communities initiative is a community-based program designed to enhance the business environment for entrepreneurs and encourage the inclusion of entrepreneurial and small business strategies into a region's overall economic development strategy. [37] This program, early in its development, offers promise to the economic gardening effort for the state because it establishes a programmatic and staffing framework upon which to convey a variety of useful services and solutions geared to the target market.

The EF initiative includes a seven-step process which, when completed, allows a qualified community to access specific state resources and services useful to resident entrepreneurs (Chart 6.6).

Connectivity

While the ESBCN and the EF communities initiative both provide a degree of connectivity in the conventional sense, from an economic gardening point of view, connectivity relates to improving the density and frequency of direct links among target entrepreneurs, their peers, and related support organizations. The Georgia Mentor/Protégé program is an excellent example of this model. The program connects qualified entrepreneurs with their counterparts in larger firms with the intent of solving specific issues identified during an extensive interview process.[38] Participants commit to an 18-month engagement cycle designed to identify strategies for accelerating growth, securing necessary resources, and defining new target markets.

---

37   Mary Ellen McClanahan, Department of Economic Development, director, Entrepreneur and Small Business Office, interview, June 15, 2006.

38   Georgia Department of Economic Development website, Mentor-Protégé, http://www.georgia. org/Business/SmallBusiness/mentor_protege.htm.

Chart 6.6 "Entrepreneur Friendly" Communities

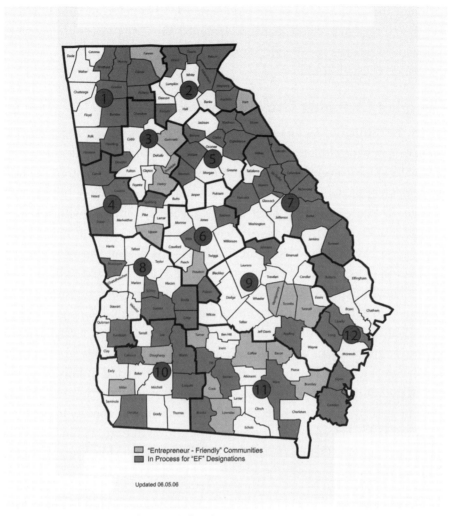

Source: Georgia Department of Economic Development.

Access to Market Information

The challenge of delivering relevant and timely market information, the cornerstone of the Littleton, Colorado, economic gardening model, becomes a daunting task when projected on a statewide basis. This is particularly true for a state as vast as Georgia. The lessons learned in Littleton, and subsequently refined when that methodology was applied to the state of Wyoming, demonstrated that the local model required adaptation for statewide delivery. In

Georgia, this adaptive process will be mitigated to a degree by a phased distribution of the service in select EF communities.[39] The EF community system and the 10 regional project managers assigned to serving local entrepreneurs will work to manage the overall volume of customers to match the capacity of the market research team.

Georgia's Changing Growth Portfolio

Given the Littleton, Colorado, state experience, does Georgia possess the ambient statewide climate conducive for nurturing economic gardening at the regional and local levels? According to the Kauffman Index of Entrepreneurial Activity, Georgia does not score as well as Colorado, but is above the national average. In 2005, Georgia's index was 0.37 percent compared with the U.S. average at 0.30 percent, ranking it 19th of 50 states. In the latest Edward Lowe Foundation Entrepreneurship Score Card, Georgia is a runner-up to the top 10 states in entrepreneurial dynamism, scoring 3 of 5 stars and ranking 13th of 50. The Entrepreneurship Score Card indicates notable improvement in Georgia's small business growth over the 2001–2005 period. Georgia is quite diversified in the size distribution of its companies and has always had an aggressive approach to attracting investment from the outside in. Over the years, with considerable support from state government and utilities, Georgia has offered attractive incentives for direct investment. Nevertheless, Georgia presents healthy scores in entrepreneurial dynamism and appears to be moving towards a balanced growth portfolio where growth from within is gaining increasing support. Georgia's scores in the Entrepreneurship Score Card are summarized in the appendix.

Most important for this chapter is how Georgia's second-stage companies have been faring in recent years. The growth in the number of firms with 10–99 employees, as well as in the jobs they created, surpassed the U.S. average in the 1990s and since the 2001 recession (Charts 6.7–6.9). Payroll growth in recent years has tracked the U.S. average closely, although it performed well above the national average in the late 1990s. On average, Georgia has not attained

---

39 Dara Barwick, Georgia Department of Economic Development, director, Regional Entrepreneur and Small Business Program, interview, May 30, 2006.

Chart 6.7 Georgia Second-Stage Employment Growth, 10–99 Employees

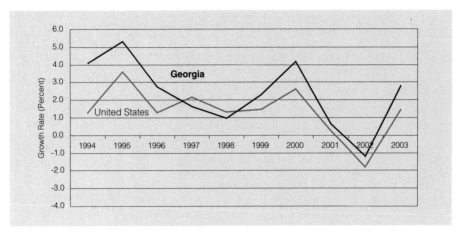

Source: U.S. Department of Commerce, Bureau of the Census, Statistics of U.S. Businesses.

Chart 6.8 Georgia Second-Stage Payroll Growth, 10–99 Employees

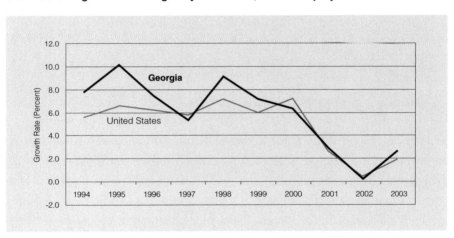

Source: U.S. Department of Commerce, Bureau of the Census, Statistics of U.S. Businesses.

the growth levels of Colorado. However, Georgia's second-stage companies are presenting more robust growth in this decade compared with Colorado.[40]

Georgia also scores reasonably well in the Nexus report mentioned earlier. In linking innovation with entrepreneurship, of the top 30 regions of 394, three were from Georgia.

---

40   U.S. Department of Commerce, Bureau of the Census, Statistics of U.S. Businesses.

Chart 6.9 Georgia Second-Stage Firm Growth, 10–99 Employees

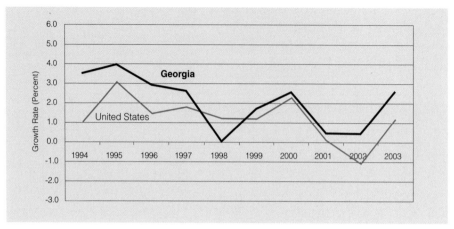

Source: U.S. Department of Commerce, Bureau of the Census, Statistics of U.S. Businesses.

It appears Georgia has strong entrepreneurial momentum and would do well to consider strategies to accelerate entrepreneurial growth as a complement to its ongoing recruitment efforts. Economic gardening offers considerable promise in Georgia.

Conclusion and Observations

The key conclusion of this report is that economic gardening, as formulated and implemented in Littleton, Colorado, has clearly passed the "beta stage" with flying colors. It is not only ready for application elsewhere; its principles and practices are being adopted rapidly based on its inherent logic and on a mounting body of supporting evidence. Most likely, gardening programs are best suited to regions and states already exhibiting healthy signs of entrepreneurial dynamism, like Georgia. Unfortunately, long-term definitive data are still scarce, but initial prospects and anecdotal evidence associated with economic gardening have been very promising. Ultimately, the prospects and future success of economic gardening practices are best expressed by the degree to which they can influence and complement existing economic development activity. Economic gardening has enough potential for spurring regional growth that industry professionals should be familiar with its principles so they can recognize situations where its best practices could be applied. Specifically, economic gardening can influence the dialogue within communities regarding the appropriate mix and allocation of economic development resources—encouraging the adoption of a balanced portfolio approach that generates long-term wealth and well-being for all citizens.

Limitations and Future Research

This report examined the origin, context and application of economic gardening principles and practices in selected U.S. locations. By design, this report was exploratory in nature and sought to identify the key themes and relative progress of this emerging practice rather than offer definitive answers to critical questions or proof of basic assumptions associated with the topic. Clearly, the next generation of research on this topic needs to quantify the assumptions and opportunity costs associated with economic gardening practices. To the degree possible, practitioners in the field currently attempt to measure the impact of economic gardening practices whenever those practices involve public sector resources or public policy review. Unfortunately, fundamental assumptions associated with economic gardening remain untested in academic circles because of the relatively recent emergence of the practice and the general absence of mainstream financial support for the topic among organizations historically associated with the funding of economic development initiatives. A short list of possible actions warranting further review includes the need to:

1. Quantify key assumptions associated with economic gardening principles, including:

   - The role and relative economic contribution of high-growth, second-stage firms
   - Any variation by region or by industry sector

2. Improve skills in measuring and assessing the receptivity and sustainability of a locale, region, or state, for economic gardening, including assessing:

   - Extant growth by firm size using a microdata file such as the National Establishment Time Series.[41]
   - The long-term political and operational challenges confronted by "gardening" programs vs. conventional economic development initiatives.

---

41 David Neumark, Junfu Zhang, and Brandon Wall, "Business Establishment Dynamics and Employment Growth" (Ewing Marion Kauffman Foundation, November 2005), 21–24.

3. Measure the comparative impact of economic gardening programs, including:

- The long-term return on investment and "total cost of ownership" of gardening programs versus conventional recruitment, expansion, and business creation strategies.

APPENDIX 6A
A Brief Description of the Entrepreneurship Score Card

In early 2005, the Small Business Association of Michigan produced the first Michigan Entrepreneurship Score Card as a way to benchmark Michigan's small business and entrepreneurship performance relative to the 49 other states. Based on constructive input from a cross-section of interested business, government, and civic leaders, the Entrepreneurship Score Card has been significantly enhanced for 2006. The Edward Lowe Foundation has taken on producing the Score Card every year both for Michigan and other interested states. The Score Card comprises 126 metrics that measure various dimensions of both the entrepreneurial economy and the broader economy that supports and sustains entrepreneurial activity.

Three key drivers that measure entrepreneurial dynamism were selected based on a comprehensive review of economic growth literature in both the United States and Europe. They are:

- Entrepreneurial Change, which measures recent improvements in number, employment, and payroll of the small and growth companies;
- Entrepreneurial Vitality, which measures the general level of entrepreneurial activity, such as small business starts, SBIR awards, etc., and
- Entrepreneurial Climate, which measures the broad economic environment under which entrepreneurship flourishes.

The three entrepreneurial drivers are aggregated, forming the composite score called Entrepreneurial Dynamism. The top 10 states for Entrepreneurial Dynamism, Change, Vitality and Climate are shown in Table 6A.1.

California and Utah score well across all three drivers, while Massachusetts, Colorado, New Mexico and Virginia score in the top 10 in two. Among a second tier of strong performers is Georgia, singled out in this chapter because of notable improvement over the past five years of Score Card data. Georgia, well

Table 6A.1 2006 Entrepreneurship Score Card

	Entrepreneurial Dynamism	Entrepreneurial Change	Entrepreneurial Vitality	Entrepreneurial Climate
1	MA	WA	MA	MA
2	CA	UT	CA	NM
3	NM	IA	CO	CA
4	VA	ID	VA	MD
5	MD	DE	MD	RI
6	WA	NM	NY	UT
7	CO	NV	UT	VA
8	UT	RI	TX	CO
9	NY	VA	MT	NY
10	RI	CA	FL	NV

Source: Edward Lowe Foundation, Small Business Foundation of Michigan, and GrowthEconomics, Inc., 2006.

versed in "outside-in" growth from business recruitment, is becoming more equally balanced by "inside-out" growth.

The Entrepreneurship Score Card scores the states on a five-point scale where 5 stars is the top 20 percent of the score range, 4 stars the next lower 20 percent of scores, etc. Both five-point scores and rankings are useful for interpreting a state's competitive position.

Georgia's summary statistics are shown in Table 6A.2. Quite notably, Georgia's progress is evident in the statistics. Georgia has held steady in Entrepreneurial Vitality but scores below the mid-range. It shows improvement in Entrepreneurial Change and Entrepreneurial Climate, and scores mid-range or above. Overall, Entrepreneurial Dynamism has improved from 2001 to 2005. In short, evidence from recent years indicates that the entrepreneurial environment in Georgia is improving. With such momentum, the state is in a good position for efforts to accelerate entrepreneurial growth and to add economic gardening to its growth strategy portfolio.

Table 6A.2 Georgia's Entrepreneurship Scores, 2001–2005

	2005	2003	2001
Entrepreneurial Change	☆☆☆☆ (ranking 18)	☆☆☆☆	☆☆
Entrepreneurial Vitality	☆☆ (ranking 20)	☆☆	☆☆
Entrepreneurial Climate	☆☆☆ (ranking 15)	☆☆☆	☆☆
Entrepreneurial Dynamism	☆☆☆ (ranking 13)	☆☆☆	☆☆

Source: Edward Lowe Foundation, Small Business Foundation of Michigan, and GrowthEconomics, Inc., 2006.

7 An Overview *of the* Regulatory Flexibility Act *and* Related Policy

Synopsis

Small business owners, aware that large firms are more able to absorb business costs because of economies of scale, have long since noted the disproportionate effects that government regulation often has on their enterprises. The Regulatory Flexibility Act of 1980 (RFA) and its subsequent refinements, including Executive Order 13272, were designed to address just that concern. Twenty-five years after the enactment of the RFA, the Small Business Administration's Office of Advocacy takes a look back and ahead at how the law and executive order are working to help improve the regulatory climate for small firms and ultimately the functioning of the U.S. economy.

In 2005, more agencies approached Advocacy requesting RFA training or seeking advice early in the rulemaking process. First-year cost savings achieved for small firms through RFA processes amounted to $6.6 billion in FY 2005. At the state level, 18 states introduced regulatory flexibility legislation, and 7 states enacted regulatory flexibility through legislation or executive order. Small entities are increasingly recognizing that working with Advocacy; with state advocacy commissions, boards, and task forces; and directly with federal and state agencies can help improve the regulatory environment. The progress made in FY 2005 suggests that the RFA compliance efforts are working, although continued monitoring of RFA compliance is needed.

The RFA: A 25-Year History

The Office of Advocacy was created in June 1976 (Table 7.1). Part of Advocacy's mandate was explicitly to "measure the direct costs and other effects of government regulation of small business concerns; and make legislative, regulatory, and nonlegislative proposals for eliminating the excessive or unnecessary regulation of small business concerns."

In 1979, a Presidential memorandum to the heads of executive departments and agencies required agencies to report on their small business burden

Table 7.1 Regulatory Flexibility Timeline

Date	Event
June 1976	President Gerald Ford signs Public Law 94-305, creating an Office of Advocacy within the U.S. Small Business Administration charged, among other things, to "measure the direct costs and other effects of federal regulation of small business concerns and make legislative, regulatory, and nonlegislative proposals for eliminating the excessive or unnecessary regulation of small business concerns."
January 1980	The first White House Conference on Small Business calls for "sunset review" and economic impact analysis of regulations, and a regulatory review board that includes small business representation.
September 1980	President Jimmy Carter signs the Regulatory Flexibility Act, requiring agencies to review the impact of proposed rules and include in published regulatory agendas those likely to have a "significant economic impact on a substantial number of small entities."
October 1981	The Office of Advocacy reports on the first year of RFA experience in testimony before the Subcommittee on Export Opportunities and Special Small Business Problems of the U.S. House Committee on Small Business.
February 1983	Advocacy publishes the first annual report on agency RFA compliance.
August 1986	Delegates to the second White House Conference on Small Business recommend strengthening the RFA by, among other things, subjecting agency compliance to judicial review.
September 1993	President Bill Clinton issues Executive Order 12866, "Regulatory Planning and Review," requiring each federal agency to "tailor its regulations to impose the least burden on society, including businesses of different sizes."
June 1995	The third White House Conference on Small Business asks for specific provisions to strengthen the RFA—including the IRS under the law, granting judicial review of agency compliance, and including small businesses in the rulemaking process.
March 1996	President Clinton signs the Small Business Regulatory Enforcement Fairness Act, giving courts jurisdiction to review agency compliance with the RFA, requiring the Environmental Protection Agency and the Occupational Safety and Health Administration to convene small business advocacy review panels, and affirming the chief counsel's authority to file amicus curiae briefs in appeals brought by small entities from final agency actions.
March 2002	President George Bush announces his Small Business Agenda, which promises to "tear down regulatory barriers to job creation for small businesses and give small business owners a voice in the complex and confusing federal regulatory process.
August 2002	President Bush issues Executive Order 13272, "Proper Consideration of Small Entities in Agency Rulemaking," which requires federal agencies to establish written procedures to measure the impact of their regulatory proposals on small businesses, to consider Advocacy comments on proposed rules, and that Advocacy train agencies in the requirements of the law.

Table 7.1 Regulatory Flexibility Timeline—continued

Date	Event
December 2002	Advocacy presents model state regulatory flexibility legislation to the American Legislative Exchange Council (ALEC) for consideration by state legislators. ALEC endorses the model legislation and states begin adopting legislation modeled on the federal law.
May 2003	Advocacy issues *A Guide for Government Agencies: How to Comply with the Regulatory Flexibility Act.*
September 2003	Advocacy presents its first report on agency compliance with E.O. 13272, noting the start of Advocacy's agency training.
September 2005	In the 25th anniversary year of the RFA, Advocacy cosponsors a symposium that looks back at the RFA's achievements and challenges and looks ahead at possible improvements. Legislation is considered in Congress to strengthen the RFA.

reduction efforts to the Office of Advocacy. By 1980, when delegates assembled for the first of three White House Conferences on Small Business, they recommended putting the onus of measuring regulatory costs on the regulatory agencies—to "require all federal agencies to analyze the cost and relevance of regulations to small businesses."

1980: The Regulatory Flexibility Act

The White House Conference recommendations helped form the impetus for the passage, in 1980, of the Regulatory Flexibility Act (RFA). The intent of the act was clearly stated:

> "It is the purpose of this act to establish as a principle of regulatory issuance that agencies shall endeavor, consistent with the objectives . . . of applicable statutes, to fit regulatory and informational requirements to the scale of businesses. . . . To achieve this principle, agencies are required to solicit and consider flexible regulatory proposals and to explain the rationale for their actions to assure that such proposals are given serious consideration."

The law directed agencies to analyze the impact of their regulatory actions and to review existing rules, planned regulatory actions, and actual proposed rules for their impacts on small entities. Agencies were required by the RFA to prepare an initial regulatory flexibility analysis (IRFA) to accompany any proposed rule and a final regulatory flexibility analysis (FRFA) with any final rule. If a proposed rule was not likely to have a "significant economic impact on a substantial number of small entities," the agency could so certify, and not be required to prepare an IRFA or FRFA.

Implementing the RFA

The Office of Advocacy was charged with monitoring agency compliance with the new law. Over the next decade and a half, the office carried out its mandate, reporting annually on agency compliance to the president and the Congress. But it was soon clear that the law was not strong enough. Small business participants in the 1995 White House Conference on Small Business recommended that the RFA be strengthened by requiring agencies to comply and by providing that agency action or inaction be subject to judicial review.

In March 1996, the Small Business Regulatory Enforcement Fairness Act (SBREFA) was signed. The new law gave the courts jurisdiction to review agency compliance with the RFA. Second, it mandated that the Environmental Protection Agency (EPA) and the Occupational Safety and Health Administration (OSHA) convene small business advocacy review panels to consult with small entities on regulations expected to have a significant impact on them, before the regulations were published for public comment. Third, it reaffirmed the authority of the chief counsel for advocacy to file amicus curiae (friend of the court) briefs in appeals brought by small entities from agency final actions.

Executive Order 13272

In March 2002, President George W. Bush announced his Small Business Agenda, giving a high priority to regulatory concerns with a goal to "tear down the regulatory barriers to job creation for small businesses and give small business owners a voice in the complex and confusing federal regulatory process." One key objective was to strengthen the Office of Advocacy by creating an executive order that would direct agencies to work closely with Advocacy in properly considering the impact of their regulations on small business.

In August 2002, President Bush issued Executive Order 13272. It requires federal agencies to establish written procedures and policies on how they would measure the impact of their regulatory proposals on small entities and to vet those policies with Advocacy; to notify Advocacy before publishing draft rules expected to have a significant small business impact; and to consider Advocacy's written comments on proposed rules and publish a response with the final rule. E.O. 13272 requires Advocacy to provide notification as well as training to all agencies on how to comply with the RFA. These steps set the stage for agencies to work closely with Advocacy in considering their rules' impacts on small entities.

The final chapter on how much small businesses and other small entities are benefiting from the RFA as amended by SBREFA and supplemented by E.O. 13272 has yet to be written. Legislation has been introduced to further enhance the RFA. Advocacy believes that as agencies adjust their regulatory development processes to accommodate the RFA and E.O. 13272's requirements, the benefits will accrue to small firms. Agencies are making strides in that direction.

The Economics of the RFA

Office of Advocacy Indicators over the Years

When the Regulatory Flexibility Act was passed in 1980, the cost of regulation was very much on the minds of economists and policymakers. Cost studies from that time period show a general consensus that small firms were being saddled with a disproportionate share of the federal regulatory burden. Then as now, one important tool for redressing the disproportionate impact on small firms was through implementation of the RFA.

As the Office of Advocacy works with federal agencies during the rulemaking process, it seeks to measure the savings of its actions in terms of the compliance costs that small firms would have had to bear had changes to regulations not been made. The first year in which cost savings were documented was 1998. Changes to rules in that year were estimated to have saved small businesses $3.2 billion. Advocacy continues to measure its accomplishments through cost savings.

Ultimately, if federal agencies institutionalize consideration of small entities in the rulemaking process, the goals of the regulatory flexibility process and Executive Order 13272 will be realized to a large degree, and the amount of foregone regulatory costs will actually diminish.

Economics has provided a framework for regulatory actions and for other public policy initiatives. What has been Advocacy's impact in influencing public policy and furthering research? Research by the Office of Advocacy and others over the past two decades has advanced the recognition that small firms are crucial to the U.S. economy.

The economy of 1980 and today differ greatly (Table 7.2). Real gross domestic product (GDP) and the number of nonfarm business tax returns have more than doubled since 1980. The unemployment rate and interest rates are much improved, and prices are higher, although inflation is significantly lower. One constant, though, is the lack of timely, relevant data on small businesses. The Office of Advocacy struggled throughout much of its early existence to measure the number of small firms accurately. The good news is that since 1988 the Census Bureau now has credible firm size data, in part because of funding from the Office of Advocacy.

Despite the data obstacles, Advocacy research shows that more women and minorities have become business owners since 1980. Small businesses are now recognized to be job generators and the source of growth and innovation. Not only are more than 99 percent of all employers small businesses, but small firms are responsible for 60 to 80 percent of all new jobs, and they are more innovative than larger firms, producing 13.5 times as many patents per employee.[1]

Research on small entities has gained more prominence, and entrepreneurs are widely acknowledged as engines of change in their regions and industries. The Office of Advocacy will continue to document the contributions and challenges of small business owners. Armed with this information, policymakers will be able to better consider how government decisions affect small businesses and the economy.

The Impact of Regulatory Costs on Small Firms

Regulatory policy involves difficult choices. Accurate data on costs are essential to a complete understanding of the tradeoffs involved. Even though the RFA first required agencies to consider small business impacts separately 25 years ago, dependable cost estimates have often been hard to come by.

---

1   See the Office of Advocacy's "Frequently Asked Questions" at http://app1.sba.gov/faqs/faqindex.cfm?areaID=24.

Table 7.2 Then and Now: Small Business Economic Indicators, 1980–2005

	1980	1985	1990	1995	2000	2005
Real gross domestic product (trillions of dollars)	5.2	6.1	7.1	8.0	9.8	11.1
Unemployment rate (percent)	7.2	7.2	5.6	5.6	4.0	5.2
Consumer price index (1982=100)	82.4	107.6	130.7	152.4	172.2	193.4
Prime bank loan rate (percent)	15.3	9.9	10.0	8.8	9.2	5.8
Employer firms (millions)	—	—	5.1	5.4	5.7	e 5.8
Nonemployer firms (millions)	—	—	—	—	16.5	e 18.6
Self-employment, unincorporated (millions)	8.6	9.3	10.1	10.5	10.2	10.5
Nonfarm business tax returns (millions)	13.0	17.0	20.2	22.6	25.1	29.0

Note: All figures are seasonally adjusted unless otherwise noted. Figures for "today" represent the latest data available; 2005 data are year-to-date.

e = Estimate

Sources: Federal Reserve Board; U.S. Department of the Treasury, Internal Revenue Service; U.S. Department of Commerce, Bureau of the Census and Bureau of Economic Analysis; U.S. Department of Labor, Bureau of Labor Statistics.

While measuring the costs of new regulations is a prerequisite for improving regulatory policy, compliance with the sum of all current regulations also places a heavy burden on small businesses. Over the past 25 years, significant gains have been made in measuring the impact of regulatory compliance on small firms. During that time, the Office of Advocacy has commissioned and produced a series of research reports on this topic, and the findings have been consistent: compliance costs small firms more per employee than large firms.

The most significant series of analyses began in the 1990s when Thomas Hopkins first estimated the costs of regulatory compliance for small firms. This research was refined by Mark Crain and Hopkins in 2001,[2] and most recently by Crain in the 2005 study, *The Impact of Regulatory Costs on Small*

---

2   See http://www.sba.gov/advo/research/rs207tot.pdf for the full report.

Firms.[3] Crain's latest estimate shows that federal regulations cost small firms nearly 45 percent more per employee than large firms. The 2005 report distinguishes itself from previous research by adopting a more rigorous methodology for its estimate on economic regulation, and it brings the information in the 2001 study up to date. The research finds that the total costs of federal regulations have further increased from the level identified in the 2001 study, as have the costs per employee. Specifically, the cost of federal regulations totals $1.1 trillion, and the updated cost per employee is now $7,647 for firms with fewer than 20 employees. The 2001 study showed small businesses with a 60 percent greater regulatory burden than their larger business counterparts. The 2005 report shows that disproportionate burden at 45 percent.[4]

Despite much progress since passage of the RFA 25 years ago, significant work remains. The hurdles include determining the total burden of rules on firms in specific industries or imposed by specific federal agencies. Estimates of these costs would help show policymakers the marginal cost of adding new rules or modifying existing ones; they would also help show the effects of repealing rules that are no longer relevant, yet still cost small business every year. Such analyses will become crucial as the mountain of federal regulations continues to rise. The future of small business will be affected by rulemaking that uses the best data available to balance the costs and benefits of regulation, while considering how additional rules will affect small businesses.

FY 2005 Federal Agency Compliance with E.O. 13272 and the RFA

Executive Order 13272 Compliance

While agency compliance with both the RFA and E.O. 13272 has improved, some agencies still do not reach out to Advocacy early enough in the rule development process to make a real difference in the impact of rules on small entities. As agencies continue to make changes to their regulatory development

---

3   See http://www.sba.gov/advo/research/rs264tot.pdf for the full report.

4   Caution should be exercised in any comparison of the cost estimates in the two studies, as the underlying methodology in the 2005 report differs slightly from that used in the 2001 report. For a brief explanation of the differences, see pages 1-4 of the 2005 report, available at http://www.sba. gov/advo/research/rs264tot.pdf.

processes to accommodate E.O. 13272's requirements, benefits to small entities will be seen. Some agencies are making strides in that direction. Advocacy continues to stress the importance of agency compliance with EO 13272 as another crucial step in consideration of the impact of their rules on small entities and is hopeful that real change as a result of the executive order will continue to be seen.

RFA Training under E.O. 13272

E.O. 13272 required Advocacy to conduct federal agency training in how to comply with the RFA and the executive order. Advocacy has trained more than half of the 66 federal agencies and independent commissions identified as promulgating regulations that affect small businesses.

Agency staff—attorneys, economists, policymakers and other employees involved in the regulation writing process—come to RFA training with varying levels of familiarity with the RFA, even though it has been in existence for 25 years. Some are well versed in the law's requirements, while others are completely unaware of what it requires an agency to do when promulgating a regulation.

Before attending the training, participants receive a training manual. The three-and-a-half-hour session consists of discussion, group assignments (in which participants review fictitious regulations for small business impact), and a question-and-answer session. Agency employees are trained through a hands-on approach to the RFA and are able to see how the law's many requirements work in a real-life regulatory setting.

RFA training under E.O. 13272 is having a real impact on agencies in a number of ways. One of the most important effects of the training is a closer relationship between the agency and the Office of Advocacy. As a result of the training, agency rule writers, economists, attorneys, and policymakers recognize that there is an office that can assist them with their RFA and E.O. 13272 compliance. This closer relationship has led to several agencies contacting Advocacy earlier in the rule development process regarding rules that may have a significant impact on a substantial number of small entities. Early intervention leads to better rules for small businesses.

Another improvement as a result of the training in a few agencies is a more detailed economic analysis. Where Advocacy once saw one-paragraph boilerplate certifications and economic analyses without any alternatives, there are now more substantiated certifications and IRFAs that at least acknowledge an attempt to identify alternatives for small businesses.

While these RFA training successes can be noted in some agencies, most have yet to jump on the E.O. 13272 compliance bandwagon. Advocacy has continued in FY 2005 to encourage agencies to comply with E.O. 13272 through its RFA training activities, including repeat training at some agencies for new employees and those who missed the initial training.

A web-based training module planned for FY 2006 will enable Advocacy to reach agencies that have not been available for training, as well as to receive electronic course feedback on what agency employees have learned. With continued training on the importance of complying with the RFA and E.O. 13272, the number of regulations written with an eye toward reducing the burden on small entities will continue to grow.

RFA Compliance

In FY 2005, small businesses continued to face a mountain of regulatory burden. However, Advocacy's involvement has had a positive impact toward reducing the load small businesses must carry. Advocacy's involvement in agency rulemakings helped secure $6.62 billion in first-year foregone regulatory cost savings and $965 million in recurring annual savings for small entities (Tables 7.3 and 7.4).

Improvements were seen in agency submission of draft rules to Advocacy for review through the increased number of draft rules sent to Advocacy's email notification system: notify.advocacy@sba.gov. Improvements in seeking assistance early in the rulemaking process were evident in the increasing number of conversations with agency rule writers willing to discuss predecisional regulatory information with Advocacy lawyers and economists in an effort to improve RFA compliance. Improvements in considering significant alternatives following discussions with Advocacy and affected small entities have occurred this year as some agency rules have contained realistic alternatives to their regulations that would benefit small entities.

Table 7.3 Regulatory Cost Savings, Fiscal Year 2005

Agency	Subject Description	Cost Savings
USDA/ APHIS	Mexican Avocado Import Program. The final rule expands existing regulations to allow distribution of Mexican Hass avocados to 47 states during all months of the year. The agency delayed distribution of the avocados to California, Florida, and Hawaii (the 3 states that have all avocado producers in the United States) for the first two years of the rule. 69 Fed. Reg. 69748 (November 30, 2004).	$34.55 million each year, for the first two years of the rule. Source: APHIS.
EPA	Cooling Water Intake. The rule requires facilities that have cooling water intake structures to install devices to protect fish and other aquatic species from being killed by the intake structures. As a result of a SBREFA review panel, EPA proposed an exemption for facilities that have a cooling water intake flow of 50 million gallons per day or less. This removes all small businesses from the cooling water intake rule. Research available to the panel indicated that cooling water intake flow volumes below the 50 million gallon per day threshold are unlikely to affect fish or other aquatic species. 69 Fed. Reg. 68444 (November 24, 2004). Note: This rule was identified in the OMB *2004 Report to Congress on the Costs and Benefits of Federal Regulations* as a candidate for regulatory reform because of its impact on small business.	$74 million over a ten-year period, and an annualized cost savings of $10.5 million. Source: EPA.
EPA	Other Solid Waste Incinerators. The rule requires new and existing incinerators at institutions such as schools, prisons, and churches to install state-of-the-art control equipment and meet costly permitting and operating requirements, or alternatively, to shut down their incinerators and send their sold waste to a landfill. EPA agreed to exempt several types of incinerators for which alternative disposal options are not feasible, including rural incinerators at institutions located more than 50 miles from an urban area where the operator can show that no other waste disposal alternative exists. 69 Fed. Reg. 71472 (December 9, 2004).	$7.5 million per year. Source: EPA.
DOD	Radio Frequency Identification Tags. DOD decided not to publish the rule as an interim final regulation. Instead the rule will go through the notice and comment process, guaranteeing small business input prior to the final rule stage. Based on DOD's analysis, it was estimated that approximately 14,000 small businesses would be affected in the first year. The rule's delay for more than a year allows small businesses greater flexibility. 70 Fed. Reg. 53955 (September 13, 2005).	$62 million. Source: DOD.

Table 7.3 Regulatory Cost Savings, Fiscal Year 2005—continued

Agency	Subject Description	Cost Savings
FCC	Restriction on Fax Advertising. Advocacy and small businesses supported legislation that would recognize a previous business relationship exemption. The Junk Fax Prevention Act of 2005 was signed into law by President Bush on July 9, 2005. Pub. L. No. 109-21, 119 Stat. 359 (2005). Note: This rule was identified in OMB's *2004 Report to Congress on the Costs and Benefits of Federal Regulations* as a candidate for regulatory reform because of its impact on small business.	$3.5 billion initially and $711 million annually. Source: FCC.
NARA	Records Center Facility Standard. The rule required extreme fire prevention and control measures at all records facilities. The 2005 final rule provides flexibility from some of the more stringent standards while still maintaining safety standards. 70 Fed. Reg. 50982 (August 29, 2005). Note: This rule was identified in the 2002 OMB *Report to Congress on the Costs and Benefits of Federal Regulations* as a candidate for reform because of its impact on small businesses.	$63 million for the first year of the rule. Source: PRISM International.
FWS	Designation of Critical Habitat for the Bull Trout. FWS submitted a draft final rule to Advocacy. The general scope of the rule was to designate certain areas as critical habitat to protect the bull trout. The final rule published by FWS included an exemption for impounded waters from the final designation of critical habitat. The exemption provided flexibility for small businesses with no impact on the species. 70 Fed. Reg. 56212 (September 26, 2005).	Not available.
MSHA	Diesel Particulate Matter Exposure in Underground Metal and Nonmetal Mines. MSHA has proposed to revise its final rule on diesel particulate matter by staggering the effective date over a five-year period to provide greater flexibility. The final rule mandated a reduced permissible exposure limit for diesel particulates in these mines from 400 micrograms per cubic meter of air to 160 micrograms per cubic meter of air. 70 Fed. Reg. 53280 (September 7, 2005).	$1.6 million per year. Source: MSHA.
DOT/ FMCSA	Hours of Service of Truckers. FMCSA amended an earlier 2003 rule that had been remanded to the agency by the U.S. Court of Appeals for the D.C. Circuit, but left in effect by Congress pending final agency action. Advocacy urged FMCSA to reduce the regulatory burdens on short-haul drivers by allowing some of them to drive two extra hours once per week (offset by rest time) as well as reducing recordkeeping requirements. FMCSA agreed to these changes. 70 Fed. Reg. 49978 (August 25, 2005). Note: This rule was identified in the 2004 OMB *Report to Congress on the Costs and Benefits of Federal Regulations* as a candidate for regulatory reform because of its impact on small business.	$200 million in first year and $200 million annually. Source: FMCSA.

Table 7.3 Regulatory Cost Savings, Fiscal Year 2005—continued

Agency	Subject Description	Cost Savings
SEC	Extension of Compliance for Periodic Reports. As required by the Sarbanes-Oxley Act of 2002, SEC published final rules June 18, 2003, requiring businesses that raise funds from public investors to report on internal controls and audit procedures. Advocacy urged SEC to delay the first compliance deadline, and the SEC extended the deadline for one year. 70 Fed. Reg. 56825 (September 29, 2005).	$2.68 billion in first year. Source: FEI.

Table 7.4 Summary of Estimated Cost Savings, FY 2005 (Dollars)

Rule / Intervention	First-Year Costs	Annual Costs
APHIS Mexican Avocado Import Program[1]	34,550,000	34,550,000
EPA Cooling Water Phase III[2]	10,500,000	10,500,000
EPA Other Solid Waste Incinerators[2]	7,600,000	7,600,000
DOD RFID[3]	62,000,000	—
FCC Do not FAX[4]	3,556,430,226	711,286,045
NARA Records Center Facility Standards[5]	63,000,000	—
FWS Bull Trout Critical Habitat Designation[6]	—	—
MSHA Diesel Particulate Matter[7]	9,274,325	1,620,869
DOT/FMCSA Hours of Service[8]	200,000,000	200,000,000
SEC Extension of Compliance[9]	2,680,000,000	—
TOTAL	**6,623,354,551**	**965,556,914**

Note: The Office of Advocacy generally bases its cost savings estimates on agency estimates. Cost savings for a given rule are captured in the fiscal year in which the agency agrees to changes in the rule as a result of Advocacy's intervention. Where possible, savings are limited to those attributable to small businesses. These are best estimates. First-year cost savings consist of either capital or annual costs that would be incurred in the rule's first year of implementation. Recurring annual cost savings are listed where applicable.

Sources:

1 Animal and Plant Health Inspection Service (APHIS).

2 Environmental Protection Agency (EPA).

3 Department of Defense (DOD).

4 U.S. Chamber of Commerce survey.

5 PRISM International and National Archives and Records Administration (NARA).

6 Note: Cost savings for this rule are not publicly available because savings were accrued during the draft stage of the rule.

7 Mine Safety and Health Administration (MSHA).

8 Federal Motor Carrier Safety Administration (FMSCA).

9 Calculations were based on data from a Financial Executives International (FEI) survey.

Model Legislation for the States

Any small business owner on Main Street will explain that the regulatory burden does not just come from Washington. The regulatory burden also comes from state capitals where state agencies are located. Sensitizing government regulators to how their mandates affect the employer community does not stop at Washington's beltway. Regulatory flexibility is a practice that must be successful at both the state and federal levels if America is to remain competitive.

The Office of Advocacy has drafted model legislation for consideration by states that mirrors the federal Regulatory Flexibility Act. Its intent is to foster a climate for entrepreneurial success in the states, so that small businesses will continue to create jobs, produce innovative new products and services, bring more Americans into the economic mainstream, and broaden the tax base. This can be done without sacrificing agency regulatory goals.

Successful state-level regulatory flexibility laws, as in the model legislation, address the following areas:

1. A small business definition that is consistent with state practices and permitting authorities;

2. A requirement that state agencies prepare a small business economic impact analysis before they regulate;

3. A requirement that state agencies consider less burdensome alternatives for small business that still meet the agency objective;

4. Judicial review of agency compliance with the rulemaking procedures; and

5. A provision that forces state governments to periodically review existing regulations.

In 2005, 18 states introduced regulatory flexibility and seven states enacted regulatory flexibility legislation or an executive order (EO) (Table 7.5). By 2005, 14 states and one territory had active regulatory flexibility statutes; 28 states have partial or partially used statutes (Chart 7.1).

A Colorado Success Story

The importance of state regulatory flexibility for small businesses is demonstrated in a "real life" example from Colorado. Under Colorado law, hotels

Table 7.5 State Regulatory Flexibility Model Legislation Activity, 2005

State	Bill Number/ Executive Order	Enacted in 2005
Alabama	HB745	
Alaska	HB33	X
Arkansas	EO	X
Hawaii	HB602/HB422	
Indiana	HB1822	X
Iowa	SB65	
Mississippi	HB1472 / SB2795	
Missouri	HB576	X
Montana	HB630	
New Jersey	A3873/ S2754	
New Mexico	HB869/ SB842	X
North Carolina	SB664	
Ohio	SB15	
Oregon	HB 3238	X
Pennsylvania	HB 236 / SB 842	
Tennessee	HB 279 / SB 1276	
Utah	HB 209	
Virginia	HB 1948 / SB 1122	X
Washington	HB 1445	

and restaurants are permitted to reseal, and allow a customer to remove from the premises, an open bottle of partially consumed wine purchased at a hotel or restaurant, with some limitations. To implement this law, the Colorado Department of Revenue proposed an amendment to a rule that would require hotels and restaurants offering resealing of opened bottles to purchase commercially manufactured stoppers and sealable containers such as bags or boxes. The overall cost of compliance for this regulatory proposal was estimated at approximately $1,771,500 to $3,275,000.[5]

According to the definition of small business under the Colorado Administrative Procedure Act (500 or fewer employees) more than 4,000 firms in the state operate with an active liquor license and would have been affected by the rule.

---

5   This number is approximate and based on the cost of a commercially manufactured stopper, corks, and overstocking charges multiplied by the number of small businesses in Colorado subject to the rule.

Chart 7.1 State Regulatory Flexibility Model Legislation Initiative as of FY 2005

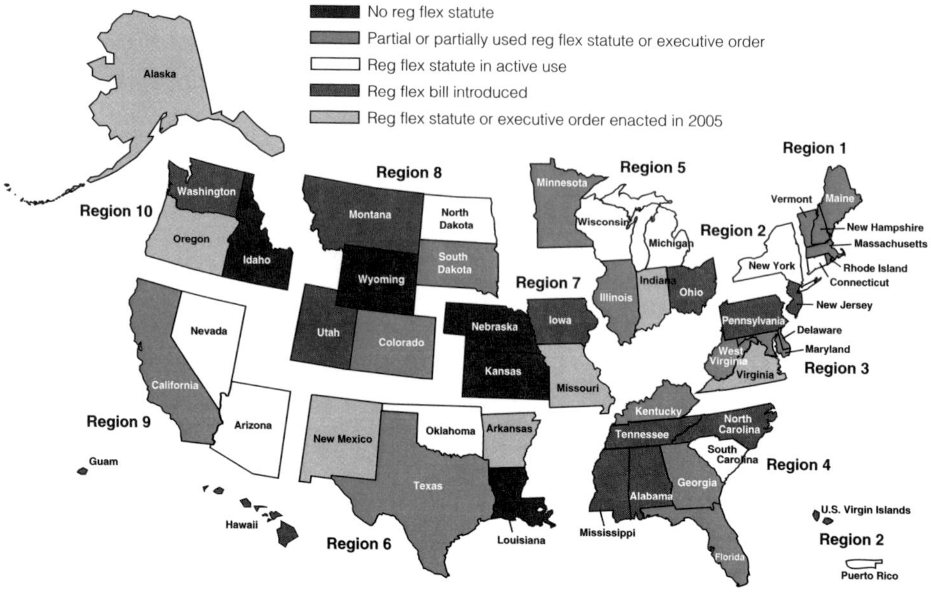

Legend:
- No reg flex statute
- Partial or partially used reg flex statute or executive order
- Reg flex statute in active use
- Reg flex bill introduced
- Reg flex statute or executive order enacted in 2005

Source: SBA Office of Advocacy

Under Colorado's regulatory flexibility structure, the Department of Regulatory Agencies (DORA) reviews proposed rules affecting small businesses and can request that an agency prepare an analysis on the economic impact of a proposed rule on small entities. In this circumstance, DORA requested that the Department of Revenue determine the cost that would be incurred by small businesses to comply with the proposed rule.

During the rule review process, DORA held that the law under which the rule was promulgated did not specify how bottles were required to be recorked, nor did it specify that sealable containers, in addition to the stoppers, are required. The Colorado Restaurant Association, on behalf of its small members, also objected to the rule on the basis that the cost of compliance would be overly burdensome to the regulated small entities.

After discussions with DORA and the Colorado Restaurant Association, and before going further with the rulemaking process, the Department of Revenue agreed to revise its initial proposal. The revised rule was a success for small business, as it provides a more economical way for them to comply with the rule by allowing the use of the original cork to recork the bottle. While they are still required to use sealable bags, they are no longer required to incur the expense of commercially manufactured stoppers and corks.

Here, the end result was a cost savings to small business without compromising the agency's objective. DORA's small business outreach was an important tool: the Department of Revenue, DORA, and small businesses worked together under Colorado's regulatory flexibility law. This example demonstrates how state agencies and small businesses can benefit by implementing a comprehensive regulatory flexibility system.

Ongoing Interaction is Key

While the first important step in creating a friendlier state regulatory environment for small businesses is to pass regulatory flexibility legislation, the hard work does not stop there. Once the legislation is passed, Advocacy works with the small business community, state legislators, and state government agencies to assist with implementation. Through its experiences, Advocacy has found that successful implementation of a state regulatory flexibility system requires: 1) agency training in the law; 2) small business activism in the rulemaking process; and 3) executive support and leadership.

On the federal level, the Office of Advocacy is responsible for training agency officials in the requirements of the federal RFA. Advocacy is able to share the successes of the federal training with the states. Similar training on the state level, whether online or in a classroom setting involving key regulatory development officials and/or agency small business ombudsmen, is a good way to provide how-to information on preparing an economic impact and regulatory flexibility analysis.

Small business owners are an important part of the regulatory process, but for small business owners to realize the benefits of a state regulatory flexibility law, they must understand it. Once they understand the benefits and the agency's responsibilities under the law, they will be better able to voice concerns about proposed rules that will adversely affect their businesses. Reaching out to small businesses early in the process is also good for agencies. Small business owners are the best source agencies can use to understand how regulations affect small businesses and what alternatives may be less burdensome. Advocacy works with trade associations, state chambers of commerce, and other groups representing small businesses—all valuable partners in reaching the small business community.

One of the most successful tools in reaching out to the small business community and in facilitating the implementation of regulatory flexibility legislation has been use of the Internet. Several states have developed a regulatory alert system that allows interested parties to sign up and receive automatic regulatory alerts by e-mail when agencies file a notice for a proposed rule that may affect their business. This system is usually developed by the state economic development department or a similar agency.

Creating a user-friendly Internet-based tool allows small business owners, trade associations, chambers of commerce, and other interested parties to stay on top of agency activities that may affect their business. It also provides an avenue through which stakeholders can voice their concerns about the adverse impact of a proposed rule and suggest regulatory alternatives that are less burdensome. Virginia is a good example of a state where, on its Regulatory Town Hall website, an interested party may sign up to receive notification of regulatory actions and to submit online comments.[6]

Advocacy helps connect the appropriate people in the states so that they share their best practices and learn from each other's experiences. The Office of Advocacy is strengthened by regional advocates located in the SBA's 10 regions across the country, who serve as a direct link to small business owners, state and local government bodies, and organizations that support the interests of small entities. The regional advocates help identify small business regulatory concerns by monitoring the impact of federal and state policies at the Main Street level. Their work goes far to develop programs and policies that encourage fair regulatory treatment of small businesses and help ensure their future growth and prosperity.

Conclusion

"The state of small business regulation has come a long way since the enactment of the Regulatory Flexibility Act in 1980," said Chief Counsel for Advocacy Thomas M. Sullivan at the Office of Advocacy's symposium on the 25th anni-

---

6   See https://www.townhall.virginia.gov/Notification/register.cfm.

versary of the Regulatory Flexibility Act, September 19, 2005. It is significant that implementation work under the RFA and E.O. 13272 continues to save small firms billions in regulatory costs, and the number of states adopting regulatory flexibility legislation continues to grow. Even more important over the long term is the change in the culture of federal and state agencies, as more officials become aware of the unintended effects of their regulations on small entities and the economy. In fiscal year 2006, Advocacy will continue to weave small entities into the fabric of regulatory decision-making at agencies. Efforts to train agencies and increased attention to small business impact analysis can change how governments treat small entities. Advocacy is seeing results from a greater working knowledge of the RFA and the administration's commitment, voiced through E.O. 13272, as well as through increased interaction among small business owners and governments at all levels.

APPENDIX A
Small Business Data

Table A.1 U.S. Business Counts and Turnover Measures, 1980–2005

Year	Business and Self-Employment Counts				Business Turnover Measures		
	Employer firms	Nonemployers	Self-employment[2] (thousands)	Nonfarm business tax returns	Employer births	Employer terminations	Business bankruptcies
2005	e 5,992,400	e 19,856,800	10,464	e 29,004,800	e 671,800	e 544,800	39,201
2004	e 5,865,400	e 19,462,300	10,431	e 28,329,900	e 642,600	e 544,300	34,317
2003	5,767,127	18,649,114	10,295	27,269,500	612,296	540,658	35,037
2002	5,697,759	17,646,062	9,926	26,347,100	569,750	586,890	38,540
2001	5,657,774	16,979,498	10,109	25,631,200	585,140	553,291	40,099
2000	5,652,544	16,529,955	10,215	25,106,900	574,300	542,831	35,472
1999	5,607,743	16,152,604	10,087	24,750,100	579,609	544,487	37,884
1998	5,579,177	15,708,727	10,303	24,285,900	589,982	540,601	44,367
1997	5,541,918	15,439,609	10,513	23,857,100	590,644	530,003	54,027
1996	5,478,047	NA	10,489	23,115,300	597,792	512,402	53,549
1995	5,369,068	NA	10,482	22,555,200	594,369	497,246	51,959
1994	5,276,964	NA	10,648	22,191,000	570,587	503,563	52,374
1993	5,193,642	NA	10,279	20,874,800	564,504	492,651	62,304
1992	5,095,356	14,325,000	9,960	20,476,800	544,596	521,606	70,643

Year							
1991	5,051,025	NA	10,274	20,498,900	541,141	546,518	71,549
1990	5,073,795	NA	10,097	20,219,400	584,892	531,400	64,853
1989	5,021,315	NA	10,008	19,560,700	NA	NA	62,449
1988	4,954,645	NA	9,917	18,619,400	NA	NA	62,845
1987	NA	NA	9,624	18,351,400	NA	NA	81,463
1986	NA	NA	9,328	17,524,600	NA	NA	79,926
1985	NA	NA	9,269	16,959,900	NA	NA	70,644
1984	NA	NA	9,338	16,077,000	NA	NA	64,211
1983	NA	NA	9,140	15,245,000	NA	NA	62,412
1982	NA	NA	8,898	14,546,000	NA	NA	69,242
1981	NA	NA	8,735	13,858,000	NA	NA	48,086
1980	NA	NA	8,642	13,021,600	NA	NA	43,252

e = estimate

NA = Not Available.

Sources: U.S. Small Business Administration, Office of Advocacy, from data provided by the following sources: employer firms from the U.S. Department of Commerce, Bureau of the Census with 2004 and 2005 estimates based on Census Bureau and U.S. Department of Labor data; nonemployers from the Census Bureau with 2004 and 2005 estimates based on U.S. Department of the Treasury, Internal Revenue Service (IRS) data; self-employment (unincorporated, primary occupation, monthly averages0 from the U.S. Department of Labor, Bureau of Labor Statistics; nonfarm business tax returns from the IRS; employer births and terminations from the Census Bureau with 2004 and 2005 estimates based on Census Bureau and Department of Labor data; bankruptcies from the Administrative Office of the U.S. Courts (business bankruptcy filings).

Table A.2 Macroeconomic Indicators, 1995–2005

	1995	2000	2004	2005	Percent change 2004–2005
Gross domestic product (GDP) (billions of dollars)[1]					
Current dollars	7,397.7	9,817.0	11,734.3	12,487.1	6.4
Constant dollars (billions of 2000 dollars)	8,031.7	9,817.0	10,755.7	11,134.8	3.5
Sales (billions of dollars)[2]					
Manufacturing	290.0	350.7	354.9	378.7	6.7
Wholesale trade	176.2	234.5	274.7	295.8	7.7
Retail trade	189.0	249.1	289.8	309.9	7.0
Income (billions of dollars)					
Compensation of employees[3]	4,193.3	5,782.7	6,687.6	7,113.1	6.4
Nonfarm proprietors' income	469.5	705.7	853.8	917.8	7.5
Farm proprietors' income	22.7	22.7	35.8	20.8	-41.9
Corporate profits[4]	696.7	817.9	1,161.5	1,351.9	16.4
Output and productivity (business sector indexes, 1992 = 100)					
Output	111.4	140.5	154.9	161.2	4.1
Hours of all persons worked	109.6	121.2	116.4	118.0	1.4
Productivity (output per hour)	101.6	115.9	133.1	136.6	2.6
Employment and compensation					
Nonfarm private employment (millions)[3]	97.9	111.0	109.8	111.7	1.7
Unemployment rate (percent)	5.6	4.0	5.5	5.1	-7.3
Total compensation cost index (Dec.) (June 1989 = 100)	126.7	150.9	175.2	180.4	3.0

Wage and salary index (Dec) (June 1989 = 100)	123.1	147.7	166.2	170.4	2.5
Employee benefits cost index (Dec.) (June 1989 = 100)	135.9	158.6	198.7	206.9	4.1
Bank loans, interest rates, and yields					
Bank commercial and industrial loans (billions of dollars)	723.8	1,085.9	926.1	1,042.4	12.6
Prime rate (percent)	8.83	9.23	4.34	6.19	42.6
U.S. Treasury 10-year bond yields (percent)	6.57	6.03	4.27	4.29	0.5
Price indices (inflation measures)					
Consumer price index (urban) (1982–84 = 100)	152.4	172.2	188.9	195.3	3.4
Producer price index (finished goods) (1982 = 100)	127.9	138.0	148.5	155.7	4.8
GDP implicit price deflator (2000 = 100)	92.1	100.0	109.1	112.1	2.8
Equity markets					
S&P composite	541.7	1,427.2	1,130.7	1,207.2	6.8
NASDAQ	925.2	3,783.7	1,986.5	2,099.3	5.7

Notes:
1 *Small Business Share of Private, Nonfarm Gross Domestic Product* by Joel Popkin and Company (study funded by the Office of Advocacy) estimates small businesses with fewer than 500 employees created 52 percent of the total nonfarm private output in 1999.

2 U.S. Census Bureau, Statistics of U.S. Business, showed that in 2002, small firms with fewer than 500 employees accounted for 24.8 percent of manufacturing, 47.6 percent of retail, and 41.2 percent of wholesale sales.

3 U.S. Census Bureau, Statistics of U.S. Businesses, showed that in 2003 small firms accounted for 45.0 percent of annual payroll and 50.7 percent of total nonfarm private employment.

4 With inventory valuation and capital consumption adjustments.

Sources: U.S. Small Business Administration, Office of Advocacy, from the U.S. Department of Commerce, Bureau of Economic Analysis, and *Economic Indicators,* March 2000 and February 2006.

Table A.3 Number of Businesses by State, 2003–2005

	Employer firms		Nonemployers	Self-employment (thousands)	
	2004	2005	2003	2004	2005
United States	e 5,865,400	e 5,992,400	18,649,114	15,636	15,780
Alabama	86,651	88,274	253,759	194	178
Alaska	16,975	16,921	48,853	43	44
Arizona	110,153	118,193	316,351	298	301
Arkansas	61,778	62,696	170,696	162	160
California	1,077,390	1,075,066	2,381,043	2,138	2,225
Colorado	146,379	152,434	369,784	350	335
Connecticut	97,311	98,067	237,465	176	181
Delaware	25,833	25,741	47,566	32	37
District of Columbia	27,424	27,656	34,518	23	23
Florida	449,070	473,936	1,272,863	1,022	1,039
Georgia	202,979	206,800	570,216	457	455
Hawaii	29,791	30,466	80,718	66	72
Idaho	43,675	46,349	95,444	109	106
Illinois	285,208	290,866	762,765	588	621
Indiana	125,746	125,532	340,365	267	255
Iowa	69,354	70,566	182,696	186	208
Kansas	69,241	69,980	168,985	175	189
Kentucky	83,046	84,988	248,394	179	194
Louisiana	96,084	97,385	268,360	221	197
Maine	40,304	41,026	107,236	94	95
Maryland	137,338	139,483	363,387	271	272
Massachusetts	178,752	183,319	442,002	340	316
Michigan	213,104	214,316	582,296	468	487
Minnesota	134,438	133,288	348,727	360	326
Mississippi	54,117	54,666	153,529	129	139
Missouri	134,448	136,516	347,644	302	304
Montana	34,570	35,597	76,401	93	85
Nebraska	46,161	47,066	109,936	121	116
Nevada	51,424	54,641	142,729	116	120
New Hampshire	40,151	40,619	99,830	77	85
New Jersey	256,863	259,273	537,932	404	409
New Mexico	42,241	43,200	107,751	111	118
New York	481,858	486,228	1,361,705	930	902
North Carolina	182,598	186,684	523,391	420	441

Table A.3 Number of Businesses by State, 2003–2005—continued

	Employer firms		Nonemployers	Self-employment (thousands)	
	2004	2005	2003	2004	2005
North Dakota	19,177	19,594	41,401	53	56
Ohio	231,374	230,799	648,904	505	501
Oklahoma	77,027	77,591	239,483	209	230
Oregon	104,114	106,820	227,156	240	257
Pennsylvania	275,853	280,394	683,294	596	552
Rhode Island	33,253	33,679	65,635	52	50
South Carolina	92,940	95,844	235,708	182	196
South Dakota	23,713	24,349	51,975	63	64
Tennessee	109,853	111,607	387,545	289	301
Texas	404,683	412,520	1,500,067	1,200	1,142
Utah	61,118	62,915	154,097	135	151
Vermont	21,335	21,451	56,646	48	52
Virginia	172,785	177,476	426,247	357	372
Washington	198,635	194,963	353,240	369	373
West Virginia	36,830	36,684	86,438	59	61
Wisconsin	125,888	127,714	297,156	312	342
Wyoming	20,071	20,721	38,785	45	45

e = estimate

Notes: State totals do not add to the U.S. figure as firms can be in more than one state. U.S. 2004 and 2005 estimates are based on U.S. Census Bureau and U.S. Department of Labor, Employment and Training Administration (ETA) data. Self-employment is based on monthly averages of primary occupation for incorporated and unincorporated status. The figures for self-employment cannot be added to the other figures.

Sources: U.S. Small Business Administration, Office of Advocacy, from data provided by the U.S. Department of Labor (ETA) and the U.S. Census Bureau, Current Population Survey, special tabulations.

Table A.4 Business Turnover by State, 2004–2005

	Firm births		Firm terminations		Business bankruptcies	
	2004	2005	2004	2005	2004	2005
U.S. Total	e 642,600	e 671,800	e 544,300	e 544,800	34,317	39,201
Alabama	9,413	10,575	10,104	10,168	325	331
Alaska	1,848	1,982	2,650	2,294	64	83
Arizona	12,421	21,339	17,553	18,249	480	525
Arkansas	7,852	7,591	6,481	7,021	376	426
California	117,016	121,482	143,115	151,944	3,748	4,236
Colorado	23,694	26,610	9,734	14,035	786	1,120
Connecticut	9,064	9,220	11,018	11,131	132	156
Delaware	3,270	3,299	3,362	3,355	276	218
District of Columbia	4,393	4,316	3,440	3,952	41	46
Florida	77,754	84,890	54,498	58,737	1,183	1,622
Georgia	29,547	29,804	27,835	29,315	2,090	2,232
Hawaii	3,698	3,763	3,754	3,794	47	81
Idaho	7,814	9,312	5,716	6,334	160	141
Illinois	28,453	30,445	33,472	32,846	912	1,042
Indiana	13,906	14,545	15,282	16,504	524	758
Iowa	5,954	6,004	7,391	6,802	360	455
Kansas	6,742	7,095	7,250	7,330	268	410
Kentucky	8,807	9,617	8,597	8,515	319	409
Louisiana	9,875	9,393	9,668	9,123	622	718
Maine	4,300	4,251	4,987	4,711	138	144

State						
Maryland	21,751	22,083	20,636	21,769	417	760
Massachusetts	18,822	19,723	20,270	18,878	315	406
Michigan	24,625	24,642	24,584	26,971	681	1,071
Minnesota	15,167	12,555	15,209	15,302	1,374	1,721
Mississippi	6,141	6,071	7,380	6,823	170	200
Missouri	16,155	17,239	17,924	20,109	354	438
Montana	4,588	4,768	4,896	4,394	109	129
Nebraska	4,849	5,127	5,051	4,982	207	296
Nevada	10,483	10,487	9,012	3,674	257	333
New Hampshire	4,865	4,758	5,401	5,406	158	586
New Jersey	35,895	33,022	50,034	32,751	684	765
New Mexico	5,683	10,648	5,592	5,670	727	828
New York	62,854	62,045	64,013	62,667	4,070	2,112
North Carolina	23,387	25,906	22,055	22,867	486	612
North Dakota	1,747	1,893	2,621	2,512	85	95
Ohio	22,725	22,542	21,328	23,429	1,432	2,099
Oklahoma	9,263	8,609	8,018	7,231	659	944
Oregon	13,481	14,445	14,407	14,804	852	1,160
Pennsylvania	33,188	38,368	34,507	38,113	1,138	1,356
Rhode Island	3,932	3,677	4,250	4,164	74	136
South Carolina	11,745	12,341	10,975	10,681	175	176
South Dakota	1,691	2,102	2,251	2,354	108	196
Tennessee	17,415	17,484	16,520	17,135	548	574
Texas	54,098	55,858	55,792	55,039	3,094	3,590

Table A.4 Business Turnover by State, 2004–2005—continued

	Firm births		Firm terminations		Business bankruptcies	
	2004	2005	2004	2005	2004	2005
Utah	11,357	11,536	11,597	11,871	440	449
Vermont	2,322	1,911	2,578	2,346	85	78
Virginia	24,134	25,061	19,919	21,359	750	476
Washington	31,955	30,353	47,141	40,944	665	786
West Virginia	3,937	3,493	5,136	4,869	247	282
Wisconsin	13,093	13,656	12,711	13,397	742	820
Wyoming	2,519	2,632	2,737	2,689	65	84

e = estimate

Notes: State birth and termination totals do not add to the U.S. figure as firms can be in more than one state. U.S. estimates are based on U.S. Census Bureau and U.S. Department of Labor, Employment and Administration data. On occasion, some state terminations result in successor firms which are not listed as new firms.

Source: U.S. Small Business Administration, Office of Advocacy, from data provided by the U.S. Department of Labor (ETA), U.S. Census Bureau, and Administrative Office of the U.S. Courts.

Table A.5 Private Firms, Establishments, Employment, Annual Payroll, and Receipts by Firm Size, 1988–2003

Item	Year	Nonemployers	Employer Totals	Employment size of firm		
				0–19*	<500	500+
Employer firms	2003	18,649,114	5,767,127	5,150,316	5,750,201	16,926
	2002	17,646,062	5,697,759	5,090,331	5,680,914	16,845
	2001	16,979,498	5,657,774	5,036,845	5,640,407	17,367
	2000	16,529,955	5,652,544	5,035,029	5,635,391	17,153
	1999	16,152,604	5,607,743	5,007,808	5,591,003	16,740
	1998	15,708,727	5,579,177	4,988,367	5,562,799	16,378
	1997	15,439,609	5,541,918	4,958,641	5,525,839	16,079
	1996	NA	5,478,047	4,909,983	5,462,431	15,616
	1995	NA	5,369,068	4,807,533	5,353,624	15,444
	1994	NA	5,276,964	4,736,317	5,261,967	14,997
	1993	NA	5,193,642	4,661,601	5,179,013	14,629
	1992	14,325,000	5,095,356	4,572,994	5,081,234	14,122
	1991	NA	5,051,025	4,528,899	5,037,048	13,977
	1990	NA	5,073,795	4,535,575	5,059,772	14,023
	1989	NA	5,021,315	4,493,875	5,007,442	13,873
	1988	NA	4,954,645	4,444,473	4,941,821	12,824
Establishments	2003	18,649,114	7,254,745	5,203,488	6,222,091	1,032,654

Table A.5 Private Firms, Establishments, Employment, Annual Payroll, and Receipts by Firm Size, 1988–2003—continued

Item	Year	Nonemployers	Employer Totals	Employment size of firm		
				0–19*	<500	500+
	2002	17,646,062	7,200,770	5,147,526	6,172,809	1,027,961
	2001	16,979,498	7,095,302	5,093,660	6,079,993	1,015,309
	2000	16,529,955	7,070,048	5,093,832	6,080,050	989,998
	1999	16,152,604	7,008,444	5,068,096	6,048,129	960,315
	1998	15,708,727	6,941,822	5,048,528	6,030,325	911,497
	1997	15,439,609	6,894,869	5,026,425	6,017,638	877,231
	1996	NA	6,738,476	4,976,014	5,892,934	845,542
	1995	NA	6,612,721	4,876,327	5,798,936	813,785
	1994	NA	6,509,065	4,809,575	5,724,681	784,384
	1993	NA	6,401,233	4,737,778	5,654,835	746,398
	1992	14,325,000	6,319,300	4,653,464	5,571,896	747,404
	1991	NA	6,200,859	4,603,523	5,457,366	743,493
	1990	NA	6,175,559	4,602,362	5,447,605	727,954
	1989	NA	6,106,922	4,563,257	5,402,086	704,836
	1988	NA	6,016,367	4,516,707	5,343,026	673,341
Employment	2003	0	113,398,043	20,830,352	57,447,570	55,950,473
	2002	0	112,400,654	20,583,371	56,366,292	56,034,362

2001	0	115,061,184	20,602,635	57,383,449	57,677,735
2000	0	114,064,976	20,587,385	57,124,044	56,940,932
1999	0	110,705,661	20,388,287	55,729,092	54,976,569
1998	0	108,117,731	20,275,405	55,064,409	53,053,322
1997	0	105,299,123	20,118,816	54,545,370	50,753,753
1996	0	102,187,297	19,881,502	53,174,502	49,012,795
1995	0	100,314,946	19,569,861	52,652,510	47,662,436
1994	0	96,721,594	19,195,318	51,007,688	45,713,906
1993	0	94,773,913	19,070,191	50,316,063	44,457,850
1992	0	92,825,797	18,772,644	49,200,841	43,624,956
1991	0	92,307,559	18,712,812	49,002,613	43,304,946
1990	0	93,469,275	18,911,906	50,166,797	43,302,478
1989	0	91,626,094	18,626,776	49,353,860	42,272,234
1988	0	87,844,303	18,319,642	47,914,723	39,929,580
Annual payroll					
2003	NA	4,040,888,841	631,221,418	1,818,493,862	2,222,394,979
2002	NA	3,943,179,606	617,583,597	1,777,049,574	2,166,130,032
2001	NA	3,989,086,323	603,848,633	1,767,546,642	2,221,539,681
2000	NA	3,879,430,052	591,123,880	1,727,114,941	2,152,315,111
1999	NA	3,554,692,909	561,547,424	1,601,129,388	1,953,563,521
1998	NA	3,309,405,533	535,184,511	1,512,769,153	1,796,636,380

Table A.5 Private Firms, Establishments, Employment, Annual Payroll, and Receipts by Firm Size, 1988–2003—continued

Item	Year	Nonemployers	Employer Totals	Employment size of firm		
				0–19*	<500	500+
	1997	NA	3,047,907,469	503,130,254	1,416,200,011	1,631,707,458
	1996	NA	2,848,623,049	481,008,640	1,330,258,327	1,518,364,722
	1995	NA	2,665,921,824	454,009,065	1,252,135,244	1,413,786,580
	1994	NA	2,487,959,727	432,791,911	1,176,418,685	1,311,541,042
	1993	NA	2,363,208,106	415,254,636	1,116,443,440	1,246,764,666
	1992	NA	2,272,392,408	399,804,694	1,066,948,306	1,205,444,102
	1991	NA	2,145,015,851	381,544,608	1,013,014,303	1,132,001,548
	1990	NA	2,103,971,179	375,313,660	1,007,156,385	1,096,814,794
	1989	NA	1,989,941,554	357,259,587	954,137,110	1,035,804,444
	1988	NA	1,858,652,147	342,168,460	902,566,839	956,085,308
Receipts	2002	770,032,328	22,062,528,196	3,126,610,830	8,558,731,333	13,503,796,863
	1997	586,315,756	18,242,632,687	2,786,839,570	7,468,211,700	10,774,420,987

NA = Not available.

Notes: A firm is as an aggregation of all establishments (locations with payroll in any quarter) owned by a parent company and employment is measured in March (startups, closures, and seasonal firms could have zero employment). This table does not show job growth as firms can annually change size classes. See www.sba. gov/advo/research/data.html for more detail.

Source: U.S. Small Business Administration, Office of Advocacy, based on data provided by the U.S. Census Bureau, Statistics of U.S. Business and Nonemployer Statistics.

Table A.6 Employer Firms and Employment by Firm Size and State, 2003

State	Employer firms Total	Employment size of firm <20	<500	Employment Total	Employment size of firm <20	<500
United States	5,767,127	5,150,316	5,750,201	113,398,043	20,830,352	57,447,570
Alabama	78,645	67,030	76,490	1,597,529	294,126	802,052
Alaska	16,315	14,393	15,824	216,807	54,832	129,729
Arizona	97,758	83,423	95,018	1,998,795	334,608	958,806
Arkansas	52,347	45,137	50,837	988,941	187,418	489,291
California	682,937	598,921	677,436	12,991,795	2,422,371	6,904,313
Colorado	121,346	106,791	118,582	1,884,500	389,748	981,726
Connecticut	77,071	65,905	75,069	1,550,867	277,148	765,240
Delaware	20,540	16,586	19,117	385,129	63,471	172,909
District of Columbia	15,883	11,877	14,796	422,918	53,822	203,591
Florida	381,651	344,987	377,527	6,549,488	1,216,874	3,004,681
Georgia	167,483	144,788	163,727	3,387,337	566,526	1,549,208
Hawaii	25,382	21,568	24,578	459,010	92,305	263,673
Idaho	34,203	29,925	33,222	466,507	116,191	268,310
Illinois	255,813	220,455	251,599	5,205,457	888,734	2,614,232
Indiana	116,481	98,843	113,687	2,540,839	433,577	1,264,992

Table A.6 Employer Firms and Employment by Firm Size and State, 2003—continued

State	Employer firms			Employment		
		Employment size of firm			Employment size of firm	
	Total	<20	<500	Total	<20	<500
Iowa	65,366	56,197	63,767	1,232,865	231,428	649,927
Kansas	61,089	52,081	59,264	1,109,869	214,537	597,742
Kentucky	71,980	60,860	69,855	1,471,878	264,868	740,556
Louisiana	82,308	69,785	80,342	1,603,922	307,638	882,064
Maine	34,807	30,691	33,932	488,973	117,316	299,340
Maryland	109,783	93,922	107,221	2,088,841	389,864	1,115,600
Massachusetts	149,266	129,214	146,417	2,974,779	518,000	1,490,506
Michigan	192,310	166,545	189,311	3,885,221	708,196	2,001,591
Minnesota	120,777	103,938	118,363	2,382,177	412,199	1,230,107
Mississippi	47,902	40,929	46,387	912,157	174,898	461,285
Missouri	122,383	105,315	119,682	2,387,761	422,158	1,198,122
Montana	29,651	26,547	28,998	302,967	99,336	214,963
Nebraska	41,638	35,744	40,356	774,913	145,787	391,633
Nevada	44,281	36,768	42,389	970,919	142,414	425,163
New Hampshire	32,652	27,753	31,593	540,306	114,069	304,902
New Jersey	204,211	180,440	201,061	3,579,076	696,606	1,806,046
New Mexico	36,049	30,517	34,686	571,381	126,432	329,103

State					
New York	433,868	388,800	429,772	7,416,680	1,436,513	3,834,223
North Carolina	166,070	143,910	162,801	3,338,231	599,495	1,605,315
North Dakota	17,224	14,705	16,645	258,940	60,195	163,596
Ohio	210,756	179,715	207,082	4,770,283	793,170	2,351,579
Oklahoma	70,429	61,126	68,628	1,184,589	248,013	642,556
Oregon	86,333	75,555	84,371	1,338,825	300,187	752,343
Pennsylvania	238,365	205,906	234,540	5,029,324	877,125	2,513,875
Rhode Island	26,019	22,183	25,132	427,455	88,243	244,561
South Carolina	79,493	68,225	77,370	1,550,604	288,499	763,098
South Dakota	21,047	18,107	20,400	299,779	72,956	190,709
Tennessee	100,620	85,086	97,773	2,299,275	368,463	1,052,520
Texas	375,922	327,089	371,028	8,051,148	1,371,459	3,840,884
Utah	50,933	43,907	49,272	900,605	168,460	449,375
Vermont	19,217	16,739	18,602	256,441	67,085	160,787
Virginia	145,624	125,517	142,529	2,932,822	521,705	1,431,739
Washington	139,984	123,079	137,436	2,293,222	481,348	1,224,800
West Virginia	32,547	27,897	31,465	561,434	119,137	304,578
Wisconsin	116,198	98,880	113,880	2,383,503	433,391	1,284,904
Wyoming	16,650	14,547	16,100	180,959	57,411	124,725

Notes: For state data, a firm is an aggregation of all establishments (locations with payroll in any quarter) owned by a parent company within a state. Startups after March, closures before March, and seasonal firms could have zero employees.

Source: U.S. Small Business Administration, Office of Advocacy, based on data provided by the U.S. Census Bureau.

Table A.7 Employer Firms and Employment by Firm Size and Industry, 2003

Industry	Nonemployers	Employers		
			Employment size of firm	
		Total	0-19	<500
Firms				
Total	18,649,114	5,767,127	5,150,316	5,750,201
Agriculture, forestry, fishing, and hunting	225,764	25,144	23,475	25,050
Mining	87,931	18,210	15,373	17,896
Utilities	13,862	7,132	5,779	6,929
Construction	2,239,310	722,818	662,786	721,873
Manufacturing	299,570	295,596	219,113	291,494
Wholesale trade	376,437	342,450	293,845	339,368
Retail trade	1,880,342	732,854	661,838	730,540
Transportation and warehousing	858,940	161,862	141,376	159,726
Information	259,942	75,786	63,960	74,598
Finance and insurance	694,953	244,657	223,161	242,924
Real estate and rental and leasing	2,045,524	270,132	255,500	268,874
Professional, scientific, and technical services	2,647,711	714,790	667,733	711,863
Management of companies and enterprises	—	27,703	6,751	20,857
Admin., support, waste mngt. and remediation srv.	1,293,822	299,383	260,729	296,041
Educational services	373,910	68,970	52,185	67,883
Health care and social assistance	1,542,907	575,089	501,914	571,409
Arts, entertainment, and recreation	888,146	106,514	91,026	105,886
Accommodation and food services	259,583	438,166	350,323	436,457
Other services (except public administration)	2,660,460	669,655	622,812	668,278
Unclassified	NA	36,497	36,369	36,496

Employment

Total	—	113,398,043	20,830,352	57,447,570
Agriculture, forestry, fishing, and hunting	—	180,673	82,797	NA
Mining	—	454,550	64,051	200,974
Utilities	—	675,938	NA	NA
Construction	—	6,381,404	2,475,859	5,487,177
Manufacturing	—	14,132,020	1,226,469	6,102,010
Wholesale trade	—	5,863,860	1,272,506	3,640,380
Retail Trade	—	14,867,825	2,864,448	6,404,638
Transportation and Warehousing	—	4,067,935	518,431	1,552,349
Information	—	3,599,902	253,793	921,522
Finance and insurance	—	6,463,706	738,291	2,064,617
Real estate and rental and leasing	—	2,044,738	732,367	1,416,087
Professional, scientific, and technical services	—	7,340,246	2,157,140	4,546,690
Management of companies and enterprises	—	2,879,156	18,105	348,209
Admin., support, waste mngt. and remediation srv.	—	8,511,138	953,568	3,465,385
Educational services	—	2,776,615	238,691	1,305,412
Health care and social assistance	—	15,472,183	2,432,929	7,459,318
Arts, entertainment, and recreation	—	1,832,985	328,029	1,236,704
Accommodation and food services	—	10,439,651	1,875,557	6,349,472
Other services (except public administration)	—	5,367,166	2,532,379	4,636,125
Unclassified	—	46,352	NA	NA

NA = Not available.

Notes: Employment is measured in March; thus some firms (start-ups after March, closures before March, and seasonal firms) will have zero employment. Firms are an aggregation of all establishments owned by a parent company within an industry. See www.sba.gov/advo/research/data.html for more detail.

Source: U.S. Small Business Administration, Office of Advocacy, based on data provided by the U.S. Census Bureau.

Table A.8 Employer Firm Births, Deaths, and Employment Changes by Employment Size of Firm, 1990–2003

Period	Type of change	Total	Beginning year employment size of firm		
			<20	<500	500+
Firms					
2002–2003	Firm births	612,296	585,552	611,976	320
	Firm deaths	540,658	514,565	540,328	330
	Net change	71,638	70,987	71,648	-10
2001–2002	Firm births	569,750	541,516	568,280	1,470
	Firm deaths	586,890	557,133	586,535	355
	Net change	-17,140	-15,617	-18,255	1,115
2000–2001	Firm births	585,140	558,037	584,837	303
	Firm deaths	553,291	523,960	552,839	452
	Net change	31,849	34,077	31,998	-149
1999–2000	Firm births	574,300	548,030	574,023	277
	Firm deaths	542,831	514,242	542,374	457
	Net change	31,469	33,788	31,649	-180
1998–1999	Firm births	579,609	554,288	579,287	322
	Firm deaths	544,487	514,293	544,040	447
	Net change	35,122	39,995	35,247	-125
1997–1998	Firm births	589,982	564,804	589,706	276
	Firm deaths	540,601	511,567	540,112	489
	Net change	49,381	53,237	49,594	-213
1996–1997	Firm births	590,644	564,197	590,335	309
	Firm deaths	530,003	500,014	529,481	522
	Net change	60,641	64,183	60,854	-213
1995–1996	Firm births	597,792	572,442	597,503	289
	Firm deaths	512,402	485,509	512,024	378
	Net change	85,390	86,933	85,479	-89
1994–1995	Firm births	594,369	568,896	594,119	250
	Firm deaths	497,246	472,441	496,874	372
	Net change	97,123	96,455	97,245	-122
1993–1994	Firm births	570,587	546,437	570,337	250
	Firm deaths	503,563	476,667	503,125	438
	Net change	67,024	69,770	67,212	-188
1992–1993	Firm births	564,504	539,601	564,093	411
	Firm deaths	492,651	466,550	492,266	385
	Net change	71,853	73,051	71,827	26

Table A.8 Employer Firm Births, Deaths, and Employment Changes by Employment Size of Firm, 1990–2003—continued

Period	Type of change	Total	Beginning year employment size of firm		
			<20	<500	500+
1991–1992	Firm births	544,596	519,014	544,278	318
	Firm deaths	521,606	492,746	521,176	430
	Net change	22,990	26,268	23,102	-112
1990–1991	Firm births	541,141	515,870	540,889	252
	Firm deaths	546,518	516,964	546,149	369
	Net change	-5,377	-1,094	-5,260	-117
Employment changes resulting from:					
2002–2003	Firm births	3,667,154	1,855,516	3,174,129	493,025
	Firm deaths	3,324,483	1,608,299	2,879,797	444,686
	Existing firm expansions	14,677,406	3,438,778	7,641,202	7,036,204
	Existing firm contractions	14,024,418	2,112,533	5,945,208	8,079,210
	Net change	995,659	1,573,462	1,990,326	-994,667
2001–2002	Firm births	3,369,930	1,748,097	3,033,734	336,196
	Firm deaths	3,660,161	1,755,255	3,256,851	403,310
	Existing firm expansions	15,385,726	3,149,876	7,587,961	7,797,765
	Existing firm contractions	17,756,053	2,289,644	7,794,376	9,961,677
	Net change	-2,660,558	853,074	-429,532	-2,231,026
2000–2001	Firm births	3,418,369	1,821,298	3,108,501	309,868
	Firm deaths	3,261,621	1,700,677	3,049,714	211,907
	Existing firm expansions	14,939,658	3,065,106	7,033,084	7,906,574
	Existing firm contractions	14,096,436	2,074,544	5,940,996	8,155,440
	Net change	999,970	1,111,183	1,150,875	-150,905
1999–2000	Firm births	3,228,804	1,792,946	3,031,079	197,725
	Firm deaths	3,176,609	1,653,694	2,946,120	230,489
	Existing firm expansions	15,857,582	3,378,838	7,744,430	8,113,152
	Existing firm contractions	12,550,358	1,924,624	5,323,677	7,226,681
	Net change	3,359,419	1,593,466	2,505,712	853,707

Table A.8 Employer Firm Births, Deaths, and Employment Changes by Employment Size of Firm, 1990–2003—continued

Period	Type of change	Total	Beginning year employment size of firm		
			<20	<500	500+
1998–1999	Firm births	3,247,335	1,763,823	3,011,400	235,935
	Firm deaths	3,267,136	1,676,282	3,052,630	214,506
	Existing firm expansions	14,843,903	3,245,218	7,266,399	7,577,504
	Existing firm contractions	12,236,364	1,969,501	5,482,142	6,754,222
	Net change	2,587,738	1,363,258	1,743,027	844,711
1997–1998	Firm births	3,205,451	1,812,103	3,002,401	203,050
	Firm deaths	3,233,412	1,661,544	2,991,722	241,690
	Existing firm expansions	14,885,560	3,238,047	7,471,622	7,413,938
	Existing firm contractions	12,044,422	2,002,313	5,747,725	6,296,697
	Net change	2,813,177	1,386,293	1,734,576	1,078,601
1996–1997	Firm births	3,227,556	1,813,539	3,029,666	197,890
	Firm deaths	3,274,604	1,620,797	2,960,814	313,790
	Existing firm expansions	16,243,424	3,400,037	8,628,839	7,614,585
	Existing firm contractions	13,092,093	2,035,083	6,343,489	6,748,604
	Net change	3,104,283	1,557,696	2,354,202	750,081
1995–1996	Firm births	3,255,676	1,844,516	3,055,596	200,080
	Firm deaths	3,099,589	1,559,598	2,808,493	291,096
	Existing firm expansions	12,937,389	3,122,066	6,725,135	6,212,254
	Existing firm contractions	11,226,231	1,971,531	5,512,726	5,713,505
	Net change	1,867,245	1,435,453	1,459,512	407,733
1994–1995	Firm births	3,322,001	1,836,153	3,049,456	272,545
	Firm deaths	2,822,627	1,516,552	2,633,587	189,040
	Existing firm expansions	13,034,649	3,235,940	7,197,705	5,836,944
	Existing firm contractions	9,942,456	1,877,758	5,000,269	4,942,187
	Net change	3,591,567	1,677,783	2,613,305	978,262

Table A.8 Employer Firm Births, Deaths, and Employment Changes by Employment Size of Firm, 1990–2003

Period	Type of change	Total	Beginning year employment size of firm		
			<20	<500	500+
1993–1994	Firm births	3,105,753	1,760,322	2,889,507	216,246
	Firm deaths	3,077,307	1,549,072	2,800,933	276,374
	Existing firm expansions	12,366,436	3,139,825	6,905,182	5,461,254
	Existing firm contractions	10,450,422	2,039,535	5,400,406	5,050,016
	Net change	1,944,460	1,311,540	1,593,350	351,110
1992–1993	Firm births	3,438,106	1,750,662	3,053,765	384,341
	Firm deaths	2,906,260	1,515,896	2,697,656	208,604
	Existing firm expansions	12,157,943	3,206,101	6,817,835	5,340,108
	Existing firm contractions	10,741,536	1,965,039	5,386,708	5,354,828
	Net change	1,948,253	1,475,828	1,787,236	161,017
1991–1992	Firm births	3,200,969	1,703,491	2,863,799	337,170
	Firm deaths	3,126,463	1,602,579	2,894,127	232,336
	Existing firm expansions	12,894,780	3,197,959	7,510,392	5,384,388
	Existing firm contractions	12,446,175	2,156,402	6,635,366	5,810,809
	Net change	523,111	1,142,469	844,698	-321,587
1990–1991	Firm births	3,105,363	1,712,856	2,907,351	198,012
	Firm deaths	3,208,099	1,723,159	3,044,470	163,629
	Existing firm expansions	11,174,786	2,855,498	6,323,224	4,851,562
	Existing firm contractions	12,233,766	2,294,270	6,893,623	5,340,143
	Net change	-1,161,716	550,925	-707,518	-454,198

Notes: The data represent activity from March of the beginning year to March of the ending year. Establishments with no employment in the first quarter of the beginning year were excluded. Firm births are classified by their first quarter employment size. New firms represent new original establishments and deaths represent closed original establishments. See www.sba.gov/advo/research/data.html for more detail.

Source: U.S. Small Business Administration, Office of Advocacy, from data provided by the U.S. Census Bureau.

Table A.9 Opening and Closing Establishments, 1992–2005 (thousands, seasonally adjusted)

Year	Quarter	Opening Establishments		Closing Establishments		Net	
		Number	Employment	Number	Employment	Number	Employment
2005	3	375	1,632	339	1,512	36	120
	2	371	1,621	340	1,485	31	136
	1	345	1,464	347	1,458	-2	6
2004	4	379	1,716	320	1,485	59	231
	3	354	1,666	345	1,645	9	21
	2	343	1,565	330	1,537	13	28
	1	349	1,514	328	1,439	21	75
2003	4	348	1,583	322	1,486	26	97
	3	328	1,499	318	1,431	10	68
	2	331	1,527	328	1,564	3	-37
	1	332	1,540	334	1,555	-2	-15
2002	4	349	1,643	329	1,610	20	33
	3	341	1,680	325	1,629	16	51
	2	348	1,804	334	1,719	14	85
	1	338	1,804	331	1,729	7	75
2001	4	352	1,838	335	1,769	17	69
	3	335	1,759	367	1,955	-32	-196
	2	339	1,815	333	1,876	6	-61

Year	Quarter						
	1	343	1,787	337	1,900	6	-113
2000	4	353	1,828	336	1,772	17	56
	3	355	1,890	348	1,859	7	31
	2	354	1,789	325	1,714	29	75
	1	357	1,918	328	1,727	29	191
1999	4	365	2,032	326	1,775	39	257
	3	346	1,946	339	1,872	7	74
	2	338	2,012	337	1,812	1	200
	1	335	2,011	318	1,898	17	113
1998	4	320	1,798	318	1,757	2	41
	3	336	1,965	316	1,719	20	246
	2	353	2,153	296	1,838	57	315
	1	347	2,155	323	1,934	24	221
1997	4	335	2,004	328	1,961	7	43
	3	328	1,913	308	1,758	20	155
	2	321	1,756	304	1,579	17	177
	1	331	1,844	299	1,593	32	251
1996	4	327	1,869	300	1,528	27	341
	3	328	1,863	293	1,559	35	304
	2	318	1,778	299	1,544	19	234
	1	321	1,753	298	1,526	23	227

Table A.9 Opening and Closing Establishments, 1992–2005 (thousands, seasonally adjusted)—continued

Year	Quarter	Opening Establishments		Closing Establishments		Net	
		Number	Employment	Number	Employment	Number	Employment
1995	4	311	1,724	294	1,536	17	188
	3	306	1,679	291	1,519	15	160
	2	306	1,697	286	1,473	20	224
	1	306	1,653	274	1,376	32	277
1994	4	295	1,632	284	1,476	11	156
	3	314	1,745	268	1,304	46	441
	2	309	1,747	285	1,491	24	256
	1	290	1,593	278	1,448	12	145
1993	4	286	1,596	263	1,375	23	221
	3	302	1,642	255	1,333	47	309
	2	293	1,536	272	1,408	21	128
	1	308	1,899	273	1,642	35	257
1992	4	289	1,636	271	1,398	18	238
	3	295	1,745	273	1,571	22	174

Note: Establishments could be new ventures or new affiliates of existing ventures.

Source: U.S. Small Business Administration, Office of Advocacy, from data provided by the U.S. Department of Labor, Bureau of Labor Statistics, Business Employment Dynamics.

Table A.10 Characteristics of Self-Employed Individuals, 1995–2004 (thousands, except as noted otherwise)

Characteristic		1995		2000		2004			1995–2004
		Number	Percent	Number	Percent	Number	Percent	Rate	Percent change
Total		13,921.9	100.0	13,832.4	100.0	15,614.6	100.0	10.2	12.2
Gender	Female	4,614.7	33.1	4,819.6	34.8	5,243.3	33.6	7.3	13.6
	Male	9,307.2	66.9	9,012.8	65.2	10,371.3	66.4	12.7	11.4
Race	Asian / American Indian	547.5	3.9	759.8	5.5	801.8	5.1	10.0	46.4
	Black	612.1	4.4	679.3	4.9	823.9	5.3	4.9	34.6
	White	12,762.4	91.7	12,393.3	89.6	13,790.3	88.3	10.9	8.1
	Multiple	NA	NA	NA	NA	198.6	1.3	9.0	NA
Origin or descent	Hispanic	698.9	5.0	775.6	5.6	1,308.8	8.4	6.7	87.3
Age	<25	501.0	3.6	375.8	2.7	504.3	3.2	2.1	0.7
	25-34	2,181.8	15.7	1,824.3	13.2	2,107.3	13.5	6.4	-3.4
	35-44	4,132.6	29.7	3,941.1	28.5	4,087.7	26.2	11.2	-1.1
	45-54	3,576.0	25.7	3,995.0	28.9	4,302.0	27.6	12.4	20.3
	55-64	2,214.3	15.9	2,274.6	16.4	3,108.4	19.9	15.8	40.4
	65+	1,316.2	9.5	1,421.6	10.3	1,504.9	9.6	23.7	14.3

Table A.10 Characteristics of Self-Employed Individuals, 1995–2004 (thousands, except as noted otherwise)—continued

Characteristic		1995 Number	1995 Percent	2000 Number	2000 Percent	2004 Number	2004 Percent	2004 Rate	1995–2004 Percent change
Educational level	High school or less	6,055.0	43.5	5,485.1	39.7	6,010.9	38.5	9.2	-0.7
	Some college	3,575.2	25.7	3,822.5	27.6	4,144.0	26.5	9.3	15.9
	Bachelor's degree	2,643.4	19.0	2,838.9	20.5	3,415.7	21.9	11.8	29.2
	Master's degree or above	1,648.3	11.8	1,685.9	12.2	2,043.9	13.1	13.9	24.0
Veteran status		2,492.5	17.9	2,029.3	14.7	1,944.4	12.5	14.8	-22.0
Disability		628.6	4.5	592.5	4.3	652.7	4.2	14.3	3.8
Born in the United States		12,411.0	89.1	12,078.8	87.3	13,390.8	85.8	10.4	7.9
Location	Central city	2,650.1	19.0	2,506.2	18.1	3,324.1	21.3	8.8	25.4
	Suburban	5,988.6	43.0	6,095.6	44.1	6,909.0	44.2	10.2	15.4
	Rural	3,382.9	24.3	3,321.5	24.0	3,090.2	19.8	12.3	-8.7
	Not identified	1,900.3	13.6	1,909.1	13.8	2,291.3	14.7	10.2	20.6

Notes: Self-employment (incorporated and unincorporated) as used here refers to an individual's primary occupation during the year. Self-employment figures presented here differ from figures that focus on monthly averages during a year. Asian / American Indian = Asian, Pacific, American Indian, and Aleut Eskimo. Disability consists of disabilities or health problems that restrict or prevent the amount or kind of work. The rate is the self-employment rate divided by the number of individuals in the category that had any job during the year.

Source: U.S. Small Business Administration, Office of Advocacy, from data provided by the U.S. Department of Commerce, Bureau of the Census, March Current Population Surveys.

Table A.11 Bank Lending Information by Size of Firm, 1991–2005 (Change in percentage of senior loan officer responses on bank lending practices)

| | | Tightening loan standards | | Stronger demand for loans | |
| | | Large and Medium | Small | Large and medium | Small |
Year	Quarter				
2005	4	-9	-5	14	9
	3	-17	-11	41	35
	2	-24	-24	37	37
	1	-24	-13	46	30
2004	4	-21	-18	26	26
	3	-20	-4	31	39
	2	-23	-20	29	38
	1	-18	-11	11	22
2003	4	0	-2	-12	-4
	3	4	4	-23	-12
	2	9	13	-39	-22
	1	22	14	-32	-21
2002	4	20	18	-53	-48
	3	21	6	-45	-36
	2	25	15	-36	-29
	1	45	42	-55	-45
2001	4	51	40	-70	-50
	3	40	32	-53	-42
	2	51	36	-40	-35
	1	60	45	-50	-30
2000	4	44	27	-23	-13
	3	34	24	-5	-4
	2	25	21	-9	5
	1	11	9	9	-2
1999	4	9	2	-2	-4
	3	5	2	0	0
	2	10	8	0	10
	1	7	4	20	11
1998	4	36	15	28	8
	3	0	-5	-9	0
	2	-7	-2	29	21
	1	2	2	26	15
1997	4	-7	-4	19	19
	3	-6	-2	13	20

Table A.11 Bank Lending Information by Size of Firm, 1991–2005 (Change in percentage of senior loan officer responses on bank lending practices)—continued

Year	Quarter	Tightening loan standards		Stronger demand for loans	
		Large and Medium	Small	Large and medium	Small
	2	-7	-4	5	11
	1	-5	-5	5	15
1996	4	-8	-12	1	4
	3	-4	-2	12	18
	2	-1	2	10	24
	1	7	4	-3	14
1995	4	-3	-2	3	7
	3	-6	-2	4	25
	2	-6	-7	29	17
	1	-7	-5	35	18
1994	4	-17	-18	31	32
	3	-7	-7	31	19
	2	-12	-9	38	38
	1	-13	-12	26	26
1993	4	-18	-9	9	17
	3	-19	-12	18	14
	2	-8	-2	0	12
	1	3	-2	20	32
1992	4	4	-5	6	-2
	3	-2	-2	-9	7
	2	1	-7	6	25
	1	5	0	-27	-12
1991	4	9	5	-30	-25
	3	12	9	NA	NA
	2	16	7	NA	NA
	1	36	32	NA	NA

NA = not available.

Notes: Figures should be used with caution because the sample size of the survey is relatively small—about 80 respondents—but they do represent a sizable portion of the market. Small firms are defined as having sales of less than $50 million. The survey asks the following question to gauge lending standards: "Over the past three months, how have your bank's credit standards for approving applications for C&I loans or credit lines—other than those to be used to finance mergers and acquisitions—to large and middle-market firms and to small firms changed?" The survey asks the following question to gauge lending demand: "Apart from normal seasonal variation, how has demand for C&I loans changed over the past three months?"

Source: U.S. Small Business Administration, Office of Advocacy, from data provided by the Federal Reserve Board.

APPENDIX B
The Regulatory Flexibility Act and Executive Order 13272

The following text of the Regulatory Flexibility Act of 1980, as amended, is taken from Title 5 of the United States Code, Sections 601–612. The Regulatory Flexibility Act was originally passed in 1980 (P.L. 96-354). The act was amended by the Small Business Regulatory Enforcement Fairness Act of 1996 (P.L. 104-121).

The Regulatory Flexibility Act of 1980 as amended

Congressional Findings and Declaration of Purpose

(a) The Congress finds and declares that—

(1) when adopting regulations to protect the health, safety and economic welfare of the Nation, Federal agencies should seek to achieve statutory goals as effectively and efficiently as possible without imposing unnecessary burdens on the public;

(2) laws and regulations designed for application to large scale entities have been applied uniformly to small businesses, small organizations, and small governmental jurisdictions even though the problems that gave rise to government action may not have been caused by those smaller entities;

(3) uniform Federal regulatory and reporting requirements have in numerous instances imposed unnecessary and disproportionately burdensome demands including legal, accounting and consulting costs upon small businesses, small organizations, and small governmental jurisdictions with limited resources;

(4) the failure to recognize differences in the scale and resources of regulated entities has in numerous instances adversely affected competition

in the marketplace, discouraged innovation and restricted improvements in productivity;

(5) unnecessary regulations create entry barriers in many industries and discourage potential entrepreneurs from introducing beneficial products and processes;

(6) the practice of treating all regulated businesses, organizations, and governmental jurisdictions as equivalent may lead to inefficient use of regulatory agency resources, enforcement problems and, in some cases, to actions inconsistent with the legislative intent of health, safety, environmental and economic welfare legislation;

(7) alternative regulatory approaches which do not conflict with the stated objectives of applicable statutes may be available which minimize the significant economic impact of rules on small businesses, small organizations, and small governmental jurisdictions;

(8) the process by which Federal regulations are developed and adopted should be reformed to require agencies to solicit the ideas and comments of small businesses, small organizations, and small governmental jurisdictions to examine the impact of proposed and existing rules on such entities, and to review the continued need for existing rules.

(b) It is the purpose of this Act [enacting this chapter and provisions set out as notes under this section] to establish as a principle of regulatory issuance that agencies shall endeavor, consistent with the objectives of the rule and of applicable statutes, to fit regulatory and informational requirements to the scale of the businesses, organizations, and governmental jurisdictions subject to regulation. To achieve this principle, agencies are required to solicit and consider flexible regulatory proposals and to explain the rationale for their actions to assure that such proposals are given serious consideration.

Regulatory Flexibility Act

§ 601   Definitions
§ 602   Regulatory agenda
§ 603   Initial regulatory flexibility analysis
§ 604   Final regulatory flexibility analysis
§ 605   Avoidance of duplicative or unnecessary analyses

§ 601 Definitions

For purposes of this chapter—

(1) the term "agency" means an agency as defined in section 551(1) of this title;

(2) the term "rule" means any rule for which the agency publishes a general notice of proposed rulemaking pursuant to section 553(b) of this title, or any other law, including any rule of general applicability governing Federal grants to State and local governments for which the agency provides an opportunity for notice and public comment, except that the term "rule" does not include a rule of particular applicability relating to rates, wages, corporate or financial structures or reorganizations thereof, prices, facilities, appliances, services, or allowances therefor or to valuations, costs or accounting, or practices relating to such rates, wages, structures, prices, appliances, services, or allowances;

(3) the term "small business" has the same meaning as the term "small business concern" under section 3 of the Small Business Act, unless an agency, after consultation with the Office of Advocacy of the Small Business Administration and after opportunity for public comment, establishes one or more definitions of such term which are appropriate to the activities of the agency and publishes such definition(s) in the *Federal Register*;

(4) the term "small organization" means any not-for-profit enterprise which is independently owned and operated and is not dominant in its field, unless an agency establishes, after opportunity for public comment, one or more definitions of such term which are appropriate to the activities of the agency and publishes such definition(s) in the *Federal Register*;

(5) the term "small governmental jurisdiction" means governments of cities, counties, towns, townships, villages, school districts, or special districts, with a population of less than fifty thousand, unless an agency establishes, after opportunity for public comment, one or more definitions of such term which are appropriate to the activities of the agency and which are based on such factors as location in rural or sparsely populated areas or limited revenues due to the population of such jurisdiction, and publishes such definition(s) in the *Federal Register*;

(6) the term "small entity" shall have the same meaning as the terms "small business," "small organization" and "small governmental jurisdiction" defined in paragraphs (3), (4) and (5) of this section; and

(7) the term "collection of information"—

> (A) means the obtaining, causing to be obtained, soliciting, or requiring the disclosure to third parties or the public, of facts or opinions by or for an agency, regardless of form or format, calling for either—
>
> > (i) answers to identical questions posed to, or identical reporting or recordkeeping requirements imposed on, 10 or more persons, other than agencies, instrumentalities, or employees of the United States; or
> >
> > (ii) answers to questions posed to agencies, instrumentalities, or employees of the United States which are to be used for general statistical purposes; and
>
> (B) shall not include a collection of information described under section 3518(c)(1) of title 44, United States Code.

(8) Recordkeeping requirement—The term "recordkeeping requirement" means a requirement imposed by an agency on persons to maintain specified records.

§ 602. Regulatory agenda

(a) During the months of October and April of each year, each agency shall publish in the *Federal Register* a regulatory flexibility agenda which shall contain—

(1) a brief description of the subject area of any rule which the agency expects to propose or promulgate which is likely to have a significant economic impact on a substantial number of small entities;

(2) a summary of the nature of any such rule under consideration for each subject area listed in the agenda pursuant to paragraph (1), the objectives and legal basis for the issuance of the rule, and an approximate schedule for completing action on any rule for which the agency has issued a general notice of proposed rulemaking, and

(3) the name and telephone number of an agency official knowledgeable concerning the items listed in paragraph (1).

(b) Each regulatory flexibility agenda shall be transmitted to the Chief Counsel for Advocacy of the Small Business Administration for comment, if any.

(c) Each agency shall endeavor to provide notice of each regulatory flexibility agenda to small entities or their representatives through direct notification or publication of the agenda in publications likely to be obtained by such small entities and shall invite comments upon each subject area on the agenda.

(d) Nothing in this section precludes an agency from considering or acting on any matter not included in a regulatory flexibility agenda, or requires an agency to consider or act on any matter listed in such agenda.

§ 603. Initial regulatory flexibility analysis

(a) Whenever an agency is required by section 553 of this title, or any other law, to publish general notice of proposed rulemaking for any proposed rule, or publishes a notice of proposed rulemaking for an interpretative rule involving the internal revenue laws of the United States, the agency shall prepare and make available for public comment an initial regulatory flexibility analysis. Such analysis shall describe the impact of the proposed rule on small entities. The initial regulatory flexibility analysis or a summary shall be published in the *Federal Register* at the time of the publication of general notice of proposed rulemaking for the rule. The agency shall transmit a copy of the initial regulatory flexibility analysis to the Chief Counsel for Advocacy of the Small Business Administration. In the case of an interpretative rule involving the internal revenue laws of the United States, this chapter applies to interpretative rules published in the *Federal Register* for codification in the Code of Federal

Regulations, but only to the extent that such interpretative rules impose on small entities a collection of information requirement.

(b) Each initial regulatory flexibility analysis required under this section shall contain—

(1) a description of the reasons why action by the agency is being considered;

(2) a succinct statement of the objectives of, and legal basis for, the proposed rule;

(3) a description of and, where feasible, an estimate of the number of small entities to which the proposed rule will apply;

(4) a description of the projected reporting, recordkeeping and other compliance requirements of the proposed rule, including an estimate of the classes of small entities which will be subject to the requirement and the type of professional skills necessary for preparation of the report or record;

(5) an identification, to the extent practicable, of all relevant Federal rules which may duplicate, overlap or conflict with the proposed rule.

(c) Each initial regulatory flexibility analysis shall also contain a description of any significant alternatives to the proposed rule which accomplish the stated objectives of applicable statutes and which minimize any significant economic impact of the proposed rule on small entities. Consistent with the stated objectives of applicable statutes, the analysis shall discuss significant alternatives such as—

(1) the establishment of differing compliance or reporting requirements or timetables that take into account the resources available to small entities;

(2) the clarification, consolidation, or simplification of compliance and reporting requirements under the rule for such small entities;

(3) the use of performance rather than design standards; and

(4) an exemption from coverage of the rule, or any part thereof, for such small entities.

§ 604. *Final regulatory flexibility analysis*

(a) When an agency promulgates a final rule under section 553 of this title, after being required by that section or any other law to publish a general notice of proposed rulemaking, or promulgates a final interpretative rule involving the internal revenue laws of the United States as described in section 603(a), the agency shall prepare a final regulatory flexibility analysis. Each final regulatory flexibility analysis shall contain—

(1) a succinct statement of the need for, and objectives of, the rule;

(2) a summary of the significant issues raised by the public comments in response to the initial regulatory flexibility analysis, a summary of the assessment of the agency of such issues, and a statement of any changes made in the proposed rule as a result of such comments;

(3) a description of and an estimate of the number of small entities to which the rule will apply or an explanation of why no such estimate is available;

(4) a description of the projected reporting, recordkeeping and other compliance requirements of the rule, including an estimate of the classes of small entities which will be subject to the requirement and the type of professional skills necessary for preparation of the report or record; and

(5) a description of the steps the agency has taken to minimize the significant economic impact on small entities consistent with the stated objectives of applicable statutes, including a statement of the factual, policy, and legal reasons for selecting the alternative adopted in the final rule and why each one of the other significant alternatives to the rule considered by the agency which affect the impact on small entities was rejected.

(b) The agency shall make copies of the final regulatory flexibility analysis available to members of the public and shall publish in the *Federal Register* such analysis or a summary thereof.

§ 605. Avoidance of duplicative or unnecessary analyses

(a) Any Federal agency may perform the analyses required by sections 602, 603, and 604 of this title in conjunction with or as a part of any other agenda or analysis required by any other law if such other analysis satisfies the provisions of such sections.

(b) Sections 603 and 604 of this title shall not apply to any proposed or final rule if the head of the agency certifies that the rule will not, if promulgated, have a significant economic impact on a substantial number of small entities. If the head of the agency makes a certification under the preceding sentence, the agency shall publish such certification in the *Federal Register* at the time of publication of general notice of proposed rulemaking for the rule or at the time of publication of the final rule, along with a statement providing the factual basis for such certification. The agency shall provide such certification and statement to the Chief Counsel for Advocacy of the Small Business Administration.

(c) In order to avoid duplicative action, an agency may consider a series of closely related rules as one rule for the purposes of sections 602, 603, 604 and 610 of this title.

§ 606. Effect on other law

The requirements of sections 603 and 604 of this title do not alter in any manner standards otherwise applicable by law to agency action.

§ 607. Preparation of analyses

In complying with the provisions of sections 603 and 604 of this title, an agency may provide either a quantifiable or numerical description of the effects of a proposed rule or alternatives to the proposed rule, or more general descriptive statements if quantification is not practicable or reliable.

§ 608. Procedure for waiver or delay of completion

(a) An agency head may waive or delay the completion of some or all of the requirements of section 603 of this title by publishing in the *Federal Register*, not later than the date of publication of the final rule, a written finding, with reasons therefor, that the final rule is being promulgated in response to an emergency that makes compliance or timely compliance with the provisions of section 603 of this title impracticable.

(b) Except as provided in section 605(b), an agency head may not waive the requirements of section 604 of this title. An agency head may delay the completion of the requirements of section 604 of this title for a period of not more than one hundred and eighty days after the date of publication in the *Federal Register* of a final rule by publishing in the *Federal Register*, not later than such date of publication, a written finding, with reasons therefor, that the final rule is being promulgated in response to an emergency that makes timely compliance with the provisions of section 604 of this title impracticable. If the agency has not prepared a final regulatory analysis pursuant to section 604 of this title within one hundred and eighty days from the date of publication of the final rule, such rule shall lapse and have no effect. Such rule shall not be repromulgated until a final regulatory flexibility analysis has been completed by the agency.

§ 609. Procedures for gathering comments

(a) When any rule is promulgated which will have a significant economic impact on a substantial number of small entities, the head of the agency promulgating the rule or the official of the agency with statutory responsibility for the promulgation of the rule shall assure that small entities have been given an opportunity to participate in the rulemaking for the rule through the reasonable use of techniques such as—

> (1) the inclusion in an advanced notice of proposed rulemaking, if issued, of a statement that the proposed rule may have a significant economic effect on a substantial number of small entities;

> (2) the publication of general notice of proposed rulemaking in publications likely to be obtained by small entities;

> (3) the direct notification of interested small entities;

> (4) the conduct of open conferences or public hearings concerning the rule for small entities including soliciting and receiving comments over computer networks; and

> (5) the adoption or modification of agency procedural rules to reduce the cost or complexity of participation in the rulemaking by small entities.

(b) Prior to publication of an initial regulatory flexibility analysis which a covered agency is required to conduct by this chapter—

(1) a covered agency shall notify the Chief Counsel for Advocacy of the Small Business Administration and provide the Chief Counsel with information on the potential impacts of the proposed rule on small entities and the type of small entities that might be affected;

(2) not later than 15 days after the date of receipt of the materials described in paragraph (1), the Chief Counsel shall identify individuals representative of affected small entities for the purpose of obtaining advice and recommendations from those individuals about the potential impacts of the proposed rule;

(3) the agency shall convene a review panel for such rule consisting wholly of full time Federal employees of the office within the agency responsible for carrying out the proposed rule, the Office of Information and Regulatory Affairs within the Office of Management and Budget, and the Chief Counsel;

(4) the panel shall review any material the agency has prepared in connection with this chapter, including any draft proposed rule, collect advice and recommendations of each individual small entity representative identified by the agency after consultation with the Chief Counsel, on issues related to subsections 603(b), paragraphs (3), (4) and (5) and 603(c);

(5) not later than 60 days after the date a covered agency convenes a review panel pursuant to paragraph (3), the review panel shall report on the comments of the small entity representatives and its findings as to issues related to subsections 603(b), paragraphs (3), (4) and (5) and 603(c), provided that such report shall be made public as part of the rulemaking record; and

(6) where appropriate, the agency shall modify the proposed rule, the initial regulatory flexibility analysis or the decision on whether an initial regulatory flexibility analysis is required.

(c) An agency may in its discretion apply subsection (b) to rules that the agency intends to certify under subsection 605(b), but the agency believes may have a greater than de minimis impact on a substantial number of small entities.

(d) For purposes of this section, the term "covered agency" means the Environmental Protection Agency and the Occupational Safety and Health Administration of the Department of Labor.

(e) The Chief Counsel for Advocacy, in consultation with the individuals identified in subsection (b)(2), and with the Administrator of the Office of Information and Regulatory Affairs within the Office of Management and Budget, may waive the requirements of subsections (b)(3), (b)(4), and (b)(5) by including in the rulemaking record a written finding, with reasons therefor, that those requirements would not advance the effective participation of small entities in the rulemaking process. For purposes of this subsection, the factors to be considered in making such a finding are as follows:

> (1) In developing a proposed rule, the extent to which the covered agency consulted with individuals representative of affected small entities with respect to the potential impacts of the rule and took such concerns into consideration.

> (2) Special circumstances requiring prompt issuance of the rule.

> (3) Whether the requirements of subsection (b) would provide the individuals identified in subsection (b)(2) with a competitive advantage relative to other small entities.

§ 610. Periodic review of rules

(a) Within one hundred and eighty days after the effective date of this chapter, each agency shall publish in the *Federal Register* a plan for the periodic review of the rules issued by the agency which have or will have a significant economic impact upon a substantial number of small entities. Such plan may be amended by the agency at any time by publishing the revision in the *Federal Register*. The purpose of the review shall be to determine whether such rules should be continued without change, or should be amended or rescinded, consistent with the stated objectives of applicable statutes, to minimize any significant economic impact of the rules upon a substantial number of such small entities. The plan shall provide for the review of all such agency rules existing on the effective date of this chapter within ten years of that date and for the review of such rules adopted after the effective date of this chapter within ten years of the publication of such rules as the final rule. If the head of the agency determines that completion of the review of existing rules is not feasible by the established date, he shall so certify in a statement published in the *Federal Register* and may extend the completion date by one year at a time for a total of not more than five years.

(b) In reviewing rules to minimize any significant economic impact of the rule on a substantial number of small entities in a manner consistent with the stated objectives of applicable statutes, the agency shall consider the following factors—

(1) the continued need for the rule;

(2) the nature of complaints or comments received concerning the rule from the public;

(3) the complexity of the rule;

(4) the extent to which the rule overlaps, duplicates or conflicts with other Federal rules, and, to the extent feasible, with State and local governmental rules; and

(5) the length of time since the rule has been evaluated or the degree to which technology, economic conditions, or other factors have changed in the area affected by the rule.

(c) Each year, each agency shall publish in the *Federal Register* a list of the rules which have a significant economic impact on a substantial number of small entities, which are to be reviewed pursuant to this section during the succeeding twelve months. The list shall include a brief description of each rule and the need for and legal basis of such rule and shall invite public comment upon the rule.

§ 611. Judicial review

(a)   (1) For any rule subject to this chapter, a small entity that is adversely affected or aggrieved by final agency action is entitled to judicial review of agency compliance with the requirements of sections 601, 604, 605(b), 608(b), and 610 in accordance with chapter 7. Agency compliance with sections 607 and 609(a) shall be judicially reviewable in connection with judicial review of section 604.

(2) Each court having jurisdiction to review such rule for compliance with section 553, or under any other provision of law, shall have jurisdiction to review any claims of noncompliance with sections 601, 604, 605(b), 608(b), and 610 in accordance with chapter 7. Agency compliance with sections 607 and 609(a) shall be judicially reviewable in connection with judicial review of section 604.

(3)   (A) A small entity may seek such review during the period beginning on the date of final agency action and ending one year later, except that where a provision of law requires that an action challenging a final agency action be commenced before the expiration of one year, such lesser period shall apply to an action for judicial review under this section.

(B) In the case where an agency delays the issuance of a final regulatory flexibility analysis pursuant to section 608(b) of this chapter, an action for judicial review under this section shall be filed not later than—

(i) one year after the date the analysis is made available to the public, or

(ii) where a provision of law requires that an action challenging a final agency regulation be commenced before the expiration of the 1-year period, the number of days specified in such provision of law that is after the date the analysis is made available to the public.

(4) In granting any relief in an action under this section, the court shall order the agency to take corrective action consistent with this chapter and chapter 7, including, but not limited to—

(A) remanding the rule to the agency, and

(B) deferring the enforcement of the rule against small entities unless the court finds that continued enforcement of the rule is in the public interest.

(5) Nothing in this subsection shall be construed to limit the authority of any court to stay the effective date of any rule or provision thereof under any other provision of law or to grant any other relief in addition to the requirements of this section.

(b) In an action for the judicial review of a rule, the regulatory flexibility analysis for such rule, including an analysis prepared or corrected pursuant to paragraph (a)(4), shall constitute part of the entire record of agency action in connection with such review.

(c) Compliance or noncompliance by an agency with the provisions of this chapter shall be subject to judicial review only in accordance with this section.

(d) Nothing in this section bars judicial review of any other impact statement or similar analysis required by any other law if judicial review of such statement or analysis is otherwise permitted by law.

§ 612. Reports and intervention rights

(a) The Chief Counsel for Advocacy of the Small Business Administration shall monitor agency compliance with this chapter and shall report at least annually thereon to the President and to the Committees on the Judiciary and Small Business of the Senate and House of Representatives.

(b) The Chief Counsel for Advocacy of the Small Business Administration is authorized to appear as amicus curiae in any action brought in a court of the United States to review a rule. In any such action, the Chief Counsel is authorized to present his or her views with respect to compliance with this chapter, the adequacy of the rulemaking record with respect to small entities and the effect of the rule on small entities.

(c) A court of the United States shall grant the application of the Chief Counsel for Advocacy of the Small Business Administration to appear in any such action for the purposes described in subsection (b).

Executive Order 13272

Federal Register

Vol. 67, No. 159

Friday, August 16, 2002

Presidential Documents

Title 3—

The President

Executive Order 13272 of August 13, 2002

Proper Consideration of Small Entities in Agency Rulemaking

By the authority vested in me as President by the Constitution and the laws of the United States of America, it is hereby ordered as follows:

Section 1. *General Requirements.* Each agency shall establish procedures and policies to promote compliance with the Regulatory Flexibility Act, as amended (5 U.S.C. 601 *et seq.*) (the "Act"). Agencies shall thoroughly review draft rules to assess and take appropriate account of the potential impact on small businesses, small governmental jurisdictions, and small organizations, as provided by the Act. The Chief Counsel for Advocacy of the Small Business Administration (Advocacy) shall remain available to advise agencies in performing that review consistent with the provisions of the Act.

Sec. 2. *Responsibilities of Advocacy.* Consistent with the requirements of the Act, other applicable law, and Executive Order 12866 of September 30, 1993, as amended, Advocacy:

(a) shall notify agency heads from time to time of the requirements of the Act, including by issuing notifications with respect to the basic requirements of the Act within 90 days of the date of this order;

(b) shall provide training to agencies on compliance with the Act; and

(c) may provide comment on draft rules to the agency that has proposed or intends to propose the rules and to the Office of Information and Regulatory Affairs of the Office of Management and Budget (OIRA).

Sec. 3. *Responsibilities of Federal Agencies.* Consistent with the requirements of the Act and applicable law, agencies shall:

(a) Within 180 days of the date of this order, issue written procedures and policies, consistent with the Act, to ensure that the potential impacts of agencies' draft rules on small businesses, small governmental jurisdictions, and small organizations are properly considered during the rulemaking process. Agency heads shall submit, no later than 90 days from the date of this order, their written procedures and policies to Advocacy for comment. Prior to issuing final procedures and policies, agencies shall consider any such comments received within 60 days from the date of the submission of the agencies' procedures and policies to Advocacy. Except to the extent otherwise specifically provided by statute or Executive Order, agencies shall make the final procedures and policies available to the public through the Internet or other easily accessible means;

(b) Notify Advocacy of any draft rules that may have a significant economic impact on a substantial number of small entities under the Act. Such notifications shall be made (i) when the agency submits a draft rule to OIRA under Executive Order 12866 if that order requires such submission, or (ii) if no submission to OIRA is so required, at a reasonable time prior to publication of the rule by the agency; and

(c) Give every appropriate consideration to any comments provided by Advocacy regarding a draft rule. Consistent with applicable law and appropriate protection of executive deliberations and legal privileges, an agency shall include, in any explanation or discussion accompanying publication in the **Federal Register** of a final rule, the agency's response to any written comments submitted by Advocacy on the proposed rule that preceded the final rule; provided, however, that such inclusion is not required if the head of the agency certifies that the public interest is not served thereby.

Agencies and Advocacy may, to the extent permitted by law, engage in an exchange of data and research, as appropriate, to foster the purposes of the Act.

Sec. 4. *Definitions.* Terms defined in section 601 of title 5, United States Code, including the term "agency," shall have the same meaning in this order.

Sec. 5. *Preservation of Authority.* Nothing in this order shall be construed to impair or affect the authority of the Administrator of the Small Business Administration to supervise the Small Business Administration as provided in the first sentence of section 2(b)(1) of Public Law 85–09536 (15 U.S.C. 633(b)(1)).

Sec. 6. *Reporting.* For the purpose of promoting compliance with this order, Advocacy shall submit a report not less than annually to the Director of the Office of Management and Budget on the extent of compliance with this order by agencies.

Sec. 7. *Confidentiality.* Consistent with existing law, Advocacy may publicly disclose information that it receives from the agencies in the course of carrying out this order only to the extent that such information already has been lawfully and publicly disclosed by OIRA or the relevant rulemaking agency.

Sec. 8. *Judicial Review.* This order is intended only to improve the internal management of the Federal Government. This order is not intended to, and does not, create any right or benefit, substantive or procedural, enforceable at law or equity, against the United States, its departments, agencies, or other entities, its officers or employees, or any other person.

THE WHITE HOUSE,
August 13, 2002.

[FR Doc. 02–21056
Filed 08–15–02; 8:45 am]
Billing code 3195–01–P

Index

importance of, 171
partnering by, 164
returns of, 167 *(box)*
self organization of, 167 *(box)*
stages of, 161, 162 *(chart)*, 163 *(chart)*
strategies of, 164
GrowthEconomics, Inc., 175
Guam and RFA legislation status, 210 *(chart)*

Hanlon, D., 123, 125, 126, 128
Harris County, Texas
women-owned businesses in, 81 *(table)*
Hawaii
RFA legislation in, 209 *(table)*
women-owned business growth in, 83
See also State data
Hawaiians as women business owners, 56
Health and Human Services, U.S.
Department of
procurement by, 44 *(table)*, 46 *(table)*, 48
Small Business Innovation Research
contracting by, 48
Health care and social assistance businesses,
72, 75 *(table)*
by firm size, 232 *(table)*
women in, 57, 60, 62 *(table)*
Health insurance coverage, 14
of labor force (by gender), 63 *(table)*
of moonlighters (by gender), 63 *(table)*
of professionals (by gender), 63 *(table)*
Heritage Foundation, 131
Hispanic American-owned businesses
dynamics of women-owned, 85,
86 *(table)*, 100 *(table)*
Hispanic Americans
number of business owners, 241 *(table)*
self-employment of, 11
as women business owners, 56, 69 *(table)*
Homeland Security, U.S. Department of
procurement by, 44 *(table)*, 46 *(table)*, 48
Hopkins, Thomas, 201
Hours worked, 218 *(table)*
See also Full-time workers, Part-time
workers
Households
borrowing by, 16, 19 *(table)*, 20
headed by men, 58, 59, 60 *(table)*
headed by women, 58, 59, 60 *(table)*
Housing and Urban Development, U.S.
Department of

procurement by, 44 *(table)*, 46 *(table)*, 48
Housing market, 15, 20
Houston, Texas
women-owned businesses in, 80 *(table)*,
82 *(table)*
HUBZone program, 50 *(table)*, 54
and transparency in procurement data, 41
Hunting, *see* Agriculture, forestry, fishing,
and hunting
Huntsville, Texas, metropolitan area
women-owned businesses in, 80 *(table)*
Hurricanes, effects on business, 8

Idaho, *see* State data
Illinois
role in entrepreneurial development, 133
See also State data
Inc. 500, 133
Income, 218 *(table)*
of financial institutions, 23
of labor force (by gender), 63 *(table)*
of moonlighters (by gender), 63 *(table)*
of noncorporate businesses, 22 *(table)*
of professionals (by gender), 62,
63 *(table)*
Indefinite delivery vehicles and procurement,
42n
Indiana
RFA legislation in, 209 *(table)*
See also State data
Industrial policy, 160
Industries
employer and nonemployers firms in,
232 *(table)*
of women-owned businesses, 57, 72,
75 *(table)*
Inflation, 9 *(table)*, 15, 16, 218 *(table)*
Information businesses, 232 *(table)*
Information technology advances, 158
Infrastructure and economic gardening, 169,
183
Initial public offerings, 28, 30 *(table)*
Initial regulatory flexibility analysis, 197
Innovation
connection to entrepreneurship, 177
in small firms, 200
Innovation Index, 176
Installation, maintenance and repair
women in, 61 *(table)*
Insurance businesses, 232 *(table)*

women-owned businesses in, 79,
81 *(table)*
Louisiana
role in entrepreneurial development, 133
women-owned business growth in, 83
See also State data
Lovatt, A., 125

Madison, Wisconsin, economic gardening,
178, 180
Maine
role in entrepreneurial development, 133
women-owned business growth in, 83
See also State data
Management
women in, 60, 62 *(table)*
Management and Budget, Office of
Circular A-76, 38
and contract bundling, 40
and RFID tags, 39
and transparency in procurement data, 41
Management and operating contracts, 39
Management businesses, 232 *(table)*
Manufacturing
businesses by firm size in, 232 *(table)*
new methods in, 158
sales in, 218 *(table)*
women business owners in, 57, 75 *(table)*
Maricopa County, Arizona
women-owned businesses in, 81 *(table)*
Marital status
of labor force (by gender), 63 *(table)*
of moonlighters (by gender), 63 *(table)*
of professionals (by gender), 62, 63 *(table)*
Market information
and economic gardening, 170, 183, 185
in Oakland, California, 179
Maryland
entrepreneurial dynamism in, 176,
192 *(table)*
role in entrepreneurial development, 133
See also State data
Massachusetts
entrepreneurial dynamism in, 176, 191,
192 *(table)*
technology successes in, 160
women-owned business growth in, 83
See also State data
Mathematics, women in, 60, 61 *(table)*,
62 *(table)*

McKibbin, L.E., 120
Media, women in, 60, 62 *(table)*
Men
as heads of household, 58, 59, 60 *(table)*
in labor force, 55, 58, 59 *(table)*
as moonlighters, 59
in the population, 58, 59 *(table)*
self-employment of, 11
See also Gender, Women in business,
Women-owned businesses
Men business owners
number of, 241 *(table)*
Mentor-Protégé program in Georgia, 183,
184
Metropolitan areas
defined, 79*n*
women-owned businesses in, 79,
80 *(table)*
Miami, Florida
women-owned businesses in, 79, 81
(table), 82 *(table)*,
Michigan
role in entrepreneurial development, 133
See also State data
Midwest, economic recessions in, 159
Millennium Challenge Corporation,
44 *(table)*
Mine Safety and Health Administration
regulatory cost savings by, 206 *(table)*,
207 *(table)*
Mining businesses, 232 *(table)*
Minnesota, *see* State data
Minorities
self-employment of, 11
as women business owners, 56, 66,
69 *(table)*
Minority-owned businesses
procurement from, 50, 50 *(table)*,
51 *(table)*
women-owned business dynamics, 84,
86 *(table)*, 100 *(table)*
Miscoding of procurement data, 40
Mississippi
Balance Agriculture with Industry
program, 159
RFA legislation in, 209 *(table)*
women-owned business growth in, 83
See also State data
Missouri
RFA legislation in, 209 *(table)*